# *Best Little Stories From The White House*

*By C. Brian Kelly*

With *First Ladies In Review* by Ingrid Smyer

**BEST LITTLE STORIES FROM THE WHITE HOUSE:** 101 vignettes drawn from the life and times of America's most famous and legendary home, written as short narratives by C. Brian Kelly and based upon a variety of sources. This book also includes *First Ladies In Review* by Ingrid Smyer, thumbnail sketches of the women who have joined the Presidents in the White House as First Ladies of the land.

First printing October 1992
Second printing March 1993

Cover design by Stephen S. Vann

Cover: Circa 1840, exaggerated view of the "President's House" as seen from Tiber Creek, south of the presidential home. Engraving based upon well-known 19th century watercolor by William Henry Bartlett (1837), now held in the official White House Collection (Library of Congress; William Allman, Office of the Curator, the White House). Presidents shown in left-hand panel, top to bottom: John F. Kennedy, Rutherford B. Hayes; Grover Cleveland; Abraham Lincoln.

Typesetting and Page Design
By Empire Press, Leesburg, Virginia

*A Cowles Media Company Affiliate*

*To our mothers,*
*Claire and Ingrid*

# Preamble

It was an Irishman from County Kilkenny, a "house carpenter," a resident of young America for all of seven years, who designed and built the White House. The latter he did twice, actually.

Apparently aprocryphal is the old saw that Thomas Jefferson submitted a design under false initials in the competition for the architectural honors—and then was passed over. One way or the other, James Hoban was the choice that emerged.

He worked under the close supervision of George Washington, with Jefferson occasionally dropping by. Washington, so involved with the creation of the Federal city bearing his name, with the plans and the site and the actual construction of the "President's House" as the first public building to begin rising in that city, never did live in it. Jefferson, on the other hand, did.

Hired slaves began the excavating in 1791, it seems. Stonecutters from Scotland later cut and finished many of the sandstone blocks making up the outer walls of the future "White House." The stone itself was native; it came from a quarry at Aquia Creek, across the Potomac River in Virginia. Hired slaves worked over there, too. And speaking of which—

What ironies, what bittersweet history, here, this one thread...blacks and the White House! At first, slaves hired out by their masters, the money for their masters' pockets, to help build it. Later, for generations and through several Presidents, slaves who worked and lived here, right under its roof. Here, too, Lincoln then agonized over the Emancipation Proclamation (with an unlikely friend's help), and here after the Civil War, paid black workers became a permanent part of the staff (mostly as servants, true). In those postwar years also, a onetime slaveowner would reside here with his daughter and son-in-law. And here, as late as 1901, Teddy Roosevelt would take heat for inviting the distinguished Booker T. Washington to dinner. And then (in the late 1920s yet!), Herbert Hoover's wife Lou thought she was being *politically correct,* if you will, was breaking all tradition, by entertaining a black congressman's wife at a small tea—small and quite separate, that is, from the one she held for the congressional wives in general. Here, in the White House also, Woodrow Wilson's housekeeper insisted that black and white staff members take their in-house meals at separate tables. Surely another extreme altogether, Eleanor Roosevelt's housekeeper fired the white domestics and replaced them with blacks.

iv

In the beginning, though, the site chosen for the mansion was a piece of the large presidential park envisioned by the Frenchman planning the entire city, Pierre L'Enfant. By 1792, however, his conception of a European-style "palace" as the presidential home had been turned down. Too grandiose by far for the young, so democratic republic. Even so, this would be the grandest home in America for many years, perhaps its largest until the Civil War.

It would be eight years under construction before its first presidential occupant, John Adams, could move in. . .and even then, its interior rooms and other many other features were far from finished. You could almost argue, in fact, that it wasn't finished, truly, until yesterday. And. . .who knows what they may do to it tomorrow, as well, it has undergone so many changes, additions, improvements and even subtractions in its 200-year history. The fact is, the White House we see today is not the White House of yore.

Just about every President or First Family has made some lasting change here, whether of small scale or large. The Benjamin Harrisons put in electricity and Chester Arthur the small elevator to the second-floor family quarters, for instance, but others contributed in more visible and far reaching ways. Jefferson it was, third President and second official White House occupant (Jefferson's political enemy John Marshall slipped in there for a while even before John Adams, just hunting for a room in the new city when he was serving as Secretary of State), who oversaw the planning and construction of the structure's early east and west wings. Nice touch, too! After the British burned the place down in 1814, leaving only a gutted shell, really, Hoban and his construction crews had to come back and build the White House all over again, with various changes from the original model. Later, much later, of course, it was Teddy Roosevelt who removed the large greenhouses that had grown at the west end— unsightly blisters, too, to judge by the photos still remaining—and added the West Wing that now houses the famous Oval Office. William Howard Taft, though, actually installed the Oval Office. . .and yet not the one so often pictured or cited today, since FDR moved Taft's creation from one side of the West Wing to the other, to face on the Rose Garden. And Jack Kennedy, speaking of the Rose Garden, redesigned and rebuilt it, with friend "Bunny" Mellon's help (Mrs. Paul Mellon). Some years before, of course, threatened with physical collapse of ceilings and other old sections, the Harry Trumans had overseen the most extensive White House restoration job since right after the British visited the Executive Mansion in 1814. So extensive was the Truman reconstruction that the entire interior was taken out, much of it piece by carefully marked piece—a truck or bulldozer could drive through the empty space inside—and then much was meticulously replaced in proper place or replicas were substituted. Important, too, steel supporting structure now replaced the old, weakening materials of the 19th century.

The result, today, of all the changes over two centuries is a stately and graceful home of 132 rooms, situated on a 18-acre "plot" in the middle of Washington, D.C., and maintained by a staff of 115. It sounds like it could be a hotel, so many employees and rooms (and under Eleanor and FDR, it sometimes *did* resemble one, so many visitors came and went all the time). It sounds by description that it could be massive and overwhelming on the one hand, and by its history, could be a jerry-built hodgepodge creation on the other hand (all those changes and additions!). But in fact it is none of the above. . .inside, it is surprisingly pleasing and *under*whelming, if you will, in its proportions. Outside, grand, yes, but no hotel, no monolith. . .rather, just about right. It is difficult to believe, in fact, that this building—where John and Abigail Adams once found six rooms to be livable—actually holds a total of 132 rooms.

But we are not come here to write only about bricks and mortar, so to speak, nor about the institution that is the White House today, that it has come to be, but rather we write about its people over the years, Presidents and First Ladies very much included! yes, but many others, too—those who lived here (and a few who died here), who worked here, visited here, even wedded or were born here. History in our small bursts, or vignettes, yes, but we hope also something of its soul becomes visible in these pages also.

From this writing, in the late summer of 1992, it is almost exactly 200 years since the laying of the White House cornerstone on October 13, 1792. It's a shame, yes, but George Washington, with business out of town, did miss it. True.

It was a Saturday. The crowd collected first at a Georgetown hostelry, the Fountain Inn. They then walked—about a mile—to the building site, led by Freemasons arranged according to Masonic rank.

James Hoban of course was there.

After the first group came those important men, the voice of authority locally, the commissioners assigned earlier to help George Washington find and lay out the 10-square-mile site for the new Federal city on the Potomac between the ports of Alexandria on the Virginia side and Georgetown, across and up the river a ways, on Maryland ground. They, the three commissioners, together with active partner Washington, also supervised the site selection, the architectural and construction contract awards and then the construction itself for the President's House.

After the Federal district's commissioners (Thomas Johnson, Daniel Carroll and David Stuart) came the local gentry, followed by workers and artisans...and all gathered, it now is thought, at the southwest corner of the recently laid-out foundation. After suitable *speechifying,* Master Mason Collen Williamson wedged the freshly mortared cornerstone into its designated niche—trapped underneath was a brass plate noting that "This first stone of the President's House..." was laid down in the 17th year of independence. It also said, in Latin, *"Vivat Respublica"*—long live the Republic!

There was no intention, it clearly can be seen, when they laid the cornerstone and began to build, to call it the White House. But once the edifice was up and standing, a large, large block in a near-naked landscape, no real city yet surrounding it, but only some farmland framed by still wild-looking countryside, and once those great chunks of hand-cut sandstone forming its walls were white-washed, it became obvious. This was, even by Jefferson's tenure as the second official occupant, the "White House." So obvious, what else to call it, really? And yet not until 100 years later was it made official. On Theodore Roosevelt's stationery and other documentation at last appeared that designation so well known today. Henceforth and forevermore. *The White House.*

C. Brian Kelly
Charlottesville, Virginia
August 1992

# 🦅 *Contents*

## I BEGINNINGS

## II MIDDLES

III   ENDS

# Beginnings

#  One Dread Moment

There was that one moment...the very first moment in the Oval Office just vacated by the man before him. Only bare furniture to greet the newcomer. Bookshelves, but no books. Walls, but no pictures. A big desk...but empty. Totally empty!

*The Nation!* The Nation was in crisis, and here he was, the new President, alone in his wheelchair. "Here he was, without even the wherewithal to make a note—if he had a note to make," wrote aide Rexford Tugwell later.

Alone in the empty, power-laden room, an awaiting world beyond the bare walls poised to hear his proclamations. And now, of all times, "for a few dreadful minutes he hadn't a single thought."

Ever since his landslide election four months before, Franklin Delano Roosevelt had been pointing toward this very moment—his first day at work as the new President.

It had been a strange and pressure-filled interregnum since Election Day of 1932.

First, he was down with the flu for about five days. Then there was a tense meeting at the White House with outgoing President Herbert Hoover just a week after the election. Discussing European hopes of cancelling huge World War I debts to the United States, Hoover directed almost all his conversation to FDR aide Raymond Moley, not to FDR himself. Hoover, indeed, found his political adversary to be "amiable, pleasant, anxious to be of service" but also "badly informed" and lacking in "vision."

FDR often nodded, wrote biographer Nathan Miller. Not in agreement, as Hoover thought, but merely to signify his understanding.

And so, they parted, with Hoover expecting FDR's endorsement of Hoover's proposals to avert the latest crisis of the Great Depression. Much to Hoover's amazement, FDR instead "went public" with contradictory views of his own. The hostility between the two only deepened as a result.

1

In those days, the lapse between Election Day and presidential inauguration stretched from early November to March 4, a hiatus of power too long for the modern world and since corrected, with inaugurations now scheduled on January 20 of the year following the presidential election.

During the long 1932-33 interregnum, FDR often gave the appearance of that "amiable, pleasant" man simply awaiting his turn at the bat. Some critics felt he should show more concern for the ailing nation, put his shoulder to the wheel and help Hoover deal with the nation's ever-growing economic crisis. As the year 1932 ended, the latest victim was the nation's faltering banking system.

Roosevelt may have appeared unconcerned, but that wasn't entirely so, added FDR biographer Miller: "Behind the scenes...Roosevelt and his advisers were working up a comprehensive legislative program that contained the basic outline of the New Deal." But a New Deal to be revealed only when FDR took office. A New Deal, some still will argue, already laid out in concept by an unpopular, ill-fated President Hoover himself.

Well into the new year, with many banks closing their doors, FDR cruised the Bahamas in Vincent Astor's yacht and came ashore in Miami, "tanned and happy," for a conference with aide Moley—and a public appearance with the mayor of Chicago, Anton Cermak. From an open touring car that evening, the President-elect delivered a few remarks in the city's Bay Front Park, then turned to greet Cermak.

"Just then I heard what I thought was a firecracker, then several more," FDR said later.

Not 20 feet away was a man shooting at FDR with a pistol...but Cermak, in the line of fire, suddenly had grown stains of blood all over his shirt. He had been shot instead.

Roosevelt wouldn't let his car speed away without gathering in the wounded Cermak first. He held Cermak in his arms as the open car raced for Jackson Memorial Hospital. He kept telling Cermak: "Tony, keep quiet—don't move. It won't hurt you if you keep quiet."

Roosevelt stayed at the hospital until Cermak came out of emergency surgery. Only then would FDR return to the Astor yacht for the night. There, members of his entourage, shaken by the evening's events, were up all night, restless, still excited...talking. But not FDR. Acting perfectly normal, he went to bed and slept with no apparent disturbance.

Cermak died a few days later, but until his inauguration, FDR continued to exude the same unflappable, confident air. With the bank crisis at high pitch by inauguration time in March, the Hoovers perfunctorily entertained the Roosevelts at the White House the afternoon before the inaugural ceremonies. While other family members sipped tea in the Red Room, Hoover and Roosevelt argued in an adjoining room over the proper response to the latest bad news. Again, FDR refused to go along with a Hoover plan, this one to act jointly in an effort to discourage the bank closings spreading across the country.

Supposedly, FDR told Hoover, "If you haven't the guts to do it yourself, I'll wait until I'm President to do it."

During the night, the governors of New York and Illinois closed the banks in each state. On Inauguration Day itself, the entire Nation's banks were closed or closing. While riding to the Capitol with his successor, Hoover wouldn't speak to him. In his inaugural address shortly afterward, the confident FDR delivered that famous, still-remembered line: "The only thing we have to fear is fear itself."

That evening, while Roosevelt family members attended the Inaugural Ball, FDR stayed "home" in the White House, his first night there, a quiet evening spent in the Lincoln study (recently decorated by Hoover's wife Lou) with old friend and aide Louis Howe.

It was the next morning that FDR reported for duty at the Oval Office for the first time. . .and felt that one, tiny moment of helplessness. But only for a moment, for in seconds, recalled his aide Tugwell later, FDR began searching the desk for a call button, and when he couldn't find it, he simply yelled.

Two staffers came running. FDR was on his way, and that very evening, he "signed the necessary documents calling Congress into session and proclaiming a four-day national bank holiday," wrote biographer Miller. The New Deal itself was off and running. The crippled country had a new man at the helm—himself crippled, but brimming with confidence.

## 🦅 *Jackie's Painful Tour*

The small elevator edged upward to the second floor. . .the family quarters. As the door slid open, the young woman inside—years younger than any First Lady of the 20th century—girded herself by taking a deep breath.

Down the hall ahead Mamie Eisenhower was waiting. And waiting. She did not advance a step as Jacqueline Kennedy emerged for a pre-inaugural tour of the private family rooms above the ceremonial and social realms of her future home, the White House.

It was not a friendly, relaxed encounter between the old and the new that December morning in 1960. For one thing, Mamie Eisenhower was determined to be alone while she showed her successor around. "Please have the rooms in order, but no servants on the upstairs floors," she had instructed Chief White House Usher J.B. West.

The time for the visit was set for noon and at 1:30 sharp, Mamie Eisenhower planned to leave the premises for another engagement. As the wife of a onetime general, college president and now President of the United States, even a lame duck, out-going President, she often could be thoroughly imperial in her manner. And now there was the outgoing "First Couple's" distinct feeling that John F. Kennedy's narrow election victory over Vice President Richard M. Nixon was a repudiation of the Eisenhower record.

While more friendly feelings emerged later, Ike was known in 1960 to consider JFK as a "young whippersnapper" and to have objected (in a letter to a friend) to any notion "that we have a new genius in our midst who is incapable of making any mistakes."

To make matters worse for the youthful Jackie Kennedy, her visit came only two weeks after her Caesarian delivery of John F. Kennedy, Jr. at nearby Georgetown Hospital. She looked thin and pale, and she had requested a wheelchair for the intimate White House tour. Obviously, someone would have to push her along.

"Oh, dear," Mamie had said at that news. "I wanted to take her around alone."

Mamie's solution was to have a wheelchair on hand but tucked out of sight. "It will be available if she asks for it," she instructed.

Jackie arrived at the South Entrance shortly before noon, seated informally in the front seat of a station wagon driven by a Secret Service agent. Chief Usher West escorted her inside—past the Diplomatic Reception Room where she entered, through the hall beyond to the elevator. Silent, she looked all around, obviously absorbing details, but also "somewhat ill-at-ease."

Upstairs, she had to advance to take Mamie Eisenhower's proffered hand. "Hello, Mrs. Kennedy," said the outgoing First Lady. "I do hope you are feeling much better now. How is the baby?"

As West bowed out of the picture, Mamie then led the way for her special guest.

An hour and a half later, two rings of the buzzer in West's office signified that the First Lady was descending in the elevator. Two First Ladies, in fact.

4

Their respective cars were waiting at the South Entrance. Mamie quickly left in her chauffeur-driven Chrysler limousine for her card game engagement, and Jackie "walked slowly" to her station wagon.

As West briefly made arrangements to send Jackie blueprints and photographs of the rooms that she soon would be redecorating, he wrote later, "I saw pain darken her face."

It wasn't until the Kennedys had settled in at the White House, weeks later, that West learned just how difficult the White House tour had been for the new First Lady. She asked him one day if he had known about the request for a wheelchair. When he told her yes, she was dumbfounded. "Then why didn't you have it for me? I was so exhausted after marching around this house for two hours that I had to go back to bed for two whole weeks!"

West explained that it had been there, hidden behind the closet door right by the elevator. "We were waiting for you to request it," he added.

Instead of pain or anger, Jackie reacted with a giggle. "I was too scared of Mrs. Eisenhower to ask," she confided.

In time, Chief Usher West would find the new mistress of his White House realm to be "elegant, aloof, dignified and regal" in public, and in private, "casual, impish and irreverent."

One thing she never was again, though, was "uncertain." Soft-spoken and subtle as she was, her voice often almost a husky whisper, "She had a will of iron, with more determination than anyone I have ever met." Younger than any First Lady whom West served in his 30 years at the White House, from the Franklin Roosevelts to the Richard Nixons, she nonetheless "had the most complex personality of them all."

# Reportage At Close Quarters

The President-elect, Mr. Lincoln, had proceeded into the capital a week in advance of his expected arrival and without prior announcement, due to the sundry plots against his person that were so widely rumored. He was presented to a young reporter in the House of Representatives, at the Capitol building itself, on the Saturday before his inauguration and, noting the fellow's youthfulness, he said: "You are not a member of the House?" To which the young man, Henry Watterson, replied: "No, sir, I only hope to be."

Then came the significant day that all were anticipating, albeit some with considerably more dread than joy—the inauguration on March 4.

5

The young man, the journalist Mr. Watterson, had been assigned to report on the inaugural events, and so he would need a copy of the newly sworn President's speech. He was told by messenger's note that very morning that a copy of Mr. Lincoln's inaugural address would be made available to him if he merely would present himself to Colonel Ward H. Lamon.

But who was Colonel Lamon? Where might he be located? Mr. Watterson had no idea. "I had never heard of him," Mr. Watterson wrote in *The Cosmopolitan* magazine in 1909. "The city was crowded with strangers. To find one of them was to look for a needle in a haystack."

The solution, however, was quite obvious. The solution was to start his search at that Mecca of Meccas in the capital city of 1861, the Willard Hotel. And so, Mr. Watterson hied himself to those very premises, and soon found himself on the second floor, before a myriad of "little dark entry-ways to the apartments facing on Pennsylvania Avenue."

He proceeded down the long corridor connecting them all, and as he did so, he saw a half-opened door. And there, just past the doorway, was Mr. Lincoln himself, "pacing to and fro, apparently reading a manuscript."

Eureka!

"I went straight in. He was alone and, as he turned and saw me, he extended his hand, called my name, and said: 'What can I do for you?'"

When Mr. Watterson explained, the President-elect was able to oblige with no further time wasted. "Why," he said, "you have come to the right shop, Lamon is in the next room. I will take you to him, and he will fix you all right."

And so it was that Mr. Watterson soon was striding to the nearby telegraph office, also at Fourteenth and Pennsylvania, but "over the way at the northeast corner," to impart to various newspapers across the Nation the contents of the day's message. The young reporter noticed the Lincoln speech "had been clumsily typeset in some country office and was considerably interlined with pencil marks."

In just two hours, the same young man—acting as an assistant to the veteran reporter L.A. Gobright—was stationed on the wooden platform erected at the East Portico of the Capitol for the Lincoln inauguration. As witness to this most historic event, our youthful journalist was so close to the principal parties that when Mr. Lincoln removed his black silk hat, "I lifted my hand to receive it...."

Not to be, however. . .Lincoln's old campaign adversary, Stephen Douglas, that is to say, *Senator* Douglas, was quicker. He reached over Mr. Watterson's arm, "took the hat and held it during the delivery of the Inaugural Address which followed."

For such auspicious occasion, it should also be noted, the President-elect wore not only the black silk hat but also a black suit and a black tie that emerged from a "turndown collar." He was "tall and ungainly;" he brandished a walking cane, with head either of silver or gold. On the wooden platform was a table holding a Bible, a pitcher of water and a glass. Mr. Lincoln pulled a manuscript from his breast pocket—the same papers that Mr. Watterson had seen him perusing at the hotel earlier—and laid his cane on it to hold down the paper.

He next took out his steel-rimmed spectacles. . .and he was ready.

For the speech that followed, "His self-possession was perfect," Mr. Watterson would write years later.

"Dignity, herself, could not have been more unexcited. His voice was a little high-pitched, but resonant, quite reaching the outer fringes of the vast crowd in front; his expression serious to the point of gravity; not a scintillation of humor. Notwithstanding the campaign pictures of Lincoln, the boor, I was prepared to expect much. It is only true to say he delivered that Inaugural Address as though he had been delivering Inaugural Addresses all his life."

The apparently disappointed Mr. Watterson derived one further fact on that fateful day. "To me it meant War."

And so it—and subsequent events—did. Indeed, the Civil War. Astonishingly enough, too, in mere weeks, the same young man who had discovered the President-elect alone in his hotel room, who then had stood so close by during the inaugural ceremonies as to reach for the presidential black silk hat. . .this same young man in just a few weeks' time was the sworn enemy of all that Mr. Lincoln represented and stood so righteously for. The Union.

For Mr. Henry Watterson, albeit he later in life did become a member of Congress, albeit he subsequently became the distinguished editor of the Louisville (Kentucky) *Courier* for many years, did raise his hand against Mr. Lincoln and his Government by joining the armies of the Confederate States of America (CSA) as a soldier in their cause.

His heart, he did later confess, never was entirely with the secessionists. But think, had it been all fire and hatred like some, what awful deed this young man, or another in his place, might have wrought on March 4, 1861. What outcome to the Nation's fate? By what fateful chance avoided then. . .and yet not in April of 1865?

7

# ⚜ *Boardinghouse Manners*

What a difference between one President's inauguration and his successor's, just eight years later! The first in this pairing came on a sun-shiny day in a still-primitive capital city boasting all of 316 Federal patronage jobs awaiting the new chief executive's pleasure. A capital city of mud and swampland, no real streets, and a handful of houses so rudimentary a contemporary called them "small, miserable huts." A capital city with an incomplete Capitol and an unfinished President's House that had a privy standing outside.

But it was a nice day for March 4 of any year, pleasant and mild enough for the Nation's third President—tall, lanky and, for all his democratic leanings, aristocratic in looks and manner—to walk from his boardinghouse quarters to the Capitol for his inauguration. He wore a gray waistcoat over green breeches and gray woolen stockings for the auspicious, long-awaited occasion.

It certainly had been long-awaited, too! Not only for Thomas Jefferson himself, but for the entire onlooking Nation. The election in November of 1800 had been only the start, rather than the expected finish, for the campaign to fill the young Nation's presidency for the third time. The ticket nominally headed by Jefferson had defeated incumbent John Adams and running-mate Thomas Pinckney, a result unexpectedly producing an awkward tie for the presidency between Jefferson and *his* running mate, Aaron Burr—73 electoral votes for each.

With that outcome, the entire matter was thrown into the House of Representatives for final disposition. And there it took 36 ballots, from February 11 to February 17 of 1801, to produce a majority vote electing one man over the other. Fortunately for the Nation, the choice in the end was Jefferson.

The distinguished Virginian, already Vice President at the time, had spent the winter of political tumult at Conrad & McMunn's tavern and boardinghouse, C Street and New Jersey Avenue, with about 30 congressmen from his own Republican party (no relation to the Republicans of today, but a supportive and convivial company for the beleaguered Jefferson, to be sure).

The day of his inauguration, Jefferson walked to the Capitol, just a block or so. With him was a minor parade of soldiers and civilians, also on foot. Ostentation there was not.

He took his oath of office in the Senate Chamber, and it was packed by nearly 1,000 persons, said one eyewitness. "The Senate chamber was so crowded I believe not another creature could enter," wrote Margaret Bayard Smith, wife of a Jeffersonian political journalist.

Conducting Jefferson's swearing-in was his old enemy John Marshall, fellow Virginian and Chief Justice of the Supreme Court. Jefferson shook hands with his recent rival (and bitter enemy, too), the scheming Aaron Burr, now Vice President. Jefferson then read his inaugural address "in a manner mild as it was firm," said Margaret Smith. An address, not so incidentally, calling for unity. "We are all republicans; we are all federalists," he said, in reference both to his party and that of his political opponents.

It was only a short walk back to the boarding-house, and that is exactly where the new President headed rather than to the future White House. The President's House, as it then was called, wasn't ready for him and he wanted to spend some time at his beloved Monticello at Charlottesville, Virginia, anyway.

He sat that night at the bottom of the communal boardinghouse table as usual. By some accounts, there was little excitement over his official ascension to the presidency that very day. Little. . .except that a visitor from Baltimore, placed right next to Jefferson, was pleased with the coincidence and wished the new President well.

Jefferson allegedly smiled in response and had a ready answer. "I would advise you," he said, "to follow my example upon nuptial occasions, when I always tell the bridegroom I will wait till the end of the year before offering my congratulations."

In sharp contrast to Jefferson's thoroughly plebian inaugural day was the inauguration just eight years later—and its setting—for fellow Virginian James Madison.

While no throwback royalist, by far, Madison rode by coach to his inaugural ceremonies at the Capitol. An estimated 10,000 visitors crowded into the fast-growing Federal city for the august occasion, which included a gay, swirling Inaugural Ball staged that night at Long's Hotel in Georgetown. Madison delivered his maiden address as President in the Hall of Representatives at the Capitol, then held a reception at his own Washington residence.

Jefferson, still holding to his constraints but clearly delighted on Madison's behalf, declined his good friend's offer to ride up Capitol Hill in the coach. Jefferson instead rode his horse in the caravan of well-wishers following the Madison party. Offered a special chair to hear Madison's inaugural address, Jefferson declined that honor, too. "This day I return to the people," he said. And with the people he sat.

Jefferson did attend both the Madison reception and the ball that night. As an interruption, earlier in the day, however, he and Madison

9

had to hurry back to the White House to appear at a surprise reception given in Jefferson's own honor as a fond farewell gesture.

The tall, white-haired widower captivated and surprised many onlookers by his obvious mood of relief and gaiety. He and Madison's colorful wife Dolley—described by Washington Irving as "a fine, portly, buxom dame who has a smile and a pleasant word for everybody"—were the real rivals for the crowd's attention at the ball, rather than the diminutive new President Madison.

Afterwards, Jefferson reverted to form—he left Washington quietly, alone on his horse, for the ride back to Monticello, about 120 miles distant. He plugged on through a severe snowstorm and arrived about mid-March, says biographer Saul Padover. On the way, however, he repeatedly encountered farmers vigorously cheering him on and drinking to his health. And in his native Albemarle County, neighbors rushed to welcome him back from the presidency of his country...of their country.

## Bless This House

Living behind these impressive, imposing, sometimes intimidating walls all these years have been real people—men, women, children, and all with very human wants, needs, triumphs and tragedies on small and personal scale. Just like all of us. And the first of these, first of them all, were John and Abigail Adams, the nation's second President and First Lady.

Like many Americans in the centuries since, they underwent a job transfer of sorts in 1800 and moved into a new house that was far from finished—the White House. They shared the visions of future grandeur for the President's House—sometimes derisively called the President's Palace—but they also had to deal with concerns such as shopping at nearby stores, putting up the laundry, keeping warm and dry, and hoping that work on the outdoor privy would be complete in time.

John Adams, that stalwart from Revolutionary days, traveled down to Washington from their home at Quincy, Massachusetts, in advance. Abigail was still recovering from one of her persistent "fevers," but her husband was required in his new place of business in the fall of 1800.

Not that he had just been elected President. Not at all...it was just that the seat of government, the entire core of the Federal government, was moving from Philadelphia to the new capital "city" of

Washington in 1800, "city" not yet the true description for the scattered edifices beginning to rise from muddy flats by the Potomac River. And so, John Adams already had been through an inauguration—he had weathered that ritual in 1797 alone, with no family present. It was held in Philadelphia, before the House of Representatives, and for the occasion Adams wore a plain grey suit in the fashion of his day. He left home the sword that he often had worn as Vice President and presiding officer of the Senate.

George Washington, of course, was just leaving the Presidency, and like any two rational men he and Adams had struck a small deal beforehand—Adams bought some of his predecessor's furniture. And already, in the Nation's infancy, the price of serving in government could be high and inadequately reimbursed. "Every one asks and every one cheats as much as he can." Adams complained of the prices in Philadelphia. In Philadelphia, too, the "President's House" had not been ready in time for his inauguration.

Then, the night before, he slept badly. The day of his inauguration he felt awful "and really did not know but I should have fainted in presence of all the world." (Shades of George Bush in Japan two centuries later!) Adams even wondered whether he should simply take his oath and then say nothing, or linger to give a speech. In the end, he did the latter. . .and was off and running in his term as the second President.

Just three years later, on November 1, 1800, he was alone again while moving into the President's House in the new capital—he would be the first of all Presidents to sleep in the great house by the Potomac. (But not the first historic figure to do so. No, sir! John Marshall, Secretary of State, in need of lodgings, had lain down his head in the unfinished White House bedrooms for some weeks during late summer.)

The next day, November 2, Adams was able to summon Abigail with a somewhat false assurance: "The building is in a state to be habitable, and now we wish for your company."

All well and good, but in fact, with winter coming on, what was "habitable" in the incomplete structure were six damp and drafty rooms. And all around was the mud of construction, worker huts, the debris of unfinished work—with leagues of wild, new land lying between Massachusetts and Washington.

For Abigail the journey of more than 550 miles would take until November 16, unhappily punctuated by a stop in New York to visit their son Charles Adams on his deathbed (he died December 1 of cirrhosis). She and her party became lost outside of Baltimore, and approaching the site of the future capital city found—"nothing but a forest & woods on the way, for 16 and 18 miles not a village; Here and there a thatched cottage. . . ."

And what she found at her destination itself was far from the grand White House and grand international city of modern times. Georgetown, one mile from the new house, was after every rain "a quagmire." Even without that drawback, it was "the very dirtyest Hole I ever saw for a place of any trade, or respectability of inhabitants."

As for the "transferred" couple's new home, it was big; bigger than anything they had ever occupied; bigger than any house in young America, in fact. "Twice as large," she wrote, as their Meeting House in Quincy, but obviously, too, "this House is built for ages to come."

To keep warm and dry, the Adamses had to keep the fireplaces roaring, "or sleep in wet & damp places," but they had trouble with another mundane detail—finding cut wood for the fires. "Surrounded by forests, can you believe that wood is not to be had, because people cannot be found to cut and cart it. . . ."

They could turn to coal, but there was the problem of having grates made to fit the fireplaces. "We have, indeed," she wrote like a frontierswoman, "come into *a new country.*"

The prosaic intruded also in terms of the family wash—the laundry. Abigail Adams had to establish a "drying room," and she settled upon an unfinished but large chamber they called the "audience room." Today, the room she chose for her laundry is known as the East Room, where the bodies of seven future presidents later would lie in state, among other historical events.

One might wonder, more immediately, though, what John Adams thought, that first night alone, the first of all Presidents to sleep in the White House. Whatever he did think, he wrote to Abigail the next day with both the message telling her to come ahead and join him and a high and noble sentiment widely quoted ever since: "I pray heaven to bestow the best blessings on this house, and all that shall hereafter inhabit it. May none but honest and wise men ever rule under this roof!"

## ꙮ *Stepping Stone President*

Fate was not kind to the "Old Hero," as William Henry Harrison was called in his day, and it may have been his own inauguration that ended his presidential career before it really began. He was in effect a stepping-stone president—first to die in office, first to usher in a Vice President as the new President, and on top of all else, holder of the shortest presidential term on record—exactly one month, from March 4, 1841, to April 4, 1841.

A stepping stone in another sense also, he was the son of the Virginia patriot Benjamin Harrison, a signer of the Declaration of Independence, and he was the grandfather of a future President, again a Benjamin Harrison.

Coming in between, William Henry Harrison, at age 68, chose to deliver an inaugural speech of an hour and 40 minutes outdoors, with no hat and no heavy coat on an unusually bitter rainy and cold March day in Washington. He rode his horse, Old Whitey, down Pennsylvania Avenue, again with no overcoat and his hat held in his hand. That he caught cold soon after is usually attributed to his inaugural appearance—and to the possibility that the old Indian-fighter was no longer quite the man who had roamed the so-called Northwest Territory, a huge area that eventually spawned the states of Indiana, Illinois, Wisconsin and Michigan.

His presidential campaign had stressed—perhaps even exaggerated—his early triumphs, such as his defeat of the Shawnee Indian chief Tecumseh on the Tippecanoe River. With fellow Virginia native John Tyler on the Whig ticket as vice presidential candidate, Harrison had campaigned in 1840 on the slogan "Tippecanoe and Tyler, too." He used log cabins and cider as symbols intended to stress the frontiersman theme. The Harrison-Tyler combine, in fact, paved the way for many a modern political campaign by trotting out promotional placards, hats, effigies, floats and like tools of the present-day political trade. It stressed the stump speech, parades, banners, torches, campaign songs...all very familiar to us today. Tyler and Harrison, however, did NOT stress their mutual status as sons of Virginia, as indeed, scions of aristocratic Virginia families mutually born to a plantation life far removed from the Northwest frontier, both in spirit and geography.

The victorious Harrison could not fight off the pneumonia that developed soon after his inauguration. He had acted quickly to appoint a distinguished-looking Cabinet, with the famed Daniel Webster as Secretary of State, but Harrison succumbed soon after (April 4) to his illness, and John Tyler became the first U.S. Vice President to take over the Presidency because of a predecessor's death in office.

To the very last, it seems, few in Washington or the country at large quite realized the seriousness of Harrison's feverish sickbed.

He, himself, may have, though. Just two days before his death, he told a woman attending him: "Ah, Fanny, I am ill, very ill, much more so than they think me."

As a footnote to his short White House tenure, it also seems that Harrison's wife, the former Anna Symmes, was fated never to spend a day or night in the White House as First Lady. Unable to leave their "frontier" home and attend his inauguration due to illness of her own, she never did reach Washington in her brief role as the President's wife. His body came back to her instead.

## ⚓ *Early Blow For Lincoln*

Abe Lincoln's first term as President had hardly begun in early 1861 when the East Room of the White House became the setting for a body lying in state—just as Lincoln's own would be four years later.

The deceased in this case was a young man, not even 30, who had been a friend to the Lincolns in Springfield, Illinois; a campaigner for the presidential nominee, and then a frequent visitor to the White House in early 1861, with the Civil War about to explode. Young Elmer Ephrain Ellsworth even accompanied the President-elect to Washington for the first Lincoln inauguration.

Previously, although an upstate New Yorker by birth, he had "read law" in Lincoln's law office in Springfield. And he was a bit of a celebrity in those pre-war years—he and his U.S. Zouave Cadets of Chicago were famous for their tour of 20 cities in 1860, he, especially, as the drill instructor and as author of a *Manual of Arms for Light Infantry*.

Quite fond of the young officer, Lincoln gave him a position in the new administration—as Adjutant and Inspector General of Militia in the War Department. With the outbreak of war, however, Ellsworth hurried to New York City, where he raised the 11th New York Volunteer Infantry, or Fire Zouaves, most of the men recruited from among the city's firemen.

They were sworn in before Lincoln himself in Washington on May 5...two days later they were busy putting out a fire, but that action was incidental to coming events.

On May 23, Virginia seceded, and across the Potomac from Washington, in Alexandria, Virginia, was a hotbed of Southern sympathizers. Visible from the White House itself was a Rebel flag, and Ellsworth—now Colonel Ellsworth—told Lincoln that he and his Zouaves would see to it that the offending flag disappeared from view.

The next day, May 24, he and his men crossed the Potomac by boat and stormed the Marshall House in downtown Alexandria, the hotel defiantly flying the Rebel standard. In the shooting that erupted, both Ellsworth and hotel proprietor James W. Jackson were killed, their violent demise often called the first real bloodshed of the great conflict to come. Ellsworth thus became the first commissioned officer to die in the Civil War, while Jackson was ballyhooed throughout the South as a martyr to the secessionist cause. And on May 25, Ellsworth's body lay in state in the East Room of the Lincoln White House.

Lincoln, in the aftermath, had to write his first letter of condolence during the war period. Addressing Ellsworth's parents, he described the slain officer as "my young friend and your brave and early fallen child."

## 🦅 *President...In Secret*

Another time, another day, a gentleman from Ohio was sworn as President of the United States in the White House itself—and in secret.

No counterfeit, nor any political neophyte, he was the well-bearded Rutherford B. Hayes, Civil War hero, former congressman, former governor of Ohio, and now...19th President.

The history books will say that he was inaugurated on Monday, March 5, 1877. And, true, he was. But, in secret, he also was sworn in as President Sunday evening, March 4, in the Red Room of the White House.

It happened during a resplendent dinner party for 38 of Washington's most distinguished "celebrities," people such as Cabinet members and Supreme Court justices. The hosts were the outgoing President and his wife, Ulysses S. and Julia Grant. The dinner, while a "cover" of sorts, was real enough, lavish enough—20 courses served, along with a variety of drink to fill the six different wine glasses at each plate.

Incoming President Hayes and wife Lucy were there, too...but was he still *incoming?* Or now *President?* Just two days before, he didn't really know if he would be President at all!

The explanation is a combination of circumstance. First, the hotly fought election of 1876—the centennial year for America—had been so close that Republican Hayes trailed his Democrat opponent Samuel Tilden in the popular vote but *might* have the edge in the all-important electoral vote. Yet, here was fresh doubt—not only because of the closeness but also for the charges of chicanery in four Southern states. An electoral commission investigating the vote count and the charges of fraud gave its nod to Hayes only at the last possible minute—March 2.

Now, enter the calendar—Grant's term would expire Sunday, March 4. By tradition, the presidential inauguration was never held on a Sunday; it must await the next day, Monday, March 5. Technically, the country would not have a President in office for 24 hours, from *noon* Sunday to noon Monday. Although it had happened twice before in the nation's early history (James Monroe and Zachary Taylor skipped the first day of their respective terms by waiting a day for their inaugurations), such a hiatus would not now be desirable. With all the bitterness engendered by the last-minute decision endorsing Hayes, with street demonstrations cropping up in Washington, Grant felt it would be safer for Hayes to take office officially, if not publicly, on Sunday.

At dinner that night, the guests obediently began their promenade from the East Room, where they had been received, to the State Dining Room for dinner. Few noticed Grant and Hayes take another route, to halt in the Red Room. There, flanked by bowers of flowers, Chief Justice Morrison R. Waite administered the oath of office to Rutherford B. Hayes.

If all else was carefully prepared for the occasion, one traditional item was missing—no one had thought to provide a Bible. With no Bible immediately available, the swearing-in proceeded after all, to be followed the very next day by a full-blown inauguration, oath-taking and all, at the Capitol.

The President-for-a-day was still President! By the logic dictating the hurried and secret oath-taking the evening before, however, the nation really did go without a President for a while. Not a full 24 hours, but for the hours between noon Sunday and the minute of the swearing-in that took place in the Red Room at evening time.

# 🦅 *Hooting At Owls*

Frolicsome is *not* how this President of dour public countenance is best remembered today, this dedicated citizen—who the morning of his inauguration took occasion in his hotel room to dance before his wife while chanting in childish sing-song: "We're going to the White House today; we're going to the White House today."

• Who, when struck by his newly appointed Postmaster General Albert Burleson's black umbrella and stiff dignity, quickly nicknamed Burleson "The Cardinal."

• Who entertained his Cabinet in their second meeting with a tired joke—a convert presiding at an especially bitter religious debate was discouraged by the eggs thrown his way, drew a pistol and said, "This damn Job business is going to last just two seconds longer!"

• Who insisted that his family life would continue as it had before. "He wanted no weaving spiders in his household," wrote Arthur Walworth in his biography of this White House occupant. "Margaret's devotion to singing and Jessie's work for good causes gave him joy; and he shared in the ecstasy of Nellie as she lost her shyness in the bustle of the new life and gave play to frivolous girlish impulses [all three his daughters]."

• Who kept other family members close as frequent visitors to his new home, often as overnight guests (but scrupulously refused any of them, even his own brother, or *especially* his own brother, even a hint of a Federal job *anywhere*).

• Who liked a snappy game of billiards in the evening.

• Who chased up and down the White House corridors playing tag with daughter Nellie. Sometimes it was "rooster-fighting," instead.

• Who, despite his intellectual renown across the breadth of the land, favored for entertainment neither opera nor ballet nor serious theatre, but...vaudeville, "where he could himself become one of 'the people' to whom he was devoting himself."

• Who, unknown to his millions of recent voters, took great delight in self-operating the presidential home's small electric elevator, a functional box made ornamental with panels of mirrors.

• Who was known to go to his bedroom window at night when awakened by the owls hooting in the magnolia tree outside, pause and then hoot right back. In the morning, he would tell those at the breakfast table he had "hooted the hooters away."

• Who, his first night at the White House, admittedly through no plan of his own, slept in the Lincoln bed "without benefit of nightclothes." (The presidential trunk had temporarily disappeared, it seems. It was delivered at 1:00 a.m., too late to be of any help *that* night.)

• This President did have his idealistic vision, or set of visions, that he thought called for earnest example and a certain public image,

17

which indeed was somewhat less fun-loving than the private man seen by intimates.

Typical of the idealism and his more serious side, he was the first President since James Madison to order *no* inaugural ball. Why? "He disliked making himself and his family the center of social and commercial aggrandizement," wrote biographer Walworth. Typically, too, the night of his election, his expression had become "grave" when the early returns indicated he would win. After he had indeed won, tears were in his eyes, he fell into silences and he spoke of feeling "a solemn responsibility." Still, the next day, he stuck to old habits and went to watch his college team at football practice.

Fierce and bristling he also was in the insistence he must now have "a chance to think." He and his family fled to Bermuda while he took that time to think (and threatened to "thrash" a photographer impudent enough to aim the camera at daughter Jessie).

His, on the other hand, was "one of the briefest inaugural addresses in the history of the nation," reported Walworth, but also, "one of the most moving".

Despite the schoolmaster's mien, he was a man casual enough to tell his Cabinet members in their first meeting with him, "Gentlemen, I thought we had better come together and talk about getting started on our way."

Soon—a week after taking his Cabinet seat—newly appointed Interior Secretary Franklin K. Lane was able to write a friend: "The President is the most charming man imaginable. . . .There had been a particularly active set of liars engaged in giving the country the impression that. . . [he] was what we call out West 'a cold nose.' He is [on the contrary] the most sympathetic, cordial and considerate presiding officer that can be imagined."

So, there you have it—even then, Woodrow Wilson hardly was known to the greater public for frolicsomeness, joviality or casualness. Nor was it yet suspected in early 1913 that his would be one of the most dramatic presidencies of all, both personally and politically, with one crushing blow after another awaiting this surprisingly joyful man.

# ⚓ *Prophetic Words Repeated*

For slandering Andrew Jackson's wife Rachel, one Charles Dickinson was sent to his grave and Jackson was left with a bullet in his chest that would stay there, next to his heart, for the rest of his life.

The old talk—Rachel, don't you know, became a legally divorced woman only *after* marrying Jackson—surfaced again in Jackson's campaign for President in 1828, and it was with difficulty that Jackson restrained his impulse toward added duels in defense of Rachel's honor.

This was the first near-popular presidential election—the first in which the voters chose the electors rather than the state legislatures choosing the electors. And the political organization that Jackson built for the election was the beginning, the foundation, of today's Democrat Party.

Rachel, though, was terrified at thoughts of herself as First Lady of the land, as hostess of the Jackson White House. "For Mr. Jackson's sake I am glad," she told one well-wisher after his election. "For my own part I never wished it."

In addition, she told a visiting young Virginian, Henry Wise: "I assure you I had rather be a doorkeeper in the house of God than to live in that palace in Washington."

As events turned out, those were prophetic words.

During the election, she had held up under the occasional slander, but soon after, "Friends noted a relinquishment of courage, a lapse into melancholy," wrote Jackson biographer Marquis James. Nearly 40 years after her marriage to Old Hickory, the hero of New Orleans and Horseshoe Bend, the onetime frontier beauty was, sad to say, grown obese. Her breath coming in a wheeze, she obviously was not well. In November 1828, a local doctor began bleeding her.

All the while, and to her consternation, plans were being laid for Jackson's triumphal trip early in 1829 to Washington and the White House.

There was thought of Rachel staying home, at the couple's beloved Hermitage outside of Nashville, Tennessee, but their best advice was to avoid any seeming retreat from lingering gossip and for both to take their rightful place in the White House.

And so unfurled the banners of preparation—suggestions of travel in a coach drawn by six white horses, of grand farewells, of balls and banquets, and Rachel was overwhelmed, engulfed. That is when she told young Wise, recently married into a Nashville family, of her heavenly preference to that palace in Washington.

Friends rallied to help the President-elect's wife prepare herself—"The poor woman submitted to be borne off to Nashville to begin the process of measuring and fitting her unstylish form to attire deemed suitable for the first lady of the land," added James in his 1937 biography, *Andrew Jackson: Portrait of a President*.

Something terrible happened on the trip into town. By some accounts, she overheard a snatch of conversation "lamenting the impossibility of rendering presentable to official society this illiterate country woman." By another account, she ran into more of the old slander about herself and Jackson. Whatever the truth, her friends found her "'crouching in a corner,' terror-stricken and hysterical."

A few days later, she was treated at The Hermitage for muscle spasms of the chest and left shoulder and "irregular action of the heart." Three quick bleedings seemed to help, and Rachel Jackson fell asleep with her pain gone.

For the next three days, with husband Andrew Jackson nearly always by her side, she seemed to be recovering, but on Sunday evening, December 22, "she sat [in a chair before the fire] too long and was put to bed with a cold and slight symptoms of pleurisy."

Her doctors brought on a sweat with hot drinks, persuaded Jackson to find sleep for himself, and all retired...except for the patient. "Twice she had her maid Hannah help her to the chair by the fire and fill a pipe with tobacco." She sat in her night dress, and shortly before 10 p.m. was heard to say once more: "I had rather be a doorkeeper in the house of God than to live in that palace." It was the last time she would say it, for 20 minutes later, she cried out, "I am fainting," then collapsed in the maid's arms.

By the time Jackson and others responded to Hannah's screams, the mistress of The Hermitage—but never of the White House— was gone.

# Lincoln's Farewell to Herndon

Lincoln's leavetaking for Washington was done in an atmosphere of foreboding. Much like Christ approaching the Last Supper, Lincoln met with various of his own disciples, and there was much thought—much talk even—of death. This was in the days immediately before boarding the train out of Springfield, Illinois, for the fateful trip east to the White House.

He went, in the first week of February 1861, to visit his step-mother, Sarah Bush Johnston Lincoln, at her homestead in Coles County, Illinois. "Here, in the little country village, he met also the surviving members of the Hanks (his mother's) and Johnston (his step-mother's) families," wrote Lincoln's law partner William Herndon. "He visited the grave of his father, old Thomas Lincoln, which had been unmarked and neglected for almost a decade, and left directions that a suitable stone should be placed there to mark the spot."

The President-elect next stopped at nearby Charleston, official seat of Coles County and site of the fourth Lincoln-Douglas debate. Staying overnight, he spoke in the "public hall," recalling "boyhood exploits." Present were many who knew him in earlier years, even "as the stalwart young ox-driver when his father's family drove into Illinois from southern Indiana [in 1830]." One fellow recounted details of the wrestling match in which a very young Lincoln, fresh from flatboating on the Mississippi with a load of hogs, bested a local champ named Daniel Needham. Also in Charleston, a man showed up with a horse that young lawyer Lincoln had recovered for him in a civil suit.

They all had some sentimental tale to tell, said Herndon, but Lincoln's farewell to his step-mother was especially moving. "The parting, when the good old woman, with tears streaming down her cheeks, gave him a mother's benediction, expressing the fear that his life might be taken by his enemies, will never be forgotten by those who witnessed it."

As for Lincoln, "deeply impressed by this farewell scene. . . [he] reluctantly withdrew from the circle of warm friends who crowded around him, and, filled with gloomy forebodings of the future, returned to Springfield."

But now came a steady stream of old friends and well-wishers there, too. Some came from New Salem, Illinois, where Lincoln spent six years as a store clerk, town postmaster, county surveyor and, toward the end, student of law. These good citizens, too, had favorite Lincolnesque stories to recall. Hannah Armstrong, whose son was the "Duff" Armstrong whom Lincoln successfully defended in a famous murder trial, came to say goodbye and was "filled with a presentiment that she would never see him alive again."

He tried to laugh off her fears, saying, "Hannah, if they do kill me, I shall never die again."

Strange sounding talk today, but in the early 1860s the country was on the brink of civil war. Lincoln's election was controversial and often resented—more than talk, there were real plots of assassination brewing even before he took his oath of office.

Preparing to leave Springfield, he of course had to settle affairs with his law partner of many years, Herndon. Lincoln held off this poignant moment until his last day in Springfield.

He appeared in the afternoon, and they went over the books and a few pending affairs of mutual interest, then Lincoln plopped down on an old sofa against one wall and stared for some time at the ceiling. Neither man spoke.

Finally, Lincoln did break the silence. "Billy, how long have we been together?"

"Over 16 years."

"We've never had a cross word during all that time, have we?"

"No, indeed, we have not!"

They talked on—actually, it was Lincoln who rambled on companionably. "He then recalled some incidents of his early practice and took great pleasure in delineating the ludicrous features of many a lawsuit on the circuit."

Lincoln also mentioned that others had tried to take Herndon's place as his partner—"weak creatures," added Herndon in his famous biography of Lincoln, "who, to use his own language, 'hoped to secure a law practice by hanging to his coat-tail.'"

Others have written that Lincoln on this same occasion made oblique reference to Herndon's reputed love of "the bottle," but did not chastise his longtime partner.

For his part, Herndon here says, "I never saw him in a more cheerful mood."

Lincoln soon gathered his papers and books and prepared to leave. First, though, "he made the strange request that the sign-board which swung on its rusty hinges at the foot of the stairway should remain." It should stay "undisturbed," said Lincoln. He then lowered his voice. "Give our clients to understand that the election of a President makes no change in the firm of Lincoln and Herndon. If I live, I'm coming right back some time, and then we'll go right on practicing law as if nothing had ever happened."

After a last look at their offices, Lincoln went into the outside hall, followed by Herndon. They went downstairs. The mood was somber. "He said the sorrow of parting from his old associates was deeper than most persons would imagine, but it was more marked in his case because of the feeling which had become irrepressible that he would never return alive."

Herndon tried to discount such wild thoughts and cheer him up, while others on the street outside frequently interrupted to say their own farewells to the remarkable local citizen going to Washington as President.

Finally, Lincoln broke away. He and Herndon shook hands warmly..."and with a fervent 'Good-bye' he disappeared down the street, and never came back to the office again."

# 🦅 *Auspicious Change*

Upon the arrival of Teddy Roosevelt, wife Edith and their six children in 1901, the White House entered an uncommonly tumultuous era—with teenager Alice, oldest of his children and born of an earlier marriage, the ringleader.

The tone may have been set when she arrived with a blue macaw called Eli Yale, famous for a mean peck "that could crack a whiskey glass," and a green snake called Emily Spinach.

The menagerie did not stop there, either. When young Quentin was ill one time, his brothers and sisters smuggled his pony Algonquin to his upstairs room by elevator. "This cheered up the ailing brother immensely but caused consternation among members of the White House staff," wrote Alice's biographer Howard Teichman many years later.

The Roosevelt clan would always be remembered by the staff for other activities, too—such as roller-skating, bicycling and even stilt-walking throughout the large home at 1600 Pennsylvania Ave.

And not only staff memories! Alice, it was reported some years later, persuaded her siblings to "attend" various state dinners—not in any ordinary and visible way, but rather by crawling along under the tables "pinching the knees of friends and begging them for food." These were memories for world leaders to keep, too.

Perhaps there was method to Alice's assignment to a large bedroom and dressing room right across the hall from her parents' bedroom suite! More seriously, Teddy Roosevelt, as one parenting penchant, told his famous daughter that she must delve into a new book every night before bedtime and learn something from it, no matter how late the hour, then tell him the *something* at breakfast the next morning. And indeed she always was well informed.

In the meantime, the Teddy Roosevelt occupancy made history even for so famous an edifice as the presidential home in Washington, D.C. Moving in on the heels of the abruptly widowed Mrs. William McKinley's departure, the Roosevelts found drabness the order of the day—an exterior of buff or gray and interior furnishings that Alice called "Late Grant and Early Pullman."

Setting to work with energy and zeal, the Roosevelts discarded potted palms, faded silk screens, old stained-glass windows, and brought in light. They painted and wallpapered. They had a master sculptor from Sicily carve the marble capitals of the outside pillars; they had the famous American architect Stanford White work his magic with the front of the stately building. They added the West Wing, now so well known for its Oval Office, created in point of fact by Teddy's successor, William Howard Taft.

Most famously of all, Teddy ordered the outside walls painted white once more. His presidential stationery was given the heading, "The White House." And so it OFFICIALLY has been ever since—the White House!

## 🦅 *Bachelor Status Ended*

Built like a well-fed shoat, the man who moved—alone—into the White House in 1885 was a sitting duck for gossipmongers, snobs and critics of all stripe. He was a middle-aged onetime sheriff, a reformer who progressed up the political ladder from sheriff to Mayor of Buffalo, New York, to Governor of New York, to President. He was the first Democrat to occupy the White House since Lincoln was first elected in 1860. He came on the heels of six Republicans in a row.

A minister's son, he recently had been forced into public acknowledgement of an illegitimate child.

A bachelor with little experience in "society," thick and brutish looking, he excited no great expectations in Washington, especially in the town's more exclusive social circles. After his inauguration, a Cleveland newsman found it interesting to write about how big a man the new President was, while Wisconsin's Senator Robert La Follette commented on the reformer's "coarse face, heavy, inert body."

With the bullyboy look went a brusque manner and a hard stare that alienated or even frightened some people. Others were unhappy to know that he had no Civil War record of service.

How could this man win over those who watch the occupants of the White House? How could this bachelor approaching 50 years of age even begin to gain the confidence and affections of his countrymen?

At first all they knew about him was that he was very businesslike; he did plunge into his new job as President and work long hours at it. He also was scrupulously honest in just about everything he did. And he brought in his sister Rose to serve as acting White House hostess for him. She a spinster, he a bachelor, they held down a very quiet White House, except for the most obligatory social events.

All so dull, dull, dull. . . .

But Rose, a feminist, teacher and writer of verse, soon won many a social lion's heart. . .even while her President brother pursued his Great Secret.

As for that matter—that secret he carried in his heart—could any of the gossipmongers have anticipated this serious, all-business, unblinking man of 48 would have a secret love? Would be planning to wed while in the White House?

Would wed a girl still in college and 27 years his junior!

But that was Grover Cleveland's plan, his earnest intention, even if he himself was afraid of the ridicule. . .of the inevitable "Beauty and the Beast" thoughts that would cross the public mind.

The demure beauty was the daughter of his late law partner Oscar Folsom—he had known Frances since her infancy, literally, and when her father had died in a carriage accident in 1875 he had been like a kindly, supportive uncle to the grieving child of 12 and her mother.

Oddly, you might say, the illegitimate son he acknowledged, a boy just about the same age as Frances, carried the name Oscar Folsom Cleveland—after both law partners. His mother was a widow. As in the case of Frances, Grover Cleveland "was there" for the youngster in the way of financial support.

But. . .back to the lonely Cleveland White House, where early in his term the new President would wake up at night "and rub my eyes and wonder if it was not all a dream."

In the meantime, he called the dark-haired Frances Folsom "Frank." She and her mother visited their friend Grover in the White House in the spring of 1885, then the young woman visited other times at the invitation of Miss Rose. The President and the college girl—for that's where she was, in college—also corresponded, with her mother's permission.

The young woman was a student at Wells College in upstate New York, due to graduate in 1886, but she moved the date up to 1885. Cleveland was delighted but regretful that she next would spend months touring in Europe. Before she could leave, he asked her hand in a letter. Secretly, that is. She said yes, and they planned a small, circumspect wedding upon her return in nine months.

A news leak now tabbed *Mrs.* Folsom as the lucky lady, but that soon was clarified. . .and the word was out. The news and gossip that initially sprung up just as quickly died down in the young woman's absence, however, and Cleveland had until June of 1886 to make his circumspect wedding plans, now turning to another sister, Mary Hoyt, for advice.

The White House would be the setting, it was decided, a scheme that at the least would keep it all private, controlled and out-of-bounds to the press—the "dirty gang," as he called reporters.

25

Frances returned from Europe aboard ship on May 27, 1886, to be met by a tugboat in the New York harbor and whisked in secret to a hotel in the city. The next day, she and her betrothed communicated by telegraph, since they couldn't yet resort to long-distance telephone calls. And that night, their engagement was announced officially.

On May 29, the future bride's hotel was a mob scene. Cleveland was on his way to New York to review parades marking Memorial Day, the 30th. He paid a call on his fiancée the evening of May 29, with more good-natured mobs cheering him on. He stayed the night at Navy Secretary William C. Whitney's home, and at the Manhattan parade the next day, he was on the reviewing stand, and she was on her hotel balcony two blocks away, and she waved her 'kerchief, and he saw, and tipped his hat. The crowds and the 19th-century "newsies" loved it all.

For the wedding June 2, Frances traveled down to Washington by train that very morning (more crowds, more press), spent the day at the White House and married the President in a 1:00 p.m. ceremony held in the Blue Room, richly banked with flowers, flowers, and more flowers. There followed dinner in the State Dining Room. They spent their honeymoon, accompanied by unwelcome minions of the press, at a mountain resort in Maryland.

The newlyweds returned to Washington in timely fashion, but not simply to the White House. By now, Cleveland had bought the big rambling farm mansion near the National Cathedral they would call Oak View. This President, first to marry in the White House itself, would have at his disposal both a private residence in Washington and the all-too public Executive Mansion.

# ✹ *Ike's First 'Crisis'*

Inauguration Day for Dwight D. Eisenhower—first Republican to come along in a long, long time, what with FDR's unprecedented four election victories and Harry Truman's unexpected election in 1948—was, naturally, a happy day. And a long day for "Ike," replete with one minor crisis.

His more public events of January 20, 1953, had begun with a church service at 9:30 am, at the National Presbyterian Church. Twenty minutes there. The ride to the Capitol with Harry Truman shortly after was a bit uncomfortable. They exchanged some sharp words.

Eisenhower took his oath of office at 12:32 p.m., it is recorded for historical posterity. He shook hands with the outgoing Truman and then crossed the platform overlooking the crowds in the east plaza of the Capitol to kiss his wife Mamie, the new First Lady. Let it be known her eyes were full of tears. Perhaps his were, too.

The inaugural parade that soon followed would have stretched for 10 miles if all units had lined up at once and stood still for posterity's measurements. In any case, it took more than five hours to pass by the Eisenhower reviewing stand.

Mamie was an appreciative audience, alternately waving, smiling, clapping, blowing kisses, even, it is said, giggling. She, late in the cold afternoon, accepted the offer by the old man next to her to share his lap robe for warmth. He was the last Republican to have occupied the White House before Ike. . .before FDR and Truman, for that matter. He had been ousted way back in 1932. He was Herbert Hoover— by now, in 1953, 78 years in age.

All this time, Ike himself had been standing to review his parade. Salutes every time a new unit passed by flourishing the proud colors. Many units, many salutes, for the general-turned-President.

Then, parade finally over, the new First Couple was driven to the White House. They entered their new quarters at an exact moment, 7:02 p.m., the day's minor crisis sneaking up to them by now.

For the next three hours, Mamie was busy in their new home preparing for the evening's two inaugural balls. She fully intended to put her best foot forward, and in Ike's eyes, she surely did. "By golly, Mamie," he said when she presented herself to him, "you're so beautiful!"

For Mamie's all-important inaugural appearance that evening, designer Nettie Rosenstein had created a Renoir-pink, rhinestone-studded gown of *peau de soie,* with an evening bag of matching pink silk adorned by rhinestones, pearls and beads within a silver frame. As further reported in *Ike and Mamie: The Story of the General and His Lady* by Lester and Irene David: "Beneath the gown's bouffant skirt were taffeta and crinoline petticoats; on her arms, almost to the shoulder, were silk gloves; on her feet, fabric shoes. Taffeta petticoats, gloves, shoes—all were of the pink silk."

Ike now was ready to get dressed, too. It was getting late, time to move on, even after such a long, demanding, exciting but wearing day. And so, finding his way about the unfamiliar quarters they had moved into, he began poking and prying about. . .searching, actually. But he couldn't find the essential item he wanted.

"Hey, Mamie," came the plea, "where the hell is my monkey suit?"

But no one knew. Neither Mamie nor his valet. "They searched the closets and the still unpacked bags without success while the new President of the United States sat on the bed in his shorts and growled that the first crisis of his administration had already occurred," summed up the Davids in their book.

The answer to the puzzle finally was supplied by Mamie, her guess right on the mark. His white tie and tails must still be on the train they took the day before to reach Washington. And surely enough, when Ike's valet and a Secret Service man "raced" to the railroad station and looked through the Eisenhower car of the day before, there was one errant suitcase awaiting its rightful owner. And it did contain the missing "monkey suit."

And so. . .one crisis averted!

Ike's next "crisis" was even more minor and easily solved. It came the next day. Early.

He rose at 7 o'clock despite the late night and the long hours of the day before and took the small White House elevator down from the second-floor family quarters to the ground floor. There he encountered Secret Service Agent Rufus Youngblood. Ike was itching to get started in his new job as President.

Only one minor problem.

"Would you show me where my office is," he had to ask. "I want to get an early start."

# ♛ *Coolidge's Favorite Prank*

The swearing in of Calvin Coolidge, like those of Harry Truman and Lyndon B. Johnson, was sudden, without pomp and totally lacking in advance planning. For hours, in fact *Vice President* Coolidge didn't even know his President and fellow Republican, Warren G. Harding, was dead.

Harding, under circumstances that some thought suspicious, died suddenly while traveling on the West Coast. In the East, Calvin and Grace Coolidge were visiting his father's humble farmhouse in Vermont—no telephone, no electricity. Coolidge was notified of his new status at 2:47 a.m. on August 3, 1923, by newspaper reporters traveling 20 miles to stir up this national story.

Wasting no time, the Coolidge family quickly gathered—in night-shirts, that is—around a table lighted by a kerosene lamp and bearing the family Bible. As a notary public, the elder Coolidge legally could swear in his son as President. Which he did.

The younger Coolidge then faced the press for the first time as President of the United States. His reaction to the night's events? "I think I can swing it," said the famously taciturn Coolidge.

The Coolidges moved into the White House after a stay at the Willard Hotel in Washington giving Mrs. Harding time to pack up and leave...but the new man was not quite as dour and reticent as he often is made out to be. His two teenaged sons, Calvin Jr. and John, gave the White House a breezy sense of youth once again—and Coolidge himself was not above an occasional prank, it seems.

"He would press all the buttons on his desk and then hide behind a door in his office. Secretaries, military and naval aides, assistants of all sorts, Secret Service men with drawn revolvers would rush in from all directions. Out from behind the door would step the President," wrote Howard Teichman in his biography of Alice Roosevelt Longworth, *Alice*.

Like presidential families before and after, the new occupants had a menagerie with them. In this case, the dogs and cats wore collars with White House name tags; a raccoon named Rebecca lived in a special cage, and a flock of chickens was kept in a coop near the august presidential mansion.

It was Coolidge's order that only his own chickens would be served at his dinner table. "His command was carried out to the letter, but the Coolidge chickens had a curious minty taste. Investigation showed the chicken coop stood atop an old mint bed planted by Alice's father [Teddy Roosevelt]. The coop was moved immediately."

## 🦅 *First In Line*

For his first inauguration as the Nation's first President, the Virginian George Washington wore brown broadcloth, a suit that was woven in Hartford, Connecticut, and he had buttons emblazoned with an eagle, its wings spread. He wore his very best white stockings of silk. Silver buckles adorned his shoes, and as befitted a general to be hailed even by Napoleon, there was a dress sword in a scabbard of steel.

Soon after his breakfast on that April 30, the city's church bells began to ring—at first cheerfully, but soon more somberly, it has been observed, since their purpose was a call to prayer.

Naturally, there were the excited crowds. The pomp and ceremony. The official escorts. The inaugural speech—as the very first, it was likely to be a trend-setter.

The swearing in and *speechifying* would be at the place where Congress met, true...but this place, in 1789, was not the scene in Washington, D.C., that we know so well today. This inauguration took place in the Federal Hall overlooking Broad Street and Wall Street. In New York City, that is, since there was no Federal City of Washington as yet—and, for the official presidential residence following the inaugural festivities, no White House as yet, either.

## 🦅 *Harry Homebody*

Throughout his career in public office—even as Senator, Vice President and President—Harry S. Truman was one to keep in close touch with family and old friends "back home." He wrote to his elderly mother every three or four days, often with pithy comments on the great issues or towering public figures of the day, and he kept up his old ties in other ways, too.

The April evening he unexpectedly became President, due to Franklin Roosevelt's sudden death, Truman had planned to play poker with his old World War I artillery compatriot Eddie McKim and others in a Washington hotel. Cancelled, of course. Just three months later, though, *President* Truman's informal activities before and during the Potsdam Conference with Stalin and Churchill were still typical of the man.

Crossing the Atlantic aboard the U.S. cruiser *Augusta,* he soon found a distant relative among the crew—"Lawrence Truman from Owensboro, Kentucky, who was the great-grandson of Grandfather Truman's brother," reports daughter Margaret in her biography simply titled *Harry S. Truman.* But that brief encounter would not be the full extent of her presidential father's extracurricular interests at Potsdam, it seems.

Using a "scrambler" phone, he called Margaret and her mother, Bess, in their hometown of Independence, Missouri, almost every one of the 17 days he spent with Stalin, Churchill (and Churchill's successor as British Prime Minister, Clement Atlee). "He never mentioned affairs of state. It was just family chit-chat. Even when he was trying to settle the problems of the world, he kept in touch with his family in Missouri," wrote Margaret years later.

At Potsdam also, Truman issued a presidential order stopping U.S. Army Sergeant Harry Truman—the President's nephew—from boarding a troopship on his way home from war-devastated Europe. The same order "whisked him [the nephew] to Potsdam for several days of high-style relaxation."

Truman also was able to visit his cousin Ralph's son Louis—Colonel Louis Truman. By family "networking," he then found himself a White House doctor. "He heard that Wallace Graham, son of his old family doctor of the same name, was stationed near Potsdam, and invited him over for a visit."

Truman was so impressed with the young man, he asked him forthwith to be the White House physician. But the "intensely idealistic" Graham tried to demur. "I want to take care of as many people as possible, not just one man."

"Even if that one man is the President of your country?"

"I've got a hospital full of men who've shed their blood for their country. I can't leave them."

In the end, they worked out a Missouri compromise. Doctor Graham stayed with his Army hospital unit until all his wounded patients had left for Stateside wards or had recovered. He later reported to his new White House post with Truman's agreement that the good doctor could keep up his surgical duties at Walter Reed Army Hospital in Washington.

Potsdam was Truman's first big international conference as President, an occasion of "instant" friendship kindled between Truman and Churchill, but tough confrontation and disillusionment with wartime ally Stalin. Serious issues, such as prosecution of the war with Japan and the fate of post-war Europe, were on the table, but still there were light moments to break the tension—one of them supplied by another old Truman pal.

Back in Washington earlier, U.S. Treasury Secretary Henry Morgenthau had resigned his post because Truman refused to include him in the Potsdam entourage for various political reasons. The party that did go of course was studded with many others of highest possible rank...but it also included "an old Missouri follower, Fred Canfil."

Who was Fred Canfil? Stalin's aides and even the KGB must have searched their dossiers on American officialdom long and hard to find this obviously very important American's pedigree. Who was he, then? "Fred had been a county courthouse employee when Dad was elected county judge, and he attached himself to Harry Truman with total devotion and loyalty," wrote Margaret. "Built like a bull," the old courthouse retainer from Missouri "had a voice which could shatter glass at a hundred paces."

For Canfil, the trip to Potsdam in such exalted company no doubt was the thrill of a lifetime, especially the moment when old friend Harry Truman called Canfil over to meet Stalin himself. "Marshall Stalin," said Truman, "I want you to meet Marshal Canfil."

Due to a certain President's recent appointive action, Fred Canfil indeed was a "marshal," not the all-important Soviet-style marshal, but a U.S. Federal Marshal. Truman, of course, saw no reason to explain it all to Stalin and *his* entourage. "From that moment forward," said Margaret, "the Russian delegation treated Fred with enormous respect."


# 🦅 *Press Conference Tactics*

When JFK replaced Ike in the White House, the minions of the press had to change press conference tactics to suit the new man's personality and style. For the reporters, the name of the game was to be noticed by the President. And, of course, to have a pithy question at the ready for the moment the presidential lightning struck. *Might strike,* that is.

The stalwarts of the *New York Times* had it pretty well doped out back in the early '60s.

Dwight David Eisenhower, a more elderly man than successor John F. Kennedy, tended to start on one side of the press conference site— and stay there.

The first question, therefore, very nearly decided which side of the room would get in all the questions. Purely a random guess in advance. At the same time, there was a protocol that granted *some* favors—the "wires," for instance, Associated Press, United Press, Reuter, and so on, provided nearly instant access to an audience of millions. They had White House respect.

Beyond the lopsided room ploy, Ike had three other quirks worth noting, each often dictating journalistic strategy.

Quirk No. 1: He didn't recognize too many reporters by name, so he would give the nod to "you with the glasses there" or "that man with the bald head."

Quirk No. 2: His mangled syntax, of course, was notorious— almost as well known as Casey Stengel's. Not known for their reverence, the post war reporters covering Ike had a cruel jibe for him (and/or his speechwriters) on the occasion of a globe-circling presidential trip—"Around the World in 80 Platitudes."

Quirk No. 3: Nor were there any sympathetic tears shed when poor Ike ran afoul of Sarah McClendon in his press conferences as President. Here, far from the battlefields of Europe, was a challenge utterly foreign to Ike. Neither West Point nor the Crusade in Europe had quite prepared him.

Wrote *Times* reporter W.E. Kenworthy:

"There was one sure way of getting in a question with Eisenhower. That was to wait until Sarah McClendon asked one of her outrageous questions. Amidst the ensuing laughter, Eisenhower, red-faced and suffocating with exasperation, would practically embrace the reporter who at that moment rescued him by jumping up and saying, 'Mr. President.'"

With the advent of the JFK years, the *Times'* Washington Bureau adopted new tactics to suit the new man's style.

For one thing, his eye roved across both sides of the room. That meant dispersing the troops. Tom Wicker, the paper's White House beat man, had an automatic seat front and center, first row. He was "certain to be recognized," along with the wires, also up front.

Kennedy could be expected to rove up and down the first three or four rows—but how, even then, to catch his eye? "With Kennedy," wrote *Times*man Kenworthy, "it's strictly a matter of timing—you must begin to rise as his finger begins to fall, and just as it is wagging his afterthought you must come in fast and he will say, 'Yes?'."

The typical JFK press conference called for careful planning, especially late in the day and close to the morning paper's early-evening deadline. For the *Times*men, longtime columnist and political savant James ("Scotty") Reston in those days was "presiding inquisitor" in the strategy huddle held in his Washington Bureau office.

The strategy was to eschew the obvious and most basic questions, since they quickly would be disposed of by the news-agency reps. What the *Times*men instead must pose were the follow-ups, the less obvious issues. They developed a list of perhaps six or more questions. They even calculated the right wording "to entice or force a responsive answer." (With Ike, but no longer with JFK, it had been necessary to set the stage for the question with background information as a reminder.)

The questions assigned in advance, the *Times'* crew of five to seven reporters would arrive in a large black limousine for the JFK press conference, usually held in the State Department auditorium before at least 250 onlooker-reporters. With JFK's arrival after his own staff briefing session, the questions would fly fast and furious. Then, it was off to meet the deadline. First, though, a copy boy had obtained the first few pages of the official White House transcript of the press conference—the rest of the session's every utterance to be ready in less than 30 minutes from the closing "Thank You, Mr. President."

Armed with these first pages (the copy boy staying behind to retrieve the rest) and their own notes, the *Times* reporters flew back to the bureau offices in the same limo—usually all together, still in a pack.

The man to write the lead had been selected, and the early transcript pages were his meat, especially if the lead stemmed from a presidential announcement. In the seven-minute run back to the Bureau, the *Times*men divided their spoils, their news editor up front in the limo and facing the passengers in the rear.

"He flips through his notes, conferring with Scotty," wrote Kenworthy." The lead is obvious—nuclear test ban. 'John, you take that.' 'Tom—politics.' 'Tony, civil rights.' 'Max, Laos and wrap the rest of the foreign stuff with paramarks.' 'Jack—McClellan and the TFX.' So it goes. By the time the car reaches the office, the conference is cut up." And so...another presidential press conference, far different from the onetime gatherings of a few familiars at the presidential desk in the Oval Office, has made history.

## 🦅 *Lincoln Escapes A Trap*

Desperate, bizarre—but no more so than shooting a man in a crowded theatre. This plot, too, was aimed at that most controversial of American Presidents, Abraham Lincoln. Just elected, he had to go to Washington to take his "seat," did he not? Traveling east from his home state of Illinois, the country lawyer-turned-President was committed to a number of speaking engagements.

In the late winter of 1861, the country was in turmoil over the slavery-secession issue. Civil War loomed, and the rail route from Pennsylvania to Washington would take Lincoln straight through a hotbed town of Southern sympathy—Baltimore.

Was Lincoln himself concerned? Was there real danger? In Philadelphia, discussing the Jeffersonian commitment to equality in the Declaration of Independence, Lincoln said: "I was about to say I would rather be assassinated on the spot than surrender it [the equality provision]."

34

He made the remark at Independence Hall the morning of February 22, 1861—and assassination *was* on his mind, unavoidably so. Just the night before, he had refused entreaties to head for Washington right away, rather than to maintain his planned speaking engagements. Lincoln said no, he would appear both in Philadelphia and before the Pennsylvania legislature in Harrisburg prior to resuming his rambling trip.

He had been en route to Washington for days and days, actually, with well-advertised stops at a train conductor's litany of towns— Indianapolis, Cincinnati, Columbus, Steubenville, Pittsburgh, Cleveland, Buffalo, Albany, New York City. He had been traveling since a poignant farewell to his hometown of Springfield, Illinois, on February 11. After telling his neighbors he was leaving them "for how long I know not," Lincoln, his trademark beard only recently grown, stood in the rear door of the rear car as his train gathered head for the trip east. It was "his last view of Springfield," noted his law partner and biographer William Herndon.

"The journey had been as well advertised as it had been carefully planned, and therefore, at every town along the route, and at every stop, great crowds were gathered to catch a glimpse of the President-elect," said Herndon also.

But that was in the North, and in the South, Lincoln already was a hated man; in the South, delegates from the secessionist states already had met in Montgomery, Alabama, to form a provisional Confederate States of America.

In the meantime, officials of the Philadelphia, Wilmington and Baltimore Railroad had been hearing rumors of sabotage and other threats to their railroad by Southern sympathizers hoping to cut off Washington, the Federal capital, from the North. The railroad hired detective Allan Pinkerton to investigate; Pinkerton and his operatives soon focused upon Baltimore, where even the police chief was known as a Rebel at heart.

In short order, posing as a broker—and Rebel sympathizer—from Charleston, South Carolina, Pinkerton visited Baltimore in person. He and his aides heard a Baltimore local drunkenly reveal the outlines of an advanced assassination plot. To wit: Lincoln would arrive by one train at the city's Calvert Street station, and while carriages took his party across town to the Baltimore and Ohio station for the train to Washington, the killers would strike. Said this source: "I am ready to do the deed and then will proudly announce my name and say, 'Gentlemen, arrest me. I am the man!'"

And there was even more evidence to impart—as Lincoln worked his way toward Washington, 30 conspirators met in Baltimore the night of February 20. They were told to pull slips of paper from a hat in a dark room—whoever emerged with *the* red ballot was the man to do the job, and no one else would ever know which one he was. Ominously for Lincoln, the leaders of this group cheated by placing eight red ballots in the hat, rather than just one. Since all 30 had taken an oath to carry out the killing, that would mean eight sworn killers on Lincoln's trail, rather than just one.

Still other details being reported to the Lincoln party pointed to the Havre de Grace ferry carrying the Lincoln train across the Susquehanna River as an obvious place for an outright attack.

Informed of the growing conspiratorial atmosphere, Lincoln nonetheless insisted upon going through with his plans for February 22. Thus, he made his appearance at Independence Hall in the morning, then journeyed to the state capital of Harrisburg for visits with both branches of the legislature and dinner with the governor of Pennsylvania, Andrew Curtin.

Lincoln was stubborn...but he wasn't about to be foolhardy. Lincoln would go through with the Philadelphia and Harrisburg schedules, he told his lifetime friend and advisor Norman B. Judd, but, "After this, if you, Judd, think there is positive danger in my attempting to go through Baltimore openly according to the published program, I will place myself in your hands."

And so it was that instead of spending the night of February 22 at the Jones House hotel in Harrisburg, Lincoln was spirited out of town in a single-car train. He was in the very able company of Ward H. Lamon, a burly, heavily armed Virginia-born lawyer who was a close friend from the Illinois courts. Judd in the meantime, had arranged to intercept all telegraph and railroad wires leading out of Harrisburg.

The escape route first took Lincoln to Philadelphia, and there he boarded a sleeper on the regular Washington-bound express—but in a disguise. Joined by Pinkerton and his operatives, Lincoln boarded the rear of the sleeping car posing as a sick man. He and his companions then rode through the rest of the night in three adjoining rooms, with Lincoln, Lamon and Pinkerton seated together in the center one. Delays forced the train to lay over in Baltimore for a tense hour, but they passed through with no change in trains. Before that, the ferry crossing-point was successfully negotiated. Pinkerton men were everywhere on the route south, flashing signal lanterns to show that all was in order immediately ahead.

Lincoln's enemies apparently never did guess that he was on the night train, and he arrived in Washington at 6:30 a.m., February 23, hours ahead of the publicly announced schedule. All the while, it seems, Lincoln had been regaling his tense companions with typically Lincolnesque homespun stories. Pinkerton later said, "I could not then, nor have I since been able to understand how anyone in like circumstances could have exhibited such composure."

History in time would reveal Baltimore as the place where local hotheads *did* attack Union soldiers passing through town in April of 1861, killing several; as the place where hostile men concocted and set in motion still another plot that *would* result in Lincoln's assassination—in a crowded theatre just four years later.

In the meantime, though, at this journey's end in 1861, the famously imperturbable Lincoln rose from his sleeper-car seat and told his worn, somewhat frayed companions of the long night, "Well, boys, thank God this prayer-meeting is over." Two weeks later, Abraham Lincoln was inaugurated as President of the United States.

## 🦅 *Daily Mission Accomplished*

Issuing forth from the great house morning upon morning was a determined young man on a mission for the President and his household. It would be embarrassing if he failed...and a culinary delight when he succeeded.

He prowled pathways destined to become today's streets, alleys and avenues in his search. Then, back then in 1801, they were woodland paths or trails across open fields, or perhaps muddy roads meandering through shrub. And the young man, soon to establish himself as one of the all-time great explorers, was Thomas Jefferson's private secretary, Meriwether Lewis, that young protege who also hailed from Albemarle County where Jefferson had built his beloved Monticello.

They were close enough that Lewis arrived at the unfinished White House soon after Jefferson's inauguration of March 4, 1801, and took up his duties in his employer's *absence*. For Jefferson had retreated to Monticello for about 30 days when Captain Lewis of the U.S. Army led his pack horses overland from Detroit to take up his posting at the side of the third President. The White House was so far from finished even after John Adams had decamped that Jefferson stayed on at his boarding house in Washington for 15 days after his inauguration, then left for his month-long stay at Monticello. Further work on the White House was to be completed by the time he returned. And one thing he wanted done quickly as possible, if not by the 30-day deadline, was to remove that outdoor privy the Adamses had installed, for all the world to see, and replace it with a pair of more private and seemly water closets installed *inside* the President's House.

Lewis, though, already used to rough and ready ways, would "rough it" as a White House aide, confidant, messenger and secretary to Jefferson. He would be given space screened off in the large public room later known as the East Room. There, makeshift partitions provided a small bed chamber and a small office space for the young man. Jefferson's own office, habitually used after he returned from Albemarle, was at the opposite end of the house, at the west end of the long transverse hall.

This Lewis was the same, yes, who with William Clark would set off on a three-year exploratory journey across the continent that opened up the West as no other single event. The famous Lewis and Clark Expedition proved the feasibility of overland travel all the way to the West Coast.

Young Lewis already was an outdoors type before his sojourn in the White House—he had hunted 'coon and 'possom alone in the Virginia woods at night at the age of eight. And now, even, in such sophisticated a setting as the President's House, he was able to keep up his outdoorsman skills in one vital aspect—it was his daily mission, leaving the White House in the early-morning mists, to hunt down and kill game for the household, hunting on land today covered over with brick and tar and concrete, streets and edifices, in the teeming universal-center city surrounding the President's House of a simpler day.

# 🦅 *Public Housing*

At 7 a.m. the day *after* his swearing-in, wife Betty recorded in her diary, "the President of the United States, in baby-blue short pajamas, appears on his doorstep looking for the morning paper, then goes back inside to fix his orange juice and English muffin. Before leaving for his office, he signs autographs on his lawn."

It will be nine or ten days before they move into the White House. In the meantime, they'll continue to live in their suburban just-us-folks house on Crown View Drive in Alexandria, Virginia, across the Potomac (and then some) from Washington.

Normal life will *not* resume, however. "At 10 a.m., an aide from the White House phones the wife of the President of the United States in Alexandria, and says, 'What are you going to do about the state dinner?'"

State dinner? Who, when?

Just a visiting king, it turns out, Jordan's King Hussein. And in six days.

Staggering thought...but then, hasn't it all been somewhat staggering? First the mid-term appointment to Vice President in October 1973, replacing a resigning Spiro T. Agnew. Then, before even moving into the official vice-presidential residence in town, Richard M. Nixon's sudden and unprecedented resignation from office on August 9, 1974. As a result, longterm Michigan Representative (and House minority leader) Gerald Ford vaulted in just months from his suburban Alexandria neighborhood to the White House.

Except, as new First Lady Betty Ford recorded in her diary that tumultuous summer, it all happened so fast...and they wouldn't be moving into the White House until young David Eisenhower and wife Julie Nixon Eisenhower could finish packing up the Nixon belongings. "They must have labored morning, noon and night," to get the job done in just ten days, wrote Betty Ford later, but they did it.

In the interim, she did play official hostess at the state dinner for King Hussein and his American-born queen. Betty Ford also toured the White House on August 13 and picked a second-floor bedroom for herself and Gerald Ford, while daughter Susan chose the third-floor bedroom, sitting room and bath that David and Julie usually stayed in when visiting the Nixons. On moving day itself, August 19, both President and Mrs. Ford flew to Chicago on Air Force One for his speech before the Veterans of Foreign Wars, then returned to Washington.

"When we get to Andrews Air Force Base, a helicopter picks us up and takes us directly to the White House," adds her present-tense diary at this point. "It's the first time, and it's a very strange feeling."

In the meantime, there had been that fuss over Betty Ford's statement that "Jerry and I were *not* going to have separate bedrooms at the White House and that we were going to take our own bed with us." That caused "a good deal of whooping and hollering," she acknowledged in her later book, *The Times of My Life* (written with Chris Chase).

That night, the first night there, she and "Jerry" crawled into their controversial common bed..."and Jerry looks around and laughs. 'It's the best public housing I've ever seen,' he says."

# 🦅 Born There

They were born in the White House itself.

• Unnamed slave child, Thomas Jefferson term, born 1806 and died 1808. Born 11 months earlier, perhaps the first of all, was a grandson to Jefferson, James Madison Randolph.

• Another presidential grandchild was Mary Louisa Adams, born December 2, 1828, to John Adams II, son of President John Quincy Adams (and grandson, himself, of a President, his own namesake John Adams).

• Soon after, during widower Andrew Jackson's term, four children were born in the White House to Jack and Emily Donelson, he a nephew of the late Rachel Jackson and secretary to the President; and she, cousin Emily, a niece of Rachel and official hostess of the White House in her Aunt Rachel's place.

• Next, in March 1840, Martin Van Buren's daughter-in-law Angelica had a difficult delivery with infant daughter Rebecca. Angelica, a cousin to Dolley Madison, recovered, but the infant daughter died in the fall of 1840.

• Then, during the Mexican War and the James K. Polk administration of the 1840s, presidential nephew and secretary James Knox Walker moved into the White House with his wife and two children—they promptly had two more while living at the White House.

• Five decades later came an occasion never to be matched before or since, a President's child born in the White House. To Grover and Frances ("Frank") Cleveland, little Esther, born September 9, 1893...and so zealously protected from the public eye that no attempt was made to scotch the story that Esther was deformed.

• Another grandchild born in the White House was Francis B. Sayre, Jr., born to Woodrow Wilson's daughter Jessie on January 17, 1915, half a year after Ellen Wilson's death in the White House. Jessie Sayre at the time was living in New England, but she returned to the White House for her baby's birth. This was where she once had lived...it also was where she was married to her attorney husband in an elaborate White House wedding in late 1913.

# *Middles*

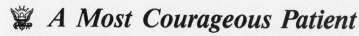 # A Most Courageous Patient

With the country in a financial panic, the stricken President's surgery should be carried out quickly and secretly, it was felt in the White House. And that is the way it was done—on a yacht cruising the East River in New York City, with the doctors on board ducking out of sight to avoid recognition by some sharp-eyed intern at Bellevue Hospital on the Manhattan side of the river.

The story begins on May 5, 1893, when President Grover Cleveland, fresh in a second White House term, first noticed an odd "rough spot" on the roof of his mouth. He didn't do anything about it at first, but by mid-June it was bothering him and he called in the White House physician, Dr. Robert M. O'Reilly.

What O'Reilly found was very serious indeed—a cancerous growth extending from Cleveland's upper teeth on the left side to nearly the center of his mouth. A surgeon called into the case, Dr. Joseph Bryant, urged fast action. "Were it in my mouth," he told the portly Cleveland, "I would have it removed at once."

At the time, however, the country was gripped by economic crisis, the Panic of 1893, a period of railroad failures, mortgage foreclosures, collapsing stocks and dangerously low gold reserves. And then, on June 27, the New York Stock Market crashed. Cleveland called for a special session of Congress to deal with the crisis—but he had to delay the date until August 7 to allow time for the secret operation on his mouth.

Was such secrecy really necessary? According to Cleveland biographer Allan Nevins, "the knowledge that Cleveland's life was in danger would have precipitated a new and far greater panic." A strong, healthy and confident Cleveland was needed for the fight against the Sherman Silver Purchase Act, seen as a major cause of the depleted gold reserves. "The whole strength of the assault upon the Sherman silver-purchase clauses lay, as everyone realized, in the grim determination of Cleveland's purpose. His weight of character could force enough members of the party [Democrat] into line, and nothing else could. Even temporary incapacitation might be fatal to his aims, while if any accident suddenly removed him from the scene, all would be lost; for the Vice President, Adlai E. Stevenson, would infallibly bring the nation to the silver standard."

And so, the well-meaning conspirators laid their plans. Bryant lined up a medical team for the oral surgery to be performed upon the President: Dr. W.W. Keen of Philadelphia, an eminent surgeon; Dr.

43

E.G. Janeway, general practitioner, and Dr. Ferdinand Hasbrouck, dentist, both of New York, along with Bryant's own assistant, Dr. John F. Erdmann. Bryant coordinated the details with White House doctor O'Reilly and Daniel Lamont, Cleveland's former private secretary and now the Nation's Secretary of War.

In the meantime, E.C. Benedict, close friend and New York City neighbor to Cleveland between his two Presidential terms (1885-1889, 1893-1897), agreed to provide his yacht the *Oneida* for the surreptitious enterprise.

Lamont and his wife accompanied the presidential party to New York on June 30, traveling by car. The group boarded "Commodore" Benedict's yacht at Pier A—quite openly, since it would be no surprise for Cleveland to enjoy Benedict's sea-going hospitality. He had done so before.

After all were aboard, including the various doctors and their equipage, the yacht remained anchored for the night in Bellevue Bay on the East River. It was here that Bryant "warned the medical staff to keep out of sight, lest they be recognized by the interns at Bellevue Hospital."

Cleveland was a good patient and apparently resigned to placing his fate in the hands of those aboard the yacht. He had asked earlier if he would *look* markedly different after his surgery; he was told the major sign of his secret operation would be a speech defect, but he would not look abnormal.

Any surgery under a general anesthetic of course carried risks, but with Cleveland the doctors were more than normally concerned about how he would react to the anesthetics involved—nitrous oxide and ether. He seemed to be strong and healthy, but he was 56, "very corpulent...and of just the build and age for a stroke of apoplexy," to say nothing of the stress he had had to face since moving into the White House for a second time just four months earlier.

Whatever fears Cleveland may have had personally, he sat in a deck chair and "chatted until nearly midnight" the evening of June 30, then slept in his berth without the help of sedatives, reported Nevins in his two-volume biography, *Grover Cleveland: A Study In Courage.*

The next morning to all outward appearances began quite normally for a presidential sojourn aboard a friend's yacht—"newspapers were taken aboard and there was a leisurely breakfast."

But soon the staff cleared out the salon to make room for the operation, and the yacht raised anchor. At half speed or so, it cruised up the East River. "The anxious Dr. Bryant told the captain, 'If you hit a rock, hit it good and hard, so that we'll all go to the bottom!'"

Cleveland, propped up in a chair against the mast, "went under the anesthetics after some innate resistance."

After the dentist Hasbrouck removed two left upper bicuspid teeth, Bryant began the surgery on the roof of Cleveland's mouth. In 31 minutes, adds the Nevins' account, "they removed the entire left upper jaw from the first bicuspid tooth to just beyond the last molar, and took out a part of the palate; this extensive operation being necessary, writes Dr. Keen, 'because we found that the antrum—the large hollow cavity in the upper jaw—was partly filled with a gelatinous mass, evidently a sarcoma.'" Actually, writes Nevins, "it was a carcinoma."

With no external incisions necessary nor any of the surgery affecting his eyeball, Cleveland would appear fairly normal, but he later would need an artificial jaw of vulcanized rubber to maintain normal appearance (and speech).

The surgery ended at 1:55 p.m., and Cleveland was given a shot of morphine to help him rest comfortably in the immediate aftermath. "What a sigh of intense relief we surgeons breathed when the patient was once more safe in bed hardly can be imagined," wrote surgeon Keen later.

Two days later, Cleveland was on his feet again while Benedict's yacht continued on its course for Buzzards Bay on Cape Cod, where Cleveland kept a summer retreat called Gray Gables. "And when on July 5 the *Oneida* after five days of cruising, dropped anchor in Buzzards Bay, he was able to walk from the launch to Gray Gables with little apparent effort. On July 17, there was a second brief operation to remove some suspicious tissue, from which Cleveland quickly recovered. Dr. Keen pronounced him the most docile and courageous patient he ever had the pleasure of attending."

A recovering Cleveland then did press his fight for repeal of the Silver Purchase Act. . .and won! The country nonetheless did suffer four years of severe depression. In the meantime, the public "gradually learned something of the ordeal he [Cleveland] had been through."

Not for "almost a quarter century," however, would all the salient facts be known in what Nevins called "one of the dramatic minor episodes of American history."

# 🦅 *Writing the Great Document*

In December of 1861, Lincoln spoke that word, that thought, to Senator Charles Sumner, Massachusetts abolitionist, but with the caution: "Don't say a word about that." And no wonder...in a country already badly rent by civil war it was an issue that could tear even more. He would have to creep up on its blind side, even though, and perhaps *because,* others already were tossing around that word and fighting over it.

Various Senators in fact urged Lincoln to take his stand, make his move...even the Confederacy, it was feared, might take the dramatic step, if only to win recognition from England and France.

Always, though not yet time, it was in Lincoln's mind. And finally, in the summer of 1862, when things were going dismally for the Union armies in the field, he wrote a draft. He presented it to his Cabinet, and his thinking on the timing of the great event was this: "Things had gone from bad to worse, until I felt that we had reached the end of our rope on the plan of operations we had been pursuing; that we had about played our last card, and must change our tactics, or lose the game...I now determined upon the adoption of the emancipation policy, and without consultation with or the knowledge of the Cabinet, I prepared the original draft of the proclamation, and after much anxious thought, called a Cabinet meeting upon the subject." *Emancipation*!

Rarely, though, had Lincoln been so wrong in his political instincts. And it was Secretary of State William Henry Seward who pointed out the problem. Such a moment *after* a string of military defeats for the Union was no time to attempt such bold step. "His [Seward's] idea was that it would be considered our last *shriek,* on the retreat." Far better, argued Seward, to wait for military success, then issue the dramatic policy statement.

And so, Lincoln did "put the draft of the proclamation aside." And thankfully so, since right after, John Pope lost the second Battle of Bull Run. But then, late in the summer, came the Battle of Antietam, a fearful slaughter also close outside of Washington, yet this time with a Northern tilt to the outcome. Lincoln was then staying at the Soldiers' Home three miles out of town, and there he finished writing a second draft. He invited his Vice President, Hannibal Hamlin, for a supper at the Soldiers' Home one night after Antietam, then took him behind closed doors in the library and read Hamlin the document. "Now listen while I read this paper," said the recent circuit-rider from Illinois. "We will correct it together as I go on." He did, they did, and the Cabinet heard the results on September 22, 1862.

At that meeting, the course of the great document's development and issuance was determined, and that is the real-life story behind it...except for one little detail—a man, an old friend, named Swett, Leonard Swett, attorney-at-law back home in Illinois.

Still in the throes of finding his path, the right path, some months before, Lincoln had sent to Bloomington, a two-day train trip away, for his old friend and fellow trial lawyer from a legal circuit so rustic they occasionally had been required to share the same bed when traveling to try cases. Told by Carl Sandburg in his *Abraham Lincoln: The War Years,* the tale is that the President took Swett into the Cabinet Room at the White House, talked for a moment or two about mutual friends, then got down to the business at hand—emancipation. Yes, *that,* and yet, it wasn't much of a discussion, really. Or perhaps it was—but a one-sided discussion, in which Lincoln did all the *discussing.*

He pulled out first one letter (pro-emancipation), read it aloud to Swett, then another (anti), and yet a third (also anti). Lincoln then "began a discussion of emancipation in all its phases." As Swett listened, Lincoln went on and on. "He turned it inside out and outside in," wrote Sandburg. "He reasoned as though he did not care about convincing Swett, but as though he needed to think out loud in the presence of an old-timer he knew and could trust."

After an hour or so, Lincoln stopped, wished Swett and their mutual friends back home well and ended the interview. He never asked his friend for any comment, but it was only *after* this session that the Great Emancipator laid his historic decree before his Cabinet, the country...the world. *The Emancipation Proclamation.*

## 🗽 *End to An Affair*

As ambassador to England in the 1850s, James Buchanan employed a colorful aide named Dan Sickles as secretary of the U.S. Legation, a controversial choice since Sickles, among other indiscretions, once refused to rise for the entrance of Queen Victoria at a formal dinner.

In Washington just a few years later, "Old Buck" was President and the prickly Sickles was a House member from New York City. Married to a very young bride, and with little visible signs of support, Sickles indulged in a grand residence on Lafayette Square, across the street from his old boss, mentor and friend Buchanan in the White House.

Few would have guessed, despite Sickles' many, many past indiscretions, that he one day would shoot a man almost at Buchanan's doorstep...and "Old Buck" would urge an eyewitness to the murder to leave town in a hurry. But...it did happen that way.

After coming to Washington in 1857, Sickles, 37, plunged into politicking, and one of his first actions was to urge the reappointment of Philip Barton Key, a casual acquaintance, as U.S. Attorney for the Federal city of Washington. Even more casual, was Sickles' innocent introduction of his wife Teresa to Key at Buchanan's inaugural ball in 1857. As the pair danced no one among the onlookers thought any more of the chance meeting.

In the months ahead, life in the Nation's capital was a whirlwind of activity, political and social, for the impetuous young congressman. His wife Teresa was more privy to the social entertainments than the political, and since her congressman-husband was often busy with more serious business, she often was escorted by the dashing U.S. Attorney, son of Francis Scott Key. In the fall, wanting to entertain on a more lavish style than their hotel quarters permitted, Sickles leased the fine Stockton Mansion on Lafayette Square, that very upscale address across Pennsylvania Avenue from "Old Buck."

Sickles never hesitated to drop in on his friend the President, while also staffing, furnishing and stocking his fine home in a manner far beyond his obvious financial means. The Sickles couple entertained frequently in their new quarters—with Key a frequent guest.

Key's presence in fact caused social comment, not because he was the handsome widower thrown in with the extraordinarily young wife of the busy congressman, but because he represented Southern aristocracy at a time when the grand house of the Union was developing cracks and fissures over the slavery and states' rights issues. It just seemed odd that such an intimate of so many Southerners in the capital would spend so much time in the company of a brash Yankee congressman of somewhat dubious reputation. In the next two years, though, Key did spend time...more and more of it.

As Sickles won a second House term, the nation's political stew was close to boiling—and Sickles seemed closely aligned with the Southern bloc in the House.

At his own house in the Square, however, other things were coming to a boil, and rumor to that effect brought a confrontation with Keys and wounded denials. Sickles appeared fully assured. "I like Keys," he told a confidant. "This thing shocked me when I first heard about it, and I am glad to have the scurrilous business cleared up."

But it wasn't. Only two blocks from the white-brick mansion in Lafayette Square was the intersection of Fifteenth Street and Vermont Avenue, and on Fifteenth Street, in a rundown neighborhood near that corner, was an empty brick house, No. 383. The man renting the innocuous abode in the fall of 1858 was Key, and the furtive,

48

shawl-wrapped woman who sometimes met him there was Teresa. Except for their clandestine meetings, the house remained empty.

The neighbors noticed and one of them eventually found out the woman was Mrs. Sickles. At Teresa's home, the servants also were becoming aware of the affair. Not only did Key visit or escort the lady of the house on social calls, quite frequently, but he signalled her from points in the Square with a white handkerchief.

"By midwinter," writes Sickles' biographer W.A. Swanberg (*Sickles the Incredible*), "the 'secret affair' was known, though perhaps not to its full extent, by almost everybody in Washington except for one person—Daniel Sickles."

An anonymous tipster took care of that omission with a note disclosing the existence—and purpose—of the house of Fifteenth Street. There came a night of confrontation in the mansion, accompanied by sobs and unearthly groans from Sickles. A servant and a visiting friend were called in to witness Teresa's full written confession.

The next morning, a Sunday, Sickles managed to shave, but he was "seized with paroxysms of sobbing." He sent for two friends and greeted them with bloodshot eyes.

He told them the facts, and all three debated what he should do, personally—and of course politically, since such scandal could be absolutely ruinous. Sickles, pacing the floor, stopped at a window and looked out, unthinkingly.

His two companions saw him pause, speechless. Across the way was Philip Barton Key himself, handsomely dressed as usual and waving his white handkerchief at the upper windows of the Sickles house.

For Key, it was incredibly bad timing.

"That villain," shouted Sickles, "is out there now, making signals!"

Sickles grabbed a pistol and dashed out. He accosted Key before more than a dozen witnesses. "Key, you scoundrel," yelled Sickles. "You have dishonored my bed—you must die!"

The wronged congressman took aim, fired and missed. Key ducked behind a tree. "Don't shoot," he entreated. He hurled his opera glass at Sickles, to no avail.

The congressman fired again. Struck this time, Key tumbled into the gutter with a scream, begging for mercy. "Sickles fired again—some witnesses said twice again," reported Swanberg. "Then he walked up to the prostrate figure, aimed the weapon pointblank at Key's head, and pulled the trigger. But the gun misfired, and suddenly several passersby came to their senses and stayed his hand."

Samuel Butterworth, one of the two friends conferring with Sickles moments before, took the congressman by the arm to lead him away. But not before Sickles asked, "Is the damned scoundrel dead yet?"

A witness to the shooting was a White House page, J.H.W. Bonitz of Wilmington, North Carolina.

"Old Buck's" first thought, of course, was shock when the young man raced into the White House to tell him what had just happened in the Square outside. But then Buchanan rallied and suggested that his page should leave town.

"He told young Bonitz that as an eyewitness he would be held in jail without bond unless he left Washington immediately. He presented Bonitz with a razor as a personal memento, and a sum of money for more practical purposes, and advised him to clear out of town...Unacquainted with the law, he [Bonitz] did not know that he would not have been jailed, nor did it occur to him that Buchanan's motives might have been to remove a witness whose story could be damaging to Sickles."

So reported biographer Swanberg, but hardly anything could have been more damaging to Sickles than his own actions and words before many of other witnesses. And yet, in modern parlance, he "got off," fully acquitted of a killing he made no attempt to deny. It wasn't merely that the prosecution, deprived of its "first-string" in the form of Key, had to rely upon a fumbling substitute. Nor was it entirely the embankment of eight "high-ranking" lawyers representing Sickles in his murder trial. What saved Sickles was not even having Edwin Stanton, the future Secretary of War, among his many attorneys (although Stanton treated the often sobbing and emotional Sickles "with the greatest solicitude even as he heaped ridicule on the prosecution, browbeat the judge, and spoke with feeling of the sanctity of the home"). Rather, the successful defense in Sickles' case was a legal "first"—an early and apparently unprecedented use of temporary insanity as grounds for dismissal.

And so, the hot-tempered congressman was set free; Buchanan in 1861 gave way to Lincoln, and in the Civil War that followed, Sickles reappeared on the national scene as a minor Union general...but one quite honorably wounded at Gettysburg.

#  A Swim in the Potomac

The U.S. Navy, at the start of World War II, didn't have much use for the large but rather unseaworthy yacht it had bought from wealthy businessman Hugh Chisholm. She had no watertight compartments, was a bit unstable and couldn't carry heavy guns. No surprise, then, that she was "beached" for the duration.

Even so, the *Williamsburg,* steadied considerably by the addition of pig iron in her bilges as ballast, would find glory of sorts in postwar years, a bit inland and upstream from her lonely berth in Norfolk, Virginia.

She cruised and she cruised, in her element at last, up and down and across the Potomac River off Washington, D.C., for the most part. She now had a full crew, upright pianos, and a dining room with tables that could handle 30 persons. She had a lounge and two bedroom suites with bath, plus sitting room, and of course many lower-deck compartments for added passengers.

Almost everywhere she went, she had an escorting "fleet" of two smaller yachts, the *Margery* and the *Lenore.* It was the *Lenore* that carried the Secret Service fellows, and of course the patron to whom the *Williamsburg* owed new life and fame was President Harry S. Truman.

"President Truman loved this yacht and used it to full advantage," recalled its former skipper, Rear Admiral Donald J. MacDonald, at the time a commander by rank. "He often told me, 'It's just wonderful. In ten minutes I'm away from everything.' Several times a week he'd call me—he had a direct line—and say he'd be coming to lunch."

If Truman didn't bring guests, he simply asked MacDonald to join him. The future admiral thus had a ringside seat for many of Truman's major decisions as President. One time, while debating what to do about headstrong General Douglas MacArthur's actions in Korea, Truman, obviously "bothered," asked MacDonald what *he* thought.

"Well, Mr. President," said the Navy man, "you can't be boss in a military organization and have people not carry out the orders, or you lose control."

As events proved, Truman obviously came to the same conclusion—he fired MacArthur.

They also discussed Truman's tough, wartime decision to use the atomic bomb against Japan. "He seemed a bit haunted by the power he'd unleashed, but it was just another one of those momentous decisions he had to make."

An Army man all the way (he served in the U.S. Army Field artillery in France during World War I), Truman thought Chief of Staff George Marshall, whom he made Secretary of State, was great. "And he thought that since General Eisenhower was Army, he must be great, too."

As Truman thought about the pending end of his second term, he had high hopes for Ike—hopes that *he* would run for President as a fellow Democrat. "He said he wanted to groom Eisenhower to follow him," and, "it just about broke his heart when, all of a sudden, Eisenhower shifted to the Republican Party."

Mainly, however, Truman repaired to his yacht as an escape from the pressures of the White House. He would rise early in the day, spend the morning at his work ashore—at 1600 Pennsylvania Avenue—then arrive at the yacht at the Washington Navy Yard (then called the Naval Gun Factory) in time for lunch. Next came a nap on board. And afterward a rubdown by a Navy pharmacist's mate who was a masseur. Finally, back to the White House about 4:30 p.m.

The *Williamsburg,* while seldom bracing the ocean itself, was not strictly a dockside yacht, it should be emphasized. There were the weekends. There were the poker games. And there were the weekend poker *extravaganzas.* "Sometimes he'd come down on Thursday. He'd have poker parties that night, still at the dock, and then about midnight some of the people would leave, and the rest of the players would continue on down the river with him."

MacDonald would guide his craft and its coterie of Truman guests about the Potomac River, usually stopping off Quantico or Blakistone Island. A seaplane often zoomed in with papers and mail demanding fast presidential attention. Sometimes, the seaplane unloaded a fresh squad of poker players!

Truman, it seems, had essentially three sets of poker friends, and all three groups had their own kind of game. The "high-flyers," personages such as Chief Justice Fred Vinson, or Agricultural Secretary Clint Anderson or George Allen, head of the Works Project Administration, played high stakes—no limit. Secondarily, "there was a sort of $700-limit group." And lastly, "when no one else was available," Truman played with staff members, aides, and other old friends, with a $100 limit usually in force.

Whatever the case: "He loved to play and he often won. It relaxed him."

Unbelievably, that was a period of such calm innocence that the President of the United States could pop into the Potomac and take a swim, undisturbed and usually uncontaminated by pollution.

"When we used to anchor off Blakistone Island and Mr. Truman wanted to go in for a swim, who'd be standing to watch him but me and my executive officer. The Secret Service would be standing up on the deck, but they wouldn't be in a position to go in and save him. Truman wore his glasses all the time that he was swimming. He'd keep his head up while he was paddling around."

As for the pollution possibility, "Before he went in I'd take samples of the water, because even then the pollution was drifting down the Potomac."

It was all so different, as MacDonald said in an interview years later for the U.S. Naval Institute's oral history program. "When he wasn't napping or playing cards, President Truman was often up on the bridge with us, or sitting on the deck. Boats would come alongside and wave to him, which he seemed to enjoy. The boaters were just thrilled to see him. It was a different time, and no one thought of taking a pot shot at him."

So very different....

# 🦅 *All the Way With LBJ*

Traveling with LBJ could be entirely unpredictable.

The Australian Prime Minister, Harold Holt, had drowned. It was shortly before Christmas in 1967, and LBJ decided he would attend the funeral. In Australia, naturally. He took along advisers McGeorge Bundy and Walt Rowstow—obviously Vietnam could be a possible stop on the way back from that part of the world.

And that *is* what LBJ had in mind, yes. But there would be more to the unannounced and unplanned itinerary. Why not see the President of Pakistan, too? Why not visit the Pope at his Vatican in Rome on the way back from the Down Under funeral of the Australian Prime Minister as well?

Why not indeed? Air Force One pilot James Cross was first alerted as the White House entourage hit Australia for Stop One. "As we arrived at Canberra just a little after daylight," recalled Cross later, "the President came in the cockpit. He said, 'Cross, we'll leave here in about 36 hours. You make some plans to go maybe up to Vietnam....'"

Maybe Thailand, too, Johnson said. Maybe Ayub Khan...and maybe a little Christmas doings with the Pope—the unsuspecting Pope—in Rome, too.

"But now don't go telling anyone."

At the end of the 36 hours, the President of the United States more or less had vanished from sight, so far as the world could tell. He now was on *unannounced* travel—first to visit American Air Force personnel in Thailand, then to spread Christmas cheer among the troops at Cam Ranh Bay in Vietnam itself. The next stop was Karachi, for the visit with Ayub Kahn.

In Rome, meanwhile, the crowds already were gathering for the annual and solemn pageantry of Christmas. And Cross, still operating on the "QT," was doing his best to line up "fuel and ground communications, as well as ground transportation, so that we could go into Rome without tipping our hand that we were going."

The idea of all the secrecy was to avoid a Communist demonstration, apparently, and indeed, "the Communists never realized we were there."

On Air Force One itself, in the meantime, LBJ kept denying his plans. He sat on his exercise bicycle, bigger than life as usual and said: "I ain't going to Rome. I don't know what you're talking about."

He sat on the exercise bike, which was bolted to the floor, and kept denying the plan, recalled *Time-Life* correspondent Hugh Sidney. "Only Johnson could conceive that on Christmas Eve [not quite the 24th, actually—it was the 23rd still] he would drop in unannounced on the Pope."

In the end, in Rome, he did concede that was the plan. In the end, without telling his own American Embassy, Johnson did whirl into the Eternal City, literally whirled by helicopter into the Vatican gardens, and did visit Pope Paul VI. One point was to ask papal help on behalf of the American POWs held by Hanoi and another point, more generally, was to dramatize the U.S. desire for peace in Vietnam.

The onlooking reporters were bemused, and more, as Johnson and the Pope exchanged gifts—the Pope had been able on short notice to produce a Renaissance oil painting, while Johnson presented His Holiness with a large package wrapped in plain brown paper and tied with thick rope.

When the Pope couldn't pull the rope loose, Johnson came up with a jackknife, Sidney also recalled. "He flicks open the blade, rips the package, excelsior springs out all over the Oriental rugs and everything else. The press is over in the corner and by this time we are in a state of shock."

In seconds, the Johnsonian Christmas present to the Pope was out in full view—a bust of LBJ himself!

Johnson and his entourage were back in Washington—he of course at the White House—well in time for Christmas Eve, 1967, after 4½ days of whirling, unannounced for the most part, around the globe.

# 🦅 *Rebel in the House*

Unrepentant and unreconstructed was the old Confederate-loving codger who lived in one corner of the White House, who regaled the press with his "inside" stories, who sat next to the President's wife at dinner, who even then could be scathing in his remarks and unawed by any company—especially that of the President. Who in fact was his own son-in-law.

Old "Colonel" Frederick Dent was not about to change his spots—or dispense with his mint juleps—just because he, a Democrat from Missouri, was moving into the White House a decade after the Civil War with daughter Julia and her Republican President-husband, Ulysses S. Grant, surely the most *Yankee* Yankee of them all.

He not only was a White House fixture after the Grants moved in, he accompanied them on family vacations and even on an ooca-sional political foray.

He could say very embarrassing things regardless of who was present at the presidential dinner table, and one of his favorite victims apparently was the President's own father, Jesse Grant. Dent called him "that old gentleman" and once complained in the elder Grant's presence, "he is feeble and deaf as a post, and yet you permit him to wander all over Washington alone."

Ten years younger than the 80-plus Rebel, and a bit sharp-tongued himself, the elder Grant heard and replied: "I hope I shall not live to become as old and infirm as…Grandfather Dent."

Jesse Grant usually passed up a White House guestroom and took a local hotel room instead, saying the presidential home held too many from "that tribe of Dents."

Indeed, the "Colonel" or "Judge," as he alternately was called, had a space all his own in the office suite on the second floor. It was here, indeed, that he often held forth for visitors from the gossip-hungry world of the press. (It was also at the dinner table, even at his beloved daughter's very elbow, that he often espoused his more embarrassing opinions.)

He occupied a bedroom close to the North Portico. And there he died one night in his own bed. His coffin then rested for a time in the "Yankee" White House, final stopping place for an ex-slaveowner from Missouri.

# ♔ *Poker Players, Do Your Duty*

Winston Churchill's famous Iron Curtain speech took place in Fulton, Missouri, and thereby hangs a tale of presidential travel by train (Harry S. Truman), really serious poker and a factor in Anglo-American relations to be determined by the fall of the cards (or, more accurately, the kindly disposition of the card-players).

The "factor," one to be handled with awe, reverence, respect *and kid gloves,* was Winston Churchill himself, recently the political hero and stout leader of his country during World War II but now displaced as Prime Minister by the British electorate, although due to serve again just short years ahead.

The presidential train left Union Station in Washington in early afternoon of March 4, 1946, for the overnight trip that would place Churchill at the podium of Westminster College in Fulton, Missouri—Harry Truman's home state—the next evening. Traveling quite comfortably in Truman's private railroad car, sofas and easy chairs at their disposal, were not only Truman and Churchill, but U.S. Admiral William D. Leahy, General Harry Vaughan, Clark Clifford, Charlie Ross, all Truman aides, confidants and advisors, plus Colonel Wallace Graham, the President's physician.

Truman and Churchill already had settled the matter of calling each other by first names, had shared drinks (no ice in his Scotch for Winston) and were having dinner when the subject of poker came up. According to Clark Clifford's autobiography *Counsel to the President* (written with Richard Holbrooke), it was Churchill who broke the ice by saying: "Harry, I understand from the press that you like to play poker."

And Truman allowed that such a report could be true, yes. "I have played a great deal of poker in my life," he acknowledged.

Churchill, claiming to have started *his* poker while covering the Boer War as a newspaper correspondent, was just delighted. When he suggested they all get up a game, Truman acceded with a warning—"the fellows around you are all serious poker players."

Churchill hustled off to change into something more comfortable— "his famous World War II zippered blue siren suit." Truman took advantage of the visitor's absence to enjoin his troops. Just as Nelson at Trafalgar signalled his fleet that England expected every man to do his duty, Truman now told his American colleagues that they faced a serious challenge. "Men," he said, "we have an important task ahead of us. This man is cagey and is probably an excellent player.

The reputation of American poker is at stake and I expect every man to do his duty."

In the game that ensued, it turned out that Churchill "was not very good at the game" after all. Perhaps a whiz at gin or bridge, he was to poker as a lamb is to wolves, it seems. In fact, in present company, he *was* a lamb among wolves.

In an hour, he had lost about $300. Then, as Churchill excused himself for a moment, Truman had to back up and tell his associates they were not treating Winston very well.

Vaughan snorted: "This guy's a pigeon" and said, "If you want us to give it our best, we'll have his underwear." But Truman delivered fresh marching orders: "I don't want him to think we are pushovers, but at the same time, let's not treat him badly."

And so, Churchill was allowed to win a few hands that evening. At one point, in a game of stud poker, Charlie Ross had an ace showing on the board and a second one in his hand.

Churchill had only a jack showing but kept on betting despite the one visible ace, clearly outranking his jack. "Then," wrote Clifford, "at the end, Churchill bet a substantial amount of money right into this ace. Charlie studied what he knew had to be a winning hand, looked over at the President, gave what I thought sounded like a sigh, and folded."

By evening's end, his American hosts pressing a bit harder, Churchill may have lost about $250 all told—and apparently was happy. "He had enjoyed himself thoroughly, but had dropped just enough money so that he could not go back to London and brag that he had beaten the Americans at poker."

He did, of course, impress his American "cousins" in Fulton the next day with his 45-minute speech that kept the audience riveted. He had worked on it during interludes on the train, and now a young Clark Clifford saw and heard the orator Churchill in full throat. "From the point of view of high rhetoric, I had never heard anything like it before. As a demonstration of the power of ideas, it was an astonishing tour de force."

The speech at Fulton, Truman on the podium in black academic robe and Churchill in scarlet, was the past and future Prime Minister's famous "Iron Curtain" speech, the one in which he warned the world that across continental Europe, dividing the West from an East under Soviet domination, had descended an iron curtain—the same barrier, of course, that then lasted for another 4½ decades.

# 🦅 *Three Days of Oratory*

The lifestyle of a President, the gold-plated spoons he found already in use at the White House and his own "pretty, tapering, soft, white lily fingers" were the subject of a famous and scathing congressional speech in the early 19th century.

The victim of Whig Rep. William Ogle's "Gold Spoon Speech" was Martin Van Buren, a widowed father of four sons who indeed had brought an effete and elegant air to the presidential mansion in comparison to his more plebeian predecessor, Andrew Jackson. And it was Van Buren's unfortunate lot, politically, to preside over the Nation's first real depression.

He first "cleaned house" by auctioning off the more worn or gaudy of the Jackson furnishings, even if Jackson had been his political ally and mentor. He next refurbished and installed new rugs, china-ware, upholstery and the like—the gold-plated spoons that Ogle soon would castigate apparently were a legacy from President James Monroe, and not Van Buren's very own affectation.

But Van Buren definitely did create a more aristocratic, less democratic atmosphere at the White House. He favored a continental menu for his elegant little dinner parties. He didn't balk at attending the widely ballyhooed wedding of the aging Russian minister to Washington, Count Bodisco, to a Georgetown school girl, all of 14 years in age. But then...neither did most of Washington society.

Dolley Madison, meanwhile, returning to her beloved Washington in 1837, had taken up residence across Lafayette Square from her old abode and she set out to find Van Buren a hostess, since he and his four sons were not quite the same thing, no matter how hard they might try.

The happy result was the Dolley-maneuvered introduction of her own distant relative, Angelica Singleton of South Carolina, to Van Buren's oldest son Abraham (also his father's private secretary). In short order, they fell in love, they married in South Carolina and moved into the White House. There, in proper time, Angelica gave birth to a baby girl, but the infant died soon after.

More happily, Angelica was a lively success in her role as hostess of the White House. Her first such outing, on New Year's Day of 1839, set off a Washington tradition that would last for many years. After visiting the White House New Year's reception, the social lions of the capital would move on to Dolley Madison's house across the famous square.

One who had dined at the Van Buren White House often enough himself was the famed Pennsylvania orator William Ogle but, with the presidential election of 1840 looming, that did not stop him from castigating Van Buren for a long list of White House frills, many of them not even of Van Buren's doing.

The presidential home, Ogle said, "glitters with all imaginable luxuries and gaudy ornaments."

How could the citizenry support "their chief servant in a Palace as splendid as that of the Caesars and as richly adorned as the proudest Asiatic mansion?"

Finger bowls, *pate de fois gras,* golden knives and forks, silver plates and a silver soup tureen, foreign-cut wine coolers, and "golden chains to hang golden labels around the necks of barrel-shaped flute decanters with cone stoppers"—all came under Ogle's attack. The food served at Van Buren's White House, of course, would never do either, offerings like *"dinde dessosse and salade a la volille."* Where, oh where, admonished Ogle, were the good old "fried meat and gravy, or hog and hominy."

Fastidious, dapper, and small, the sinful Van Buren really was not so extravagant, but this time of shaky national economy was no moment for indulgences that *might* be misconstrued, no matter how reasonable. Such as new curtains for the Blue Room ($1,307.50 for three). Such as foreign-made carpeting.

Overall, though, Van Buren only had cleaned and scrubbed, upholstered, papered and painted. Later made out to be overly indulgent in his White House spending, wrote White House historian William Seale, "Van Buren actually spent less than half of what Andrew Jackson had put out on the house, approximately the same amount of the second Adams, and not half as much as the first Adams."

Two steps that Van Buren did take were well worth the effort if not the expense—he added shower baths and copper bathtubs to the bathing facilities of the East Wing (but no running water for the second floor), and he took steps to replace and improve upon the heating system installed by Madison but destroyed by the British in 1814. Van Buren emplaced a hot-air heating system for the first floor and the great hall upstairs. The upstairs rooms still would be heated strictly by individual fireplaces tended by "fireman" servants.

Van Buren's mistake was to allow appearances that made him vulnerable to charges of elitism and antipathy to truly democratic thought. His coach, with its silver trim and matching four, was the "finest seen in the capital since General Washington's," said Seale.

His son John, after visiting Queen Victoria, acquired the nickname "Prince John," and daughter-in-law Angelica as White House hostess might have thought better of receiving guests seated on a platform...like Queen Victoria herself!

Unable to fix the nation's economy, unwilling to mend his small affectations, Van Buren was a tempting target for political bullies, and Ogle was so glad to play the part that he kept up his "Gold Spoon" speech for three days while the entire House sat as a committee of the whole and the crowds in the galleries grew ever larger and more gleeful.

Ogle's exaggerations were typical of the year's "Log Cabin" campaign that elected William Henry Harrison in Van Buren's stead.

Harrison was an old Indian fighter, an Ohio resident, a colorful and heroic figure who might have spent *some* time at frontier log cabins in the past, but he also was the scion of an aristocratic Virginia family, and he had lived in grand homes in both the Indiana territory and in Ohio.

If Van Buren held the election outcome against Harrison in any way, he hid his feelings quite well. When the President-elect visited Washington a month before his inauguration on March 4, 1841, he visited Van Buren at the White House, and Van Buren visited him at Gadsby's Hotel. The outgoing President even invited Harrison to move into the White House *before* the inaugural activities for a bit of rest and to get away from harassing job-seekers.

Harrison instead visited his daughter in Virginia, but thanks to Martin Van Buren, a somewhat dressier—and certainly better-heated White House—could have been his *before* he became President.

# ⚜ 'This Damned Old House'

The White House—Executive Mansion, still—that Abraham Lincoln took over in 1861 in many ways was like a state capitol in a state capital. For one thing, inconceivable now, its hallways thronged with people—it was a public building open to the public. And filled with the public.

To go home (to his private quarters) for lunch, Lincoln had to push his way through the crowds jamming the hallways.

His normal routine was to rise at 7 a.m. and work for about two quiet hours, then have breakfast with his family in the private quarters allotted to the President—west end of the second floor.

Then, he "went to work," to his office at the east end, same floor, a room that also doubled as the Cabinet Room. He kept a large desk with pigeonholes containing various papers, but he did his paperwork at a table nearby. In the winter, he would be warmed by a fire beneath a marble mantel. An oil portrait of an earlier frontiersman looked on silently—Andrew Jackson.

Other decorations were sparse, unless you count the maps pinned to the walls or lying on the lengthy Cabinet table.

The Cabinet met at noon on Tuesdays and Fridays, but even without that complication, Lincoln soon found as President that he could not maintain his original idea of having unlimited visiting hours. So he fixed those times as 10 a.m. to 1 p.m., Monday, Wednesday and Thursday, during which hours even unannounced, ordinary citizens could see him if willing to wait long enough.

A guard kept order in the jammed hall outside his office and took visitors' cards; a private secretary, John G. Nicolay, did screen the pressing visitors. Lincoln accomplished his office work with the help of three secretaries through most of the Civil War period. The daily staff in the "business" section of the White House also included a doorman.

By 1864, new interior modeling would permit Lincoln access to his family quarters without pushing through the awaiting throngs.

His routine, in the meantime, also called for a daily outing in a carriage with Mrs. Lincoln, usually at 4 p.m., and walks. Since the White House had no telegraph of its own in those days, Lincoln had to go to the nearby War Department every night to see the day's Civil War dispatches. It wasn't until late in 1864 that a Washington police officer, in plainclothes but armed, was assigned to accompany Lincoln on such outings on foot. (He would be, after all, the *first* U.S. President to be assassinated.)

The dinner hour was usually 6 p.m., but state dinners began a bit later—at 7:30 p.m. In time, the Lincolns held public receptions on Tuesday evenings and Saturday afternoons. It is said that souvenir hunters snatched away bits of drapery and carpet all the time.

Since the place did look tattered from the day they moved in, Mary Todd Lincoln was given a $20,000 congressional appropriation to spruce up the presidential home. She spent the money in no time on carpets, drapes, furniture, chinaware (666 pieces of Limoge!) and in fact ran up a deficit of another $6,000. Her husband was mortified and, in perhaps their best-known domestic tiff, later complained to Benjamin Brown, commissioner of public buildings, that "it would stink in the nostrils of the American people to have it said that the

President of the United States had approved a bill overrunning an appropriation of $20,000 for *flub dubs,* for this damned old house, when the soldiers cannot have blankets.''

The President's own salary, meanwhile was an annual $25,000, and, amazingly, he apparently was able to put much of that sum aside for a rainy day—he entered the White House worth $15,000 and when he was assassinated four years later his estate had grown to $85,000. He kept his money at the Riggs bank in Washington.

Certainly earning his salary, he on most days in the White House went back to work in his office after dinner. He would quit his labors at about 11 p.m.

The Lincolns did not enjoy a very active social life in their new city of Washington, traditionally and still dominated by a Southern social elite and hostile in mood to all that Lincoln represented. There were fears, when he first arrived as President-elect, of plots to seize the Capitol—still lacking its dome—and he had been inaugurated with Federal cavalry spotted at key points in the city and riflemen on the rooftops.

No surprise, then, that the Lincolns seldom went ''out,'' except to the opera and the theatre.

They did entertain, however, holding Friday evening ''levees'' or dances, during which Mary Todd Lincoln would stand slightly behind her husband in the receiving line rather than shake every hand. Their son Willie's death from a fever early in 1862 took her from the social scene for at least a year. Lincoln's assassination in 1865 ended it all for the Lincolns...except for the grief and the memories of an unbalanced Mary Todd Lincoln and her two surviving boys.

## 🦅 *White House Honeymoon*

And then there was the time a young lady living in the White House broke off her engagement to a onetime resident of the presidential home in order to marry a third member of the President's household, the first young man's own brother. Which she then did—marry the second young man. In the Blue Room. And the President in question, John Quincy Adams, danced at their wedding. By his own account, ''a Virginia reel with great spirit.''

Not that everybody in the family was so pleased with the union of presidential son John Adams II and his bride Mary Catherine Hellen. In fact, neither of John's two brothers attended the wedding on February 25, 1828.

The White House triangle among cousins began, you might say, with the death of Nancy Hellen, eldest sister of the President's wife, Louisa Catherine Johnson Adams. The "First Family" that resided in the White House in the latter 1820s thus included Nancy's three orphaned children, Mary Catherine, Thomas and Johnson, in addition to the three Adams' boys—Charles, George and John II. And Mary Catherine soon was a tempting apple in the eye of one Adams brother after another. Charles, for one, willingly or not, escaped her net with a sour comment in his diary labelling her "one of the most capricious women" of a "capricious race."

Also falling under her spell was George Adams, who became engaged to the wily young woman as early as 1823—the Hellen children had moved in with the Adamses in 1817 and simply went on to the White House with John Quincy in 1825. George had studied at Harvard and was pursuing his career as a lawyer in Boston. He became a Massachusetts state legislator in 1826. It was his plan to be well launched on his professional career before taking the engagement to its final point of marriage. Four, five, six years, apparently seemed a reasonable waiting period to him.

But not to his prospective bride, who rarely saw her proper young man from Boston, and who *did* see another young man practically every day at the White House. That was young John, who had been tossed from the Harvard ranks in 1823 and who now served his father as private secretary.

In the meantime, Charles, the third Adams brother, already had noticed the storm signals. Also a budding lawyer in Massachusetts, he recorded after one visit to Washington that his brother George's winsome fiancée "has some alluring ways which are apt to make every man forget himself."

*Poor George.* He would be "in a perfect fever and sickness if he was to imagine that she had encouraged me in the least," wrote his brother Charles.

George, it must be said, did not exactly press his long-distance courtship, so busy was he up there in Boston.

In another visit, brother Charles discovered brother John apparently had fallen "victim of her arts." The young woman was "behaving unworthily" of George, and the family obviously was upset—"My Mother [Louisa Adams] is half inclined to the marriage [with George] and half opposed, my Father tacitly opposed." And Charles was "sorry for" John, caught in her alleged snares.

In the end, predictably, Mary Catherine broke her engagement with George (he was distraught, despite the lukewarm nature of their romance) and married John, whose mother Louisa then wrote to Charles: "I shall...only announce to you the fact that the wedding is over, that Madame is cool, easy, and indifferent as ever and that John looks already as if he had had all the cares of the world upon his shoulders and my heart tells me that there is much to fear."

The honeymoon, no great change for the newlyweds themselves, nonetheless was a rarity—it was spent at the White House. And their first child, Mary Louisa Adams, completed the cycle by her birth at the White House, on December 2, 1828.

As for Louisa Adams' "much to fear," it is sad but true that both Adams' sons who were seriously involved with Mary Catherine had many problems, became heavy drinkers and died young. That is not to say their shared fate was the fault of Mary Catherine, who, in fact later in life provided comfort and care to her infirm mother-in-law Louisa through the latter's final years as a widow...until her death in Washington in 1852.

## ☙ *Righteous Crusade Sabotaged*

*Rats, rats, rats!* With the basement kitchen area and adjoining store rooms serving rats and mice as vast dining halls, Andrew Johnson's daughter Martha Patterson went on the warpath.

She was a strong-willed young woman, as evidenced by the fact that she emerged as the primary White House hostess and domestic supervisor after her father the Vice President succeeded the assassinated Abraham Lincoln in 1865. Altogether, ten Johnson family members had moved in, including the new President's wife Eliza. But she was ill, nearly an invalid, and reclusive. At first their daughters, Mary and Martha, both served as hostesses, but it was Martha, wife of David Trotter Patterson, a U.S. Senator from their home state of Tennessee, who gradually took over the social stewardship of the White House. (A rarity in the history of the White House was the spectacle of a Senator also living in the presidential quarters, yes.)

And so, as one of her crusades to spruce up the hotel-like Executive Mansion, Martha declared her war against the vermin infesting the venerable and historic walls.

Little did she know, it seems, that her every effort was being foiled by another resident of the self-same house, by sabotage at the hands of another family member—her own father, the President himself!

Not that he cared for rats, one may suppose. But for mice he apparently had a soft spot.

The story comes out. While daughter Martha strenuously imported cats, scattered poisons and placed traps down in the White House bowels, Andrew Johnson was busy two floors above feeding at least the mice with white flour ground at his own farm in Tennessee.

It seems that he had noticed the nibble marks on a flour package, then he actually saw a mouse in his bedroom—not the traditional presidential bedroom on the south wall, incidentally, but a room on the north side.

After espying the mouse, Johnson placed the floor packet on the bedroom hearth to allow the mice to "get their fill."

As a result, he told an aide that he had won the confidence of "the little fellows" and not only would supply them more flour, but also "some water that they may quench their thirst."

He may have gone to a newly equipped bathroom by his bedroom for the water—it previously had held bath tubs but no real plumbing, and Johnson changed that by converting it into a full-fledged bathroom, complete with even a barber's chair.

Daughter Martha, in the meantime, proceeded not only with her war on vermin but also a clean-up of the entire White House, top to bottom, even the attic, along with redecorating and remodeling. Her efforts there included complete removal of the low-lying East Wing and its replacement by a single-story colonnade that gave the famous East Room a pleasant balcony on the roof of the new structure.

#  *Collaborators*

One or both of the two young men in the White House called their boss "The Tycoon." One liked "The Ancient" a bit better. The same, John Milton Hay, called the President's wife "Hell Cat." And one or both thought that Robert E. Lee deserved to be shot.

Come together as secretaries for Abraham Lincoln, John George Nicolay and John Hay were young, still undistinguished men, as they began interwoven careers in the White House of the Lincoln Administration. Both were, or would be, writers. Both would be diplomats. Both began their tenure with Lincoln as secretaries answering the mail, screening the visitors, even preparing a daily news summary.

Both worked long, hard hours and both slept in the White House.

Both, in future years, would spend more than 15 years collaborating on a 10-volume biography of their boss, Lincoln, that is still considered an absolutely vital source on the history of the period, on the Lincoln Administration and on Lincoln himself.

Before they came together in Washington again to work on the gigantic biography, Nicolay spent a few years as the U.S. Consul Resident in Paris. After they delivered their monumental work to the reading public (5,000 sets quickly sold), John Hay moved on...moved on to serve as the American Secretary of State under Presidents William McKinley and Theodore Roosevelt. Nicolay, for his part, much earlier had accepted a sinecure as Marshal of the U.S. Supreme Court.

The biographical work the two men composed has defied analysts in their attempts to determine which wrote which sections, since each could write well...and each certainly knew the subject matter from first-hand observation. Not content with mere observation, however, they enlisted the aid—and the papers and the authorization—of Lincoln's oldest son, Robert Todd Lincoln. They researched meticulously and were wary of accepting interviews as totally reliable source material. One further aid to their labors was a somewhat erratic diary that Hay had kept while serving as one of Lincoln's three White House secretaries. Both also had various notes and letters of their own to fall back upon, along with full knowledge of the whereabouts of other documentation.

The two had met in Illinois shortly before Lincoln's ascendancy to President. Nicolay, born in Bavaria in 1832 and most recently a newspaper editor-publisher, was a clerk in the office of the Illinois Secretary of State, Ozias M. Hatch, in Springfield, when Lincoln ran for President. Hay, born in Indiana in 1838, first encountered Nicolay while attending school in Pittsfield, Illinois, in 1851. Hay then spent his college years at a school in Springfield and at Brown University. He became reacquainted with Nicolay when he returned to Springfield in 1858 to work in an uncle's law office.

Nicolay, meanwhile, had met presidential nominee Lincoln and soon became his secretary. Later, when the mail volume of the President-elect shot past 50 letters a day, he prevailed upon Lincoln to hire Hay as well.

Both men accompanied Lincoln to Washington for his first inauguration in 1861—and stayed.

More than desk-bound secretaries, really, they ran political errands for Lincoln and went on out-of-town trouble-shooting trips for him on occasion. Obviously, he trusted their honesty and their discretion to the utmost.

Nicolay, disliked by Mrs. Lincoln, had spent his free time in the White House studying French, and he was on his way to the consul post in Paris when Lincoln was assassinated. Hay, who disliked Mrs. Lincoln, also had wangled an appointment to Paris—as Secretary of the U.S. Legation there. He also would have been gone, but he lingered to break-in a new office staff at the White House. He rushed to the Lincoln bedside the fateful night of April 14-15 and was at the beloved "Ancient's" side when he died the morning of April 15.

The two began their biographical collaboration in Washington in the 1870s, with Robert Todd Lincoln's okay. Hay found time also to publish a novel and serve as Assistant Secretary of State. Nicolay labored through family problems—an infant son's death in 1878 and his wife's death in 1885.

In that year, too, the pair agreed to allow *Century Magazine* to begin publishing their *Abraham Lincoln: A History* in serial format for $50,000. Their 10-volume work then appeared in 1890, with half of the series already run in the magazine.

Hay soon was off to serve as American Ambassador to England, but they still were able to collaborate on a two-volume production of Lincoln's own writings. Soon after that, Nicolay hoped to turn out a greatly shortened single-volume version of their Lincoln *History* but, in 1901, death came first. His name would live on in fresh form, however, after his daughter Helen produced a biography of Nicolay himself—*Lincoln's Secretary: A Biography of John G. Nicolay*.

Hay, meanwhile, was now fully devoted to his own public service. As for his view of the "Tycoon" or "Ancient" they both had served, Hay one time told another biographer, William Herndon, that Lincoln had his blind spots, surely ("absurd to call him a modest man," and so forth), but, "As Republicanism is the sole hope of a sick world, so Lincoln with all his foibles, is the greatest character since Christ."

# 🦅 *Controversy Over Dinner*

When pioneer black educator Booker T. Washington, born into slavery, was invited to sup at the White House with Teddy Roosevelt, there was instant furor. "Probably the First Negro Ever Entertained at the White House," headlined the Atlanta *Constitution*. Other papers in the South wailed, too.

Teddy Roosevelt defended his action as a perfectly innocuous attempt "to show some respect to a man whom I cordially esteem as a good citizen and a good American." But even Teddy eventually had to admit that politically, in the South especially, it had been a mistake.

The fact is, furor aside, other blacks had made appearances at the White House before the dinner of 1901. The freed slave and abolitionist Sojourner Truth once visited Lincoln, while another famous ex-slave, Frederick Douglas, played a presiding role over black performers appearing in concerts at the Rutherford B. Hayes White House. Such appearances, of course, were exceptions, were a bow to "celebrities" of one kind or another, and most blacks seen at the White House at any time during the latter 19th century, Civil War and Reconstruction notwithstanding, would have been servants. "From all indications," wrote White House historian William Seale, "no Negro received a social invitation to the White House before Booker T. Washington in 1901, nor did many thereafter for many years."

Which is not to say that the dinner with Teddy Roosevelt was Booker T. Washington's first White House visit. On the contrary, the black educator had achieved auspicious results in a visit to the Executive Mansion just three years earlier when he went there, unbidden...in hopes of gaining an audience with Roosevelt's predecessor, William McKinley.

That was in 1898, and Washington, chief founder and still head of Tuskeegee Institute in Alabama, had just found out that President McKinley would be traveling to nearby Atlanta, Georgia, to attend a "Peace Jubilee" marking the end of the Spanish-American War. Here was a chance, a heaven-sent opportunity, to persuade a President of the predominately white nation to visit its pre-eminent black school of the day, Washington realized. He wasted no time traveling to Washington. A letter request would not do—he had to see the President in person.

But how could he quickly arrange such an all-important audience? By his own account (in *Up From Slavery*), Washington said that he went to the White House unannounced. "When I got there, I found the waiting rooms full of people, and my heart began to sink for I feared there would not be much chance of my seeing the President that day, if at all."

But Washington managed to gain presidential secretary J. Addison Porter's ear, and the Booker T. Washington calling card then wafted into the inner sanctum of McKinley's own office. "...and in a few minutes word came from Mr. McKinley that he would see me."

After that, no problem. Plans for the Atlanta trip were still flexible, and McKinley was quite receptive after Washington argued the visit "would not only encourage our students and teachers, but would help the entire race." McKinley couldn't yet promise, but after a

second visit by Booker T. Washington the next month, McKinley—
the last veteran of the Civil War to serve in the White House—agreed
to go. In between the two visits by the black educator, it so happened
also, several race riots had erupted in the South. "As soon as I
saw the President [the second time], I perceived that his heart was
greatly burdened by reason of these race disturbances," wrote
Washington later.

McKinley said he wanted to show his "faith in the race," according to Washington, and Washington for his part said hardly any
gesture would "go farther in giving hope and encouragement" to
his fellow blacks "than the fact that the President of the Nation
would be willing to travel 140 miles out of his way to spend a day
at a Negro institution."

When the day came, December 10, 1898, not only blacks but many
white citizens and leaders crowded into the "little city of Tuskegee"
for the rare presidential visit. Drawn to the spot were "a host" of
newspaper correspondents, the Alabama state legislature and governor, along with McKinley's own Cabinet.

The entire student body of the black school paraded before the eminent visitors—float after float, farm animals and equipment, students
carrying a stalk of sugar cane, often with a single cotton boll attached
to one end. Speeches, of course, were made right and left, including
McKinley's own and even an oration by the Postmaster General.

It may have been Navy Secretary John D. Long who really put his
finger on what was happening, whose sentiments, if *felt* more widely,
might have avoided the furor that greeted Booker T. Washington's
social visit with Teddy Roosevelt just three years later.

The dramatic picture rendered at Tuskegee that December day in
1898, Long said, was of the Nation's President sharing the platform
with the governor of a former Confederate state on the one hand
and a black leader, Booker T. Washington, on the other. This, said
Long, was a "trinity," this was "a picture which the press of the country should spread over the land." This was a picture, *as* he said, which
should be "transmitted to future time and generations."

## ☆ *'Royal Pup' Chastised*

Alexander Hamilton was killed in 1804. Naval hero Stephen
Decatur in 1820. And, in that day and age, so were many others—
victims, one and all, of the vicious social convention called dueling.
Over offended feelings of honor, over a matter of insult, perceived

or real, "gentlemen" often settled affairs by killing, maiming or merely pinking the offender in a ritual that allowed each to take shots at the other.

It was a time when a "chip on the shoulder" could be dangerous. And so the President's son, the son of John Quincy Adams, set all the grim ritualistic wheels in motion one day when he publicly insulted a visitor to the White House.

The incident took place in the East Room during a reception on April 2, 1828, a time when young John Adams II—a newlywed—lived at the White House with his recent bride and served his father as private secretary. The second son of John Quincy Adams had not sailed an entirely smooth course as a young man about town—as, indeed, the son of a very circumspect President. He had been given the boot at Harvard, and two months before, he had married a cousin and fellow White House resident who had broken her engagement to his own brother George.

Now, at the reception in April, John bridled at the sight of journalist Russell Jarvis of the *United States Telegraph,* who had just entered the East Room with his wife, her parents and two additional women. They already had been formally received by John's mother, Louisa, with no problem.

Nor would there have been any problem, except that John recognized Jarvis as a critic of his father (as was the newspaper's editor, Duff Green). A companion asked John about one of the women, and he, in reply, loudly and unmistakably said the woman was the journalist's wife—and there, with her, "is a man who, if he had any idea of propriety in the conduct of a gentleman, ought not to show his face in this house."

The offending group promptly turned and left, but as the town plunged into the inevitable gossip, the first repercussion was not long in coming. Sent by mail, it was a challenge to duel.

Young Adams did not respond. Nor did he hide. As private secretary to his father, he continued to deliver presidential messages to Congress in its as-yet unfinished Capitol.

Denied his gentleman's "satisfaction", Jarvis waited one day—April 15, it was—in the Capitol's Rotunda for the President's son. When John Adams appeared on his usual rounds, Jarvis accosted him in no uncertain terms. He pulled the young man's nose and slapped him in the face, insults to make anybody pale, and more than enough for a duel under the unspoken rules of the day.

The President, himself an opponent of dueling, complained in a message to Congress that son John had been "waylaid and assaulted" in the legislature's own house. He called for legislation to guarantee the safety of couriers between Congress and the White House. And who knows what he said to his "courier" son?

In any case, Congress investigated with an eye to censure, calling forth both men to testify, and newspapers, pro-Adams and anti-Adams, reported and trumpeted over the unhappy matter. In the end, no duel ever did take place. Congress refused to censure Jarvis. His newspaper, the *Telegraph* could stick by its language calling the pulling of the Prince's nose "a signal" chastisement for the "Royal puppy."

# 🦅 *Early Social Doings*

President and Mrs. James Monroe thought it best, socially speaking, to have people *in* rather than to go *out*—at least not to private homes. And so they missed the major party of the season in January of 1824, a ball given by John Quincy Adams for the Hero of New Orleans, General Andrew Jackson. A thousand men and women attended—everybody who was *any*body in Washington of the day (except the sitting President and his wife).

Adams, who would succeed Monroe at the White House, thought to install additional pillars to hold up the lower floors under the expected crush in the Adams home on F Street. He was Monroe's Secretary of State at the time, and Jackson, also a future President, was a newly elected Senator. More pointedly, in 1824, both men would be presidential contenders. Against each other.

Coming in an election year, the party obviously had political undertones, overtones, in-between tones—the gamut, politically. In the end, although Jackson won the popular vote of 1824 for President, no single one of the four presidential candidates had gained a majority of the electoral votes. That development threw the final vote into the House of Representatives. It, after considerable political tumult and name-calling, selected Adams as the Nation's sixth President.

His then was a difficult presidency, fraught with political and personal problems. But the stiff New Englander and his wife Louisa nonetheless did have an active, if not flamboyant social life. Like the Madisons, they would stay *in* rather than go out. While *in,* they staged an annual New Year's reception that would attract several thousand. Their biweekly levees, receptions also, were popular as well.

A recent Harvard graduate attending a White House dinner under the Adamses found that 20 congressmen and 20 "gentlemen from different parts of the country" made up the guest list. The table was lit by "an enormous gilt waiter, with many vases, temples, and female figures in different attitudes holding candles." Dinner lasted from 6:00 p.m. to 10:00, and in the interim the guests had supped upon "every variety of fish, flesh, and fowl." Included was a boned and finely sliced canvasback duck that struck the young visitor as "cake." He also recalled the meal included macaroni, and for drink there had been "every drinkable under the sun—porter, cider, claret, sherry, Burgundy, champagne, Tokay, and the choicest madeira that ever passed my larynx."

Alone, the Adamses could turn to themselves and family members for quiet eveningtide entertainments. Louisa Adams or sons could take a turn at the harp or pianoforte. The mistress of the mansion also wrote both verse and drama, and it is thought that household members acted out Louisa Adams' scripts such as *The Wag, or Just From College: A Farce in Three Acts,* or a more serious but melodramatic piece supporting independence for Greece.

There were those who found the scholarly Adams, son of a President, veteran diplomat, cultured and urbane, a bit *dull,* while others found him to be quite *eloquent.* Both words were used by White House guests.

Whatever the case, he and his family either entertained or politically fought some astounding historical figures—Henry Clay, Secretary of State under Adams; Daniel Webster; John C. Calhoun, Vice President in tandem with the Adams term of office; and of course, Andrew Jackson, who in 1828 handily defeated Adams in a heated and scathing campaign for President.

Still destined to serve honorably and well as a House member, Adams left the White House the day before Jackson's rowdy inaugural festivities in March 1829. The Adamses moved to a house beyond the capital city, on Meridian Hill. Jackson did not make the customary courtesy call on the outgoing President, and Adams did not attend the Jackson inauguration, so bitter were their respective feelings. That day, alone, Adams rode his horse—he rode along F Street, where he had lived just before entering the White House himself.

# Unfit For A Queen

Every five minutes they vacuumed the red carpet covering the asphalt drive at the South Portico. The Queen was coming, the Queen was coming.

72

And at what a time in the Nation's history!

It was the American Bicentennial, 200 years since the dramatic events of the American Revolution, and the Queen of England was coming to the Gerald Ford White House for a state dinner, one of the most elaborate ever held in the presidential mansion. "The evening was magic," wrote White House Social Aide Stephen M. Bauer later.

Guests sat at 24 tables under a colorful tent erected in the Rose Garden. Rain and a thunderstorm had threatened to disrupt the dinner July 7, 1976, for Her Majesty, Queen Elizabeth II, until the last moment, with lightning reportedly striking trees on the nearby South Grounds. But no rain dared to sully the freshly vacuumed carpet this night.

"She wore a spectacular diamond necklace, diamond earrings and a fabulous diamond tiara," said Bauer in his book *At Ease in The White House: The Uninhibited Memoirs of a Presidential Social Aide,* written with Frances Spatz Leighton. In addition to administration officials and leaders of the Washington diplomatic corps, those hob-nobbing with the Queen and Prince Philip included celebrities Cary Grant, Barbara Walters, Julie Harris, Telly Savalas, Texas Governor John Connally and baseball star Willie Mays.

For all the elaborate planning, however, for all the historic grandeur intended, the Queen of England on this bicentennial occasion at the President's house had to endure "pop" music with lyrics that some would consider banal, tasteless ("...the Queen's face unfortunately showed she caught every syllable all too clearly.")

Next, she sat through comedian Bob Hope's stand-up appearance acknowledging the diamond tiara with the remark, "In this country when we see a crown we think of margarine."

And finally, after all had moved into the State Dining Room, came the sight of President Ford dutifully taking the visiting Queen's hand in order to lead off the gala's dancing—unfortunately this time to the music of "The Lady is a Tramp."

# ✺ *Skinny Dipper*

Very early one day in the 1820s, a gentleman from New York was in the vicinity of Tiber Creek, at its conjunction with the Potomac River, a thoroughly bucolic setting behind the new President's House. The sun had not yet risen when along came another gentleman, dressed (for the moment) in pantaloons and blue pea jacket.

He was walking "rapidly" from the White House, as indeed the President's House already was being called, and he clearly was hurrying to the river. The summer morning's encounter would have been close to today's Washington Monument, near the very foot of 17th Street.

Having recognized the man in pantaloons and pea jacket as President John Quincy Adams, the onlooking Thurlow Weed withdrew a discreet distance and watched as Adams began to shed his clothing even before he reached "a tree on the brink of the river."

Seconds later, bereft of all clothing, Adams was enjoying his frequent early-morning swim in the Potomac behind the presidential mansion. "[He] struck out 15 or 20 rods, swimming rapidly and turning occasionally upon his back, seeming as much at ease in the element as on terra firma."

Since all good things must end, Adams in a short while returned to shore and dried himself off "with napkins, which he had brought for the purpose in his hand."

Others in the early days of the capital occasionally espied Adams taking his watery constitutional, but the historians of today tend to dismiss the story that a zealous female reporter once nailed down an interview with the austere President—and son of a President—by sitting on his discarded clothes.

Fact it is, though, that in those seemingly innocent beginnings of its life as the First Family's home, the White House could not boast of any plumbing, no running water! More like a country estate, it faced a dirt road running west to Georgetown. To the east a mile was the Capitol, and Adams—as part of his physical regime—liked to walk there and back. He started out by completing the round trip in an hour and 15 minutes; he eventually knocked the time down to an hour flat. He also rode horseback in his rural setting. The White House during his term as the nation's sixth President had a stable for eight horses.

The vista from behind, down to the river, was of a farm, really. To the west beyond 16th Street, the view was of open country. From the south porch, the occupants could see past their gardens of flowers and shrubs to pasture ground for both cows and sheep all the way to the river, a stretch of several hundred yards. This, too, was where Tiber Creek came in from the east. And as it joined the Potomac after crossing the line of 15th Street, there were islands and some marshlands.

Back at the great house, there were low lying sheds, a dairy, a vegetable garden. The North Portico had not yet been built. Looking a bit bare by our image today, the presidential home still lacked tall, grand trees to soften the outline and keep its grandiose scale in proportion.

The Nation almost lost its sixth President to his fondness for the Potomac. It seems that one day he, son John and a servant named Antoine set off from the river banks on the White House side of the river in a leaky canoe. The younger Adams was swimming. His father, partially disrobed, was in the small craft, and so was Antoine, already naked and ready for the water.

In mid-river or so, the leaking boat foundered completely, leaving all three in the water. The President began swimming for the opposite shore, their goal from the outset, but he was weighted down by the long sleeves of his shirt as they filled with water. Describing the sleeves as two "56-pound weights upon my arms," Adams later wrote, he was left "struggling for life and gasping for breath. . . ."

Fortunately, he did reach the far shore, as did son John and the servant Antoine. Gathering clothes from what they had left among them, Antoine then had to walk back into town to find a carriage. They were six hours late returning to the White House. It is said they weren't even missed.

## 🦅 *Dinner With Old Hickory*

Coming into office on the heels of the cultured and urbane John Quincy Adams, the frontier hero Andrew Jackson—"Old Hickory" to his countrymen—might have been expected to serve his dinner guests far more simple fare. For the plebian, somewhat populist Jackson, perhaps a slab of smoked venison would have been appropriate and symbolic.

But not so. . .not always, at any rate.

Attending an *informal* White House dinner with the widower Jackson and several guests in 1834, a Pennsylvania lawyer found a table "very splendidly laid and illuminated." He noticed a chandelier above that held 32 candles, plus added candles on various surfaces about the room.

He and his fellow guests sat down with their host at 6:30 p.m., and then came one sophisticated course after another. "The first course was soup in the French style; then beef böuille, next wild turkey boned and dressed with brains; after that fish; then chicken cold and dressed white, interlaided with slices of tongue and garnished with dressed salad; then canvasback ducks and celery; afterward partridges with sweet breads and last pheasants and old Virginia ham."

All was accompanied by select wines—sherry and port for the soups and first meats, madeira for the turkey and fish, champagne for the later fowl courses. Then came desserts—jelly and small tarts, followed by "blanche mode and kisses with dryed fruits in them." Then preserves, followed by ice cream and grapes and oranges. The desserts came with claret.

Here, clearly, was a meal for anybody to remember for some time. And the only way to possibly consume so many foods was the methodology imposed by Jackson's "French servants," that is, to move the courses on and off the table quickly, thus affording the diners mere tastings of each offering.

The meal took until 9:00 p.m., the Pennsylvania lawyer later recalled, and afterward the party retired to a drawing room, where the guests sipped coffee and then a liqueur while the ladies played the piano and sang. The party ended at 9:30 p.m.

Lavish as it was, wrote Jackson biographer Marquis James, the dinner was, for the Jackson White House, only an "an informal affair, a degree removed from a family dinner." The added fact is, "General Jackson's state entertainments were marked by a richness and a dignity devoid of stiffness [and were] unequalled since Washington's day."

## Persistent Bodyguard

On election night of 1864, when things had been running hot and close for Abraham Lincoln in his bid for a second presidential term, a burly, Virginia-born lawyer set himself up outside Lincoln's White House door with pistols and knives. Born in the Old Dominion but later an attorney on the 8th Judicial Circuit in Illinois with Attorney Lincoln, Ward Hill Lamon was devoted disciple, it certainly did appear.

More or less appointing himself as frequent bodyguard, he accompanied the President-elect in his secret dash by nighttime train through Rebel-infested Baltimore for the first Lincoln inauguration in Washington. The new President rewarded his old friend and circuit-riding colleague by appointing him Marshal of the District of Columbia. The post, much like that of an old-time sheriff, was suitable enough for the man who had accompanied Lincoln on the train with protection gear that included brass knuckles, pistols, a knife, and the like. Now, "Hill," as he was called, could preside at special ceremonies and run the local prison.

He found Virginia troops to follow his banner early in the Civil War—as Union men, of course. Later, when Lincoln spoke at Gettysburg, Lamon was marshal-in-chief for the ceremonial parade into the cemetery to be dedicated. He later introduced a speaker—his old colleague Lincoln.

Still, times were rough and he worried over Lincoln's safety. The President at least once had been shot at in public (a hole apparently shot in his hat one day when he journeyed the four miles from the real White House downtown to the "summer White House" at the Soldier's Home).

He kept warning Lincoln of possible betrayers right in the White House, suggesting a screening system for anyone asking to see the President. He once proposed the arrest of a seditious-*sounding* congressman and during the heated campaign of 1864 began spending the night at the White House to keep Lincoln safe. He warned Lincoln repeatedly to be more careful in public, and even after the election he was terribly upset to hear that Lincoln went to the theatre one night with a foreign diplomat and Senator Charles Sumner of Massachusetts. . .and no one else. Neither of Lincoln's companions on that outing, asserted Lamon, "could defend themselves against an assault from any able-bodied woman in this City."

He begged Lincoln's secretary and aide John G. Nicolay to make sure that Lincoln never left the White House alone, "either in the day or night time."

One night in April 1865, Lincoln attended the theatre again—Ford's Theatre. He wasn't alone, he was under guard, but he was shot and fatally wounded anyway. One has to wonder what might have been the result if Lincoln, himself, had not sent Lamon to Richmond, fallen capital of the fallen Confederacy, just three days before to report on conditions in Virginia and the prospects for reconstruction. Lamon came hurrying back. . .he came back and was marshal of the state funeral for his old friend.

One has to wonder also why Lamon, seven years later, lent his name to a biography of Lincoln that was perceived at the time as being overly critical and "vulgar." Lincoln's parents never married, it seemed to hint, and Lincoln himself wasn't really so pious, and he liked dirty jokes. The book apparently was written by a law partner's son, Chauncy Black, based on Lamon's recollections and notes from onetime Lincoln law partner William Herndon.

In happier days, one has to recall, Lincoln had called Lamon "my particular friend."

# 🦅 Alice's Bad Idol

For a White House gathering, it apparently was an uneasy and dreary dinner party this night before an inauguration when the Teddy Roosevelts had in the William Howard Tafts as a friendly gesture, one set of Republicans to another.

Although Teddy Roosevelt had hand-picked his successor rather than run in 1908, his usually ebullient daughter Alice Roosevelt Longworth was not at all happy with such a turn of events—even among political friends. Indeed, who *was* entirely happy? The Roosevelts, were sad at leaving, the Tafts fidgeting and anxious to move in the next day.

Already, word had seeped through official Washington that Taft, far from overcome by gratitude, was planning to give many of Teddy's political appointees the boot, from Cabinet on down. Alice was annoyed also to be offered a ticket to Taft's White House reception following the next day's inauguration.

Imagine! A ticket to get in! And never mind that it was Taft's kindly wife Nellie who made the offer. Alice was not yet ready to relinquish her claims to the White House. "I! I, who had wandered in and out for eight happy years!" she later anguished.

How serious Alice may have been at the thought of her family leaving the White House is difficult to judge now. After all, she was by this time a married woman whose husband, Rep. Nicholas Longworth, had his own career in politics (he one day would be Speaker of the House), and in 1909 she no longer lived at the White House.

But...who knows? After all, it was Alice who slipped into the garden that evening and buried "a bad little idol" there in the dirt. And with dire incantations, it is said, with a girlish, flippant curse on future occupants of the grand old structure.

The next day, a howling storm of rain, sleet and snow drove the inaugural ceremony indoors—into the Senate chamber of the Capitol, the floor and galleries elbow-to-elbow with onlookers. Nellie Taft then broke tradition by riding next to her President-husband in his horse-drawn carriage—the first time a First Lady had ridden in the inaugural parade down Pennsylvania Avenue from the Capitol. "After getting 'Will' to pressure Congress to appropriate money for four autos, she felt she had earned a place on the seat next to him," wrote Alice's biographer Howard Teichman. And that night they traveled to the Inaugural Ball by motorcar.

In the meantime, the weather was so bad that in the outdoor festivities the band players found their brass mouthpieces frozen...."valves closed, reeds split."

Taft himself now apparently changed...or revealed his true self. He came in from the day's festivities, dumped his gloves, silk hat and greatcoat and "threw himself" on a sofa with the announcement: "I'm President now and I'm tired of being kicked around!"

Until that very moment, "Mr. Taft had been the jolliest, friendliest visitor the Roosevelts ever had entertained," said Teichman. "With that statement, his speech and his attitudes toward the servants and staff members changed radically. He snapped, he scowled, he snarled."

In another change, the very corpulent Taft ordered a new bathtub. At more than 300 pounds, it seems he could hardly squeeze into the tub that had served so many other Presidents for decades.

Taft's wife Helen (nickname, Nellie) contributed to other changes, too. Nearly all the Teddy Roosevelt servants and staff were replaced. The new First Lady hired a housekeeper and a chef—"entertainment grew lavish." She also was a confidante and adviser to her husband on political and policy matters, it seems—more openly so than many of her predecessors. She even attended his political meetings. And then, just ten weeks or so into their presidential term, she suffered a terrible stroke. "Will spent the rest of the days of his Presidency teaching his wife how to speak and walk again."

Still another unhappy experience for Taft was...*the ghost.*

True or untrue, the story is that an aide pecked at his office door one day and reported a kitchen worker was quitting suddenly. Worse, other White House domestics were considering the same drastic action.

But why?, Taft wanted to know, his ire already on the rise.

Well, Sir, it seems they are afraid of the ghost.

Ghost!?

Well, said the bearer of this unfortunate news, more than one maid and houseman had seen a gossamer figure or felt a frigid hand on their shoulders. A couple of the maids couldn't keep from screaming. Sometimes they left their tasks, burst into sobs, and ran for more populated areas such as the kitchen.

Taft immediately saw the obvious danger here—the story would leak out to the newspapers! "I won't have it," he warned direly. "...I forbid anyone who works in this house ever to mention the subject to me or anyone else again."

But then he thought of the obvious question. Whose ghost?

"Abraham Lincoln's youngest son," was the sad answer.

"Tell them it's nonsense, and never again do I want that story repeated."

But somebody did. Alice heard it and commented, "There are worse things than ghosts—bad Presidents in the White House are worse than apparitions."

## ✌ Slaves in the Attic

Others had done it before him, but "Old Zach" had his doubts, what with the country already arguing over the slavery issue. Others, Southern Presidents before him, had brought slaves into the White House...but now, at the halfway point of the 19th century, this was an issue aboil, and perhaps discretion should be the order of the day.

Taylor, former general and hero of the recently concluded Mexican War, moved up to Washington and its Federal White House from Louisiana. He owned slaves.

As he and Mrs. Taylor settled in, the White House staff they kept or assembled would consist of James K. Polk's old steward, Henry Bowman, followed in the same post by German immigrant Ignatius Ruppert; one Swedish, two Irish housemaids; a butler, Charles Beale of Virginia; the perennial doorkeeper and messenger and...15 Zachary Taylor "house slaves" carried up to Washington from Louisiana.

Taylor worried over having highly visible slaves tending to White House chores, even if the practice did save money and help the family budget. So, he kept them "invisible." They were steered away from the public rooms on the first floor and told to do their work upstairs in the private family territory. According to pre-eminent White House historian William Seale: "They must have slept in the eight attic rooms." And it is his suggestion that Taylor was acutely aware that allowing them to move about their duties in full view of the "hundreds" passing through the public rooms every week "might have invited incident." By 1850, Seale notes, "Northerners in Washington were increasingly uncomfortable about the presence of slaves."

After all, in Taylor's day, the major debate in Congress was over the slavery-fostered Compromise of 1850. And the Civil War itself was only about 10 years away.

As a Southerner (and native of Virginia), Taylor was not unique in carrying slaves to the White House—indeed his immediate predecessor, President Polk, fired paid White House servants to replace them with *his* slaves. Unbelievable as it may sound today, Polk not only imported his own slaves from his home base in Tennessee, he actually *bought* slaves while serving as President, and then housed them all in the basement servant quarters of the White House.

Another President who installed his slaves in White House quarters was Thomas Jefferson, the very man who had lost the battle in the Continental Congress to incorporate an anti-slavery line in the Declaration of Independence. *His* Declaration.

As the nation's third President, Jefferson brought with him household slaves from Monticello, although he once complained that he preferred to have white servants, "who, when they misbehave, can be exchanged." His slaves didn't always get along with Jefferson's French-speaking White House steward, Etienne Lemaire, but it is largely from Lemaire and his notes that we know today of a baby slave born and died at the White House under Thomas Jefferson. The infant was born to slaves named Fanny and Eddy, probably in late 1806, and then became ill in the summer of 1808, with nurses helping to tend to the child. By November, Lemaire's daybook notes say, it was necessary to build a small coffin for *"l' enfant de fany."* Apparently spending his or her entire lifetime at the White House, the slave child would have been almost two in age.

Slaves also were a "normal" fixture to be seen at the White House under James Madison and Andrew Jackson. A Madison slave, in fact, once returned to the White House several of its silver items—urns, trays, candelabra—after the mansion was looted and burned during the British occupation of Washington in the War of 1812. And a Madison slave, Paul Jennings, would produce the first known *insider* memoir from the White House.

His own slaves notwithstanding, it also should be noted here, President Zachary Taylor was a stalwart defender of the United States as a union, not to be split asunder by the action of rebellious states. When three Southern congressmen sought his support one day during the raging Compromise debate, they made the mistake of saying that if California were admitted to the Union as a free state, the Southern states might seize New Mexico as added slavery territory.

Taylor, shouting and raging, practically chased the trio from his second-floor office and down the White House stairs.

Abraham Lincoln's future Vice President (before Andrew Johnson) Hannibal Hamlin found Taylor moments later "rushing around like a caged lion" and calling the departed congressmen "those damned traitors.

#  Public Audience Room

Oh, yes, if these old walls could only speak...or did they when Lincoln dreamed that he, himself, was there, dead, lying in state? Which, poor man, he was, just a few weeks later. In the storied East Room of the White House.

What volumes these walls could speak to! And not only of the seven Presidents in all who have lain in state here, but also of the joyous times, the frivolous moments, the incidental and unimportant yet captivating moments.

For here is where the first White House occupants hung their laundry to dry. Where Thomas Jefferson threw up partitions to provide living quarters for his private secretary Meriwether Lewis, future explorer of the West (Lewis and Clark Expedition). Where the ceiling fell in during the Jeffersonian term. Where, 100 years later, Teddy Roosevelt's children allegedly roller-skated. Where, no doubt about it, his daughter Alice was married to Nicolas Longworth, the congressman and future Speaker of the House for whom today's Longworth House Office Building is named.

Here, too, were married Ulysses S. Grant's daughter Nellie and Lyndon B. Johnson's daughter Lynda (to future Virginia Governor and U.S. Senator Charles S. Robb). Here, Lincoln before his death by assassination, gave a reception early in 1864 for his new master of the Union armies, the same U.S. Grant.

The East Room in the beginning was conceived as the "Public Audience Room"—from the very start, White House architect James Hoban envisioned the large, airy chamber at the east end of the White House as the Executive Mansion's primary reception room, the site of the presidential home's ranking social gatherings, and major sit-down dinners.

The large space remained an unfinished cavern for nearly 20 years after the John Adamses first occupied the White House in 1800.

Little is known of its earlier furnishings—or day-to-day uses—under the first few Presidents. John and Abigail Adams could not make much use of the room in its largely unfinished state in 1800. Jefferson, the nation's third President, not only housed Lewis in the room—until the waterlogged ceiling came down—but may also have used it as a pantry and storage room. His inventory of 1809 mentions a table and kettle used for washing "tumblers" and says that 34 chairs were kept in the "Large Unfinished Room."

James Madison held Cabinet meetings in one part of that room—at its south end. And speaking of Madison, hanging in the East Room in more recent years has been the famous Gilbert Stuart portrait of George Washington that Dolley Madison so often is credited with rescuing from the British in the War of 1812.

Remember? As the British swooped down upon Washington and the government fled...as the British approached, that moment when they set fire to the White House. But, she found, the portrait was screwed to the wall. No time to dilly-dally, with the British coming! So, she ordered the frame broken and the canvas itself to be pried out, and given into "the hands of two gentlemen from New York, for safekeeping." It was. (Former Madison slave Paul Jennings said, however, that rather than Dolley, it was two White House workers who did the rescuing.)

After the British had left town and restoration of the damaged White House was begun, the East Room underwent finishing touches—and even some furnishings. But the four sofas and two dozen chairs placed in the grand chamber had not been upholstered when John Quincy Adams, son of the mansion's first occupant, used the room for his New Year's Day receptions. Following Adams, Andrew Jackson, the frontiersman, added some very fancy furnishings that began to do the "Public Audience Room" justice. He installed wallpaper (yellow), carpeting (red-bordered), cut-glass chandeliers, black marble fireplace mantels, gilt-framed mirrors and various lighting fixtures of the non-electrical sort (since electricity was not yet domesticated for man's use). Under Jackson, too, there appeared curtains in white, blue and yellow pastels and upholstery that one visitor described as "light-blue satin-silk."

All on that day was a far cry from the busy, baroque tastes of the Victorian Age, which found U.S. Grant adding phony beams above gilded columns and Chester Arthur apparently happy with New York designer Louis Tiffany's lining for the ceiling—silver paper!

In the interim, of course, from the time of Jackson to that of Grant and Arthur, the East Room had seen other, more serious, even hard uses. The first Union officer killed in the Civil War, Ephraim Ellsworth, was brought here to lie in state in the home of his good friend, Abe Lincoln. Lincoln's own son, Willie, passed through the room in a coffin after he died of natural causes at age 12. Union troops at one historical moment were quartered in the room, and then Lincoln's body was placed here, in state, while the Nation absorbed the shock of its first presidential assassination.

On happier days, however, it was here that the Teddy Roosevelts held a memorable Day-After-Christmas Party for Washington area children—memorable because 550 children, together with mothers, nannies or nurses, responded to the invitations, the entertainment schedule ran out and the children, for a brief period, ran wild.

It was here, too, under another Roosevelt—FDR—that England's visiting King George VI received the Washington diplomatic corps one summer's day in 1939, just before the eruption of World War II in Europe. And immediately after the war, Harry S. Truman, FDR's successor, held a reception in the East Room honoring the chief architect of World War II victory in Europe, General Dwight D. Eisenhower. Only a short time before, FDR himself had passed through the East Room in a coffin, but at his own prior instruction had not actually lain in state in the chamber. Less than 20 years later, a still young WWII veteran, John F. Kennedy, *would* lie in state in the "Public Audience Room."

Like the White House itself, the East Room, restored in the latter 20th century to its early "look" of classic and yet simple elegance, has seen them all...every President and entourage but one, George Washington. And that only because the White House was not yet built; Washington, D.C., was not yet the Nation's capital city. Seen them all come and go...funerals, weddings, entertainments...if walls could only speak, what tales, what memories, what volumes!

# ⚓ *Doing Nothing*

Children don't make high policy or run for re-election, but children nonetheless have been a part of the White House ever since it first became a home. They have provided some of its happiest and/or liveliest moments. One such child, hardly recalled today, once was known throughout the land as "Baby McKee." This was Benjamin Harrison's grandchild—Benjamin also—who was among the four generations of Harrisons living at the White House between the two Grover Cleveland terms of the late 19th century.

It is said that "Baby McKee" liked to hitch up his goat cart to a pet goat nicknamed "His Whiskers," and one time the animal raced to Pennsylvania Avenue in front of the North Portico, with the President himself giving chase in formal frock coat and top hat.

Even the ill-fated Lincolns had their happy, proud and poignant moments with their sons—for instance when Tad, 7, began wearing a Union officer's uniform cut down to miniature size to fit his frame.

Secretary of War Edwin Stanton even gave him a "commission" as a colonel (but it was the older Robert Todd Lincoln who would grow up to be a future Secretary of War).

The Ulysses S. Grants in the 1870s passed a happy time in the White House with three sons and a daughter, 11 to 18 in age when the family moved in. Young Fred and brother "Buck" served their father as confidential secretaries during a second term, and their sister Nellie was married in the White House. After Fred married elsewhere in 1874, he and his bride Ida lived at the White House, and their daughter Julia, named for the First Lady, was born *in* the White House.

The "Teddy" Roosevelts *descended,* one might say, on the White House with five young children, 3 to 14 in age, plus half-sister Alice, 17, in 1900. "A nervous person had no business around the White House in those days," said Chief Usher Ike Hoover years later. The White House that had just seen William McKinley die of an assassin's bullets now rang with "howls and laughter," and "nothing was too sacred for their amusement and no place too good for a playroom."

Even the President played in the attic (with the children, of course). One time, a child turned off the lights while Teddy was chasing another of this wild crowd. And, bang!, Theodore Roosevelt, President of the United States, ran into a post in the dark.

Two decades later, the Nation was saddened by the slow death of Calvin Coolidge's son Calvin, Jr., infected with blood poisoning from a blister on his foot. But happier days came again with the sights and sounds of Franklin Roosevelt's ever-growing crowd of grandchildren—a rare gathering of all 13 for his fourth inauguration in early 1945 was the largest gathering of presidential grandchildren ever assembled at any one moment in the White House.

One of the most romantic stories to come from family life at the White House has to be the meeting of two children, both age 8, at Dwight D. Eisenhower's second inauguration, one a boy, the other a girl, and both—in the photographs—showing buck teeth.

That was in 1953, and neither child *then* lived in the White House. Later, however, the young lady did...and later, they were married, the climax of a happy, storybook romance. They, of course, were "Ike's" grandson David and Richard M. Nixon's daughter Julie, most recently, Mr. and Mrs. David Eisenhower.

A series of teen-aged girls lived at the White House after FDR died and Harry S. Truman gave way to "Ike," and Eisenhower in turn bowed to John F. Kennedy as White House occupant. They were the Lyndon B. Johnson daughters Luci and Lynda Byrd, the Nixon daughters Julie and Tricia, the Gerald Ford daughter Susan, and the Jimmy Carter daughter Amy.

Just before that hair-dryer parade, the Kennedys had moved into the White House with daughter Caroline, all of 3 years of age, and infant son John Jr. ("John-John"), 2½ months. If for no other reason, Caroline may go down in history for her answer when asked one day what her father the President was doing just then. "Oh," she said, "he's upstairs with his shoes and socks off, not doing anything."

## 🦅 Fit For Clerks or Queens

Kings and queens have slept here, a famous prime minister and even a sour-visaged Soviet foreign minister. An artist of some note slept and worked by the northern light here. Presidential secretaries traditionally made this room their home. At one time, six clerks made it their office. Another time, the door locked, it may have been the setting for a key bit of political sleuthing by Abe Lincoln.

Peel away the historical layers of the Queens' Bedroom, or Rose Guest Room, at the eastern end of the second floor, and the geological strata of American history appear, one by one.

Here, in Andrew Jackson's day, was his friend, longtime "houseguest" and artist R.E.W. Earl. A widower after marrying, and then losing, the late Rachael Jackson's niece, Earl both slept and worked in the bedroom above the East Room on the north side of the great house. He previously had stayed for long periods at Jackson's Tennessee "manse" called The Hermitage, and his portrait of Rachael now was hanging in the bereaved Andrew Jackson's own bedroom.

Later, it became traditional for the presidential secretaries to live in the same northeast room; Lincoln's two secretaries both slept in the bedroom and one, John Hay, used the small corner room next to it as his office.

The smaller room, eventually a dressing room, saw different uses over the White House eras—as office, as storage, as bedroom. And across the hall from both once were the President's own offices. In between was the very public hallway where visitors waited in hopes of gaining access to the man inside those offices. Oilcloth covered the floor as some protection against its rough usage, and spittoons were a common sight in the hallway. It was like that, with crowds lining the hallway and the nearby "business stairs" in effort to see the President, when Lincoln first took the reins of government—the

Union's government, as events turned out. He officially took office in March 1861, and in early April the Civil War had not yet erupted.

In Charleston Harbor, Fort Sumter was isolated, under threat... if Lincoln did nothing, the secessionists might regard that as weakness. To do something, on the other hand, would mean sending supplies by U.S. Navy vessels, possibly mis-read as an affront and challenge. Virginia had not yet seceded but was teetering when Lincoln received a loyalist Virginian behind locked doors in a second-floor bedroom of the White House—probably in the Rose Guest Room, historians say.

From this agent's report on events at the convention in Richmond, Lincoln deduced that the loyalist cause in Virginia was weak, probably doomed. After his informant John Baldwin left, Lincoln ordered the supply expedition to sail for Fort Sumter. If Virginia would not hold, what had he to lose, after all. He also sent courteous word to the governor of South Carolina on April 8. On April 12, Fort Sumter came under Confederate fire—the Civil War was underway. Two days later, Fort Sumter surrendered...the rest, as they say, is history.

When the smoke had cleared just a few years later, Lincoln himself was one of the many victims...and his successor, Andrew Johnson of Tennessee, had moved into the White House, where the former bedroom for the presidential secretaries now became an office for six clerks. Still later, when the wounded James Garfield lay dying in his bedroom at the west end of the second floor in 1881, the future Queen's Bedroom was for a time converted to use as an emergency telegraph office.

As the White House moved into the 20th century, the Teddy Roosevelts made sweeping changes. The eastern hall no longer housed spittoons or even offices, and Edith Kermit Roosevelt insisted upon rose as the bedroom's color. By the time of Herbert Hoover, the large, comfortable Rose Room and its dressing room in the corner were fixtures—probably the favorite guest room suite in the house. It now came complete with a four-poster, canopied bed known as "the Andrew Jackson Bed." And maybe it was.

Later still, at the advent of World War II, Winston Churchill slept in the Rose Room—and during the war, so did Stalin's unsmiling foreign minister V.M. Molotov (as in "Molotov cocktail").

By late in the 20th century, the venerable room had welcomed guests ranging from those two major figures of the world stage to a number of queens, among them Queens Elizabeth (England); Wilhelmina and Juliana (the Netherlands); Frederika (Greece). And so it is, and has been since the 1960s, "The Queens' Bedroom." And hanging on one rose-hued wall is an apt painting, a portrait of Emily Donelson, Andrew Jackson's niece who acted as a surrogate First Lady for the widower President. And the artist? Ralph E.W. Earl, the same artist and friend of Jackson who once occupied the very same room.

# 🦅 *Man Reclining On Bed*

A day in the life of the nation's only crippled President usually began about 8 a.m., with a breakfast carried to his bedroom on a tray. While partaking of his meal, he would breeze through half-a-dozen newspapers, seated half-dressed in a sweater or cape. He liked, his wife once said, no conversation during this initial hour of the day's activities.

Still not quite ready for the outside world, he would receive his chief staff aides—Press Secretary Steve Early, confidant (and chief secretary) Louis Howe, and Military Aide Edwin M. Watson, roughly from 9 to 9:30 a.m. They would brief him on the day's schedule, and then they left the field to Franklin Delano Roosevelt's personal valet Irvin McDuffie (whose wife Lizzie was a White House maid).

It was time for dressing and shaving.

He had to be wheeled into the bathroom, but once there he shaved himself. His Commerce Secretary Harold Ickes recalls conferring with him there one day. "There he was, sitting before a mirror in front of the washstand, shaving. He invited me to sit on the toilet seat while we talked...."

Next, back into the bedroom and Ickes, struck by the scene before him, watched as FDR "reclined on his bed while his valet proceeded to help him dress." What struck the onlooker at this intimate—and yet apparently commonplace moment—was "the unaffected simplicity and personal charm of the man."

Said Ickes also: "He was the President of the United States but he was also a plain human being, talking over with a friend matters of mutual interest while he shaved and dressed with the help of his valet. His disability didn't seem to concern him in the slightest degree or to disturb his urbanity."

By 10:30 a.m., FDR ordinarily would be ready to face his more public schedule for the day. That meant, first, being pushed in his wheelchair to the office suite in the West Wing, built by another Roosevelt—cousin Teddy. The way for polo-victim FDR was eased by newly constructed ramps.

Roosevelt, like many Presidents before and after, would spend most of the working day in his Oval Office (he created a new one in 1934), but this was also the spot where he had his lunch. He first would run through appointments of about 15 minutes each with people he should see, for a total of about two hours.

The former Under Secretary of the Navy had embellished the room's bare walls and its furnishings with ship models on the mantel and engravings of river settings with more watercraft by Currier and Ives, and next to his paralyzed, useless feet were likely to be his two Irish setters, and since he was a grandfather, wrote the historian Arthur M. Schlesinger Jr. *(The Coming of the New Deal),* the presidential desk bore an oddly mixed combination of government papers, books and toy pigs or donkeys, and yet nearby, but inconspicuous, were the presidential flag and the Great Seal in the ceiling. "Behind the President, light streamed softly in through great glass windows running down to the floor, and to the east, briefly glimpsed, were the quiet rose garden and the porticoes and magnolia trees."

Compared to the Washington world immediately outside, said the historian, "this bright and open room had an astonishing serenity." Another visitor and close observer, Swiss biographer Emil Ludwig, said: "You would think you were in the summer residence of the general manager of a steamship company, who has surrounded himself with mementoes of the days when he was captain."

Similarly, the bedroom FDR had left earlier in the day was most informal—more ship prints on the wall, and on the mantel there, more toy animals, plus family photos and various knick-knacks. The bed itself was of white iron, and next to it was a white table. The room in its entirety, Schlesinger found, was old-fashioned, was thrown together indiscriminately, was cluttered, was "ugly and comfortable."

But now it is time for lunch—in the Oval Office, served at the desk straight from a hotel-like portable warmer. It very well could be ham with a poached egg.

Afterward, a few more appointments, followed by one to two hours of dictation to secretary Grace Tully.

Next, at 5 o'clock, came the famous "children's hour" of FDR's White House tenure. Gathering in the office staff, it was "an interlude of relaxation and gossip," explained historian Schlesinger.

At 5:30 p.m., FDR repaired to his new White House swimming pool, financed by a fund-raising campaign started by the New York *Daily News*. Then after a 20-minute swim, came cocktail time—a martini or old-fashioned before dinner.

Dinner itself was followed by more office work in the private FDR study—located in the second floor private quarters, it was one of the three oval rooms in the White House proper. He might deal with papers here, dictate or have more meetings.

And finally, into bed before the witching hour. In just five minutes, usually, the President of the United States was sound asleep.

One thing, though. Unlike some others, this crippled occupant of the White House had a stern rule for the Secret Service. They were never, said Schlesinger, "never allowed. . .to lock the doors of his room at night."

## 🦅 *Sentimental Evenings*

Strike up the United States Marine Band in the Eisenhower White House and what do we hear? On this particular occasion, it was the Wedding March from *Lohengrin.* And entering the East Room at measured pace, veiled in white, was no nervous young bride, but Mamie Eisenhower!

And following her this evening in 1959, two more middle-aged women dressed in white also. Close friends, in fact—Mrs. Neil McElroy, wife of the Secretary of Defense, and Mrs. Leonard Heston, whose husband, a general, was commander of Walter Reed Army Medical Center in Washington.

And all walking this measured tread. And at the center of the room met by their respective husbands. And a slight readjustment as now the Marine Band played a waltz, and the couples glided and bowed around the room before onlooking friends.

And after that, all three couples assembled in front of a clergyman, who led them in repeating their marriage vows. "There were audible sobs from some of the guests," reported Lester and Irene David in their book *Ike and Mamie.*

Reason for the unusual White House "wedding"? An anniversary—the 43rd anniversary for Ike and Mamie. It also marked anniversaries for their old friends the McElroys and the Heatons. So realistic was the planning for the mock wedding that the women carried bridal bouquets.

But this was not the first such sentimental occasion noted in the Eisenhower White House. In 1954, Ike and Mamie celebrated their 38th anniversary by inviting 100 members of his 1915 West Point Class (and a few widows) to dinner at the White House, with both the Marine Band and the Air Force Symphony Orchestra playing for the President and his guests. After Ike on that evening squired Mamie through "The Anniversary Waltz," he told a friend it was their first dance in 16 years—the first since before he had gone off to war in World War II!

During the same evening, the Marine Band had played the popular songs of the 1915 era, and Ike had "distributed West Point song books and led the guests in a community sing." Apparently, on both evenings, a good, sentimental time was had by all!

## 🦅 *JFK Misses His Lunch*

For sophisticated diplomats, grizzled old pols and teary-eyed sentimentalists alike, there was one hallmark of the Kennedy White House that was special and unforgettable—children.

There were, on the one hand, two very young Kennedys, John and Caroline, always much in evidence despite the size and official function of the presidential home. "Every morning, like the merriest of tinkling chandeliers, the house resounded with the laughter of the children and their friends," recalled White House Social Secretary Letitia Baldridge years later.

Further, their childish accoutrements had become a part of the landscape. On the South Lawns, a tree house, swings, a jungle gym. Or the sight might be Caroline riding her pony, Macaroni by name. Or, upon an accommodating snowy day, "Mrs. Kennedy driving the children around the snow in an old-fashioned horse-drawn sleigh."

On most mornings, Caroline walked her "daddy" from the second-floor family apartment to his office...his Oval Office in another part of the house. The children's accoutrements did not confine themselves either to the South Lawns or the private quarters upstairs, it also seems. "No matter how stern or unbending a foreign official and his wife might be," wrote Tish Baldridge, "as I was escorting them through the Mansion, I loved to watch their faces change from sternness to enthusiasm, from seriousness to laughter, at the sight of one roller skate peeking timidly out from under a historic damask drapery—or a tricycle dumped momentarily against the marble pedestal holding Abraham Lincoln's bronze bust."

In addition to the impact of the Kennedys' own children, there was the concerted and deliberate stress on youth that was a hallmark of the Kennedy White House—concerts, performances, tours and like extravaganzas *by* young people, *for* young people. The first in a series of youthful outdoor concerts on the White House Lawn was given by the Greater Boston Youth Symphony and the Breckinridge Boys' Choir from Breckinridge, Texas—the unexpectedly chilly April day forced a change in the day's drink menu from cool lemonade to hot chocolate. But the concert established a little-known Kennedy "tradition," too.

President John F. Kennedy briefly appeared to welcome the young White House guests and to encourage their musical calling. "He apologized for not being able to stay through the concert, but promised to leave the door of his office open, so he could hear everything. The children kept looking back, and sure enough, the French doors of the Presidential office were kept open throughout, as they were for every children's concert thereafter." Kennedy, in fact, always took pains to greet his young visitors whenever he could—one day, an 11-year-old who had been eating chocolate cake found himself shaking JFK's hand. JFK, in turn, found his hand covered with sticky icing. Unperturbed, he licked his palm and told his young onlookers: "Mumm, good! I'll have to have a piece of that, too."

On another occasion, the visiting Korean Orphans' Choir, escorted by Ms. Baldridge, "bumped into Caroline and her nursery school classmates." Without prompting, the Korean tykes lined up in two rows "and burst into song right in the hallway." Caroline and her playmates stood and listened, then applauded at the end...the admittedly sentimental Social Secretary hurriedly reaching, at the same time, for her handkerchief.

Typically, too, the Korean orphans left with White House presents—PT-boat tie clips for the boys and "little link bracelets with the PT-boat charm" for the girls. "Each child had an enormous lollipop in his hand—and, of course, the precious memory of having sung for Caroline Kennedy."

Another occasion for tears was the day the Interlochen Music Camp National High School Symphony Orchestra and ballet corps appeared before an audience of handicapped and orphaned children, the Interlochen children dressed in uniforms and "looking like an army of scrubbed angels."

At one point, JFK strode forth to deliver his greeting. The children broke into a choral rendition of "Hail to the Chief." And among the onlookers, the tears really flowed ("...it was heartening to notice that even some of the Social Aides were flicking tears away from the corners of their eyes.").

Still to come, though, was the bright, sunshiny day when Tish Baldridge and her cohorts led "a wheel-chair brigade" of spastic children into the Rose Garden as part of a special, private tour for the terribly afflicted youngsters. It was not expected that they would see the President, or he, them. "The President, we knew, would be upstairs having lunch, prior to rushing to the State Department Auditorium for a televised press conference." The Rose Garden had been chosen as a stopping point to avoid disturbing the wartime commander of PT-109.

But, lo, here came a man quite suddenly, "through a French door onto the terrace." And it was. . . it was JFK, running late, but insistent on briefly visiting with each child. *Visiting* meant a snatch of conversation with each, a shake of the afflicted hands or a touch on the cheek.

Meanwhile, the clock was ticking. No time now for a presidential lunch.

Unlike everyone else, Kennedy seemed to comprehend when the spasm-tortured children talked to him. "Their speech had been so affected by their affliction, I could not understand one word," recalled Social Secretary Baldridge.

Kennedy reached one child in particular, a boy. He knelt down to hear him. "Then he dashed back into his office, returned with an old PT-boat skipper's hat he had used in the war, and plopped it down on the boy's head."

The President cf course missed his lunch that day and was late for his nationally broadcast press conference. Did it really matter? Tish Baldridge would forever remember the spastic child's reaction. "The child's face radiated a joy totally impossible to describe. I will never forget the look in his eyes." Somehow, as JFK knelt by his side, the boy had been able to explain. . .to tell about his father. As JFK himself later explained the exact situation: "His father was in PT boats, too. His father is dead."

## ⚓ *Jackie to the Rescue*

After glamorous, sophisticated Jackie Kennedy "conquered" Paris in 1961, there came an all-important summit pitting her young American President-husband from Boston against an "old pol" of the Bolshevik school, Soviet Premier Nikita Khrushchev. Typically, when Austria greeted the two heads of state with a black-tie dinner on the first night of summitry in Vienna, Khrushchev appeared with his standard bag-of-wheat suit.

At a ballet performance in the historic Schonbrunn Palace that evening, White House staffers further noticed, the Soviet premier did not always watch the graceful dancers on stage. Instead, he was seen "ogling" First Lady Jackie Kennedy, who of course was beautifully dressed for such an occasion.

While his more-than-just-plump wife Nina looked "schoolmarmish and self-conscious" in her "plainest of dark dresses," Jackie made a startling contrast, recalled Social Secretary Letitia Baldrige.

Nonetheless, the White House staffers working on summitry protocol and social arrangements behind the scenes "immediately liked" Nina Khrushchev. "She was sweet and gracious whenever we talked to her." By contrast, her husband was "diffident and difficult." Perhaps Khrushchev was conscious that in Vienna in 1961 he was "being publicly compared to the glamorous young President in a city that frankly loathed anything Soviet." In any case, his smiles that first evening were reserved for the glamorous *Mrs.* Kennedy. "Interpreters were, naturally, used all the time, but one could tell he enjoyed the extra time just to gaze at her."

Vienna's complete disenchantment with the Soviet visitor was obvious when the official motorcades took to the streets with their high-ranking passengers. The Soviets evoked "sullen silence" from the Austrian onlookers, while the Kennedy motorcade "instigated near-riots of joyous, screaming Viennese."

Meanwhile, as the husbands met officially during the second day of summitry, First Lady Jackie was all diplomat—and kindheared human being—when a minor crisis arose at a luncheon for the visiting ladies. The hostess was the Austrian President's daughter, and the luncheon was held in the Palais Pallavacini, with "an exact balance" of Austrian, Soviet and American guests.

The meal over, the party had moved to the living room for coffee. Meanwhile, a crowd of 3,000 or so onlookers had gathered in the square outside the palace. Now they began chanting—chanting Jackie's name. "In every country, the rhythm had been the same," wrote Baldrige in her book *Of Diamonds And Diplomats: An Autobiography Of A Happy Life.* The crowds would chant "Jac-kie!" over and over.

Here, though, there was an embarrassing complication. The crowd outside showed no recognition of that other "First Lady"— Nina Khrushchev. Conversation among the luncheon guests faltered as Nina sat there, "gazing sadly down at her feet, saying nothing."

The atmosphere in the room was tense, with the Austrian hostess obviously wondering how to salvage the situation. Instead of the hostess, however, it was Jackie Kennedy to the rescue.

"She went to the open window to appease the impatient crowd, smiled and waved at them. The volume of noise became an ear-splitting symphony of cheering and applause. After about one minute, she took Mme. Khrushchev gently by the arm, and led her back to the window. She held up Mme. Khrushchev's hand for a second, and then the Russian began to wave on her own."

That did it! The crowd fell into step right away. Now the roaring chant was: "Jac-kie! Nin-a! Jac-kie! Nin-a!"

## 🦅 *Old Compatriot's Visit*

There was real war talk in the air when an old fighting compatriot arrived in Andrew Jackson's capital, talk of force to make the State's Righters in the South fall into line behind the Federal government's lead...talk of armed conflict, secession, and *nullification*. Specifically, South Carolina nullified the 1828 and 1832 Federal tariffs, and Jackson wanted to use Federal troops to push South Carolina into line.

It was a bitter debate, with Jackson's own Vice President, John C. Calhoun of South Carolina, openly opposing the President, even resigning to join the battle in the Senate. So it was that Martin Van Buren ran with Jackson in 1832. And after Jackson won re-election with New Yorker Van Buren by his side, South Carolina withdrew its original nullification, only to "nullify" a congressional action authorizing use of Federal forces against the state—a denial never tested *per se,* and no satisfactory end to the growing schism between North and South that would erupt, 30 years later, in the Civil War.

Caught up in the hot political battle shortly after his re-election, Jackson heard his old "Sergeant", Sam Dale, was in town. A compatriot of Jackson's in the war against the Creek Indians and again against the British at New Orleans, Dale in the years since 1815 had advanced to the rank of general in the Mississippi militia. Still, he was "too modest" to seek an audience with Jackson. And so, Jackson sent for him, using a willing U.S. Senator as the messenger.

Dale arrived at the White House to find Jackson closeted in the upstairs study in a strategy session on the nullification issue. Among the six or seven gentlemen present was Jackson ally and U.S. Senator Thomas Hart Benton of Missouri.

Jackson obviously didn't want his old comrade-in-arms to feel awed. He pointedly included Dale in the conversation, saying: "General Dale, if this thing goes on, our country will be like a bag of meal with both ends open. Pick it up and it will run out."

Later, the political associates gone, Jackson took out a decanter of whiskey to share with his old friend and they talked. Jackson at one point told Dale he had done his duty but he was now in his advancing age and paying the price of solitude for having remained a bachelor.

Apparently this reference brought Jackson to the painful subject of his late wife Rachel, since he paced the room with his eyes suddenly full of tears.

Their discussion came back to the nullification issue. "Dale," said Jackson, the Mississippian's former commander in the field of battle, "they are trying me here; you will witness it; but, by the God in Heaven, I will uphold the laws."

Dale, of course, said he hoped all would "go right."

"They SHALL go right, sir!"

And Jackson slammed his hand on a table "so hard that he broke one of his pipes," wrote his 20th-century biographer Marquis James.

Meanwhile, before the nullification storm ran its course, Jackson sent fighting ships to Charleston harbor in South Carolina, denounced any state's right to nullify or secede, and issued his Proclamation on Nullification (December 10, 1832). One who closely read the ban against such threats to the Union was an unknown country lawyer in Illinois, Abraham Lincoln. He would consult it again when composing his inaugural address of 1861.

## ⚓ *Minor Embarrassment*

You can't be at two places at once. Not an old saw, but a real episode in the life of a President—and that of a troubled private secretary—was the time, *the creative event,* when Grover Cleveland's second-term secretary, Henry T. Thurber, otherwise sober and well-suited in every way to his job, pulled up short in judgement one day when the boss was away from the office.

In fact, that was part of the problem—the boss was away, yes, but for the unannounced if slightly frivolous purpose of fishing.

Unfortunately, a major public figure chose that very moment to die.

White House comment would be appropriate.

As the reporters gathered, Thurber was on the spot. They wanted comment. But the boss had said to keep his fishing trip quiet. No disclosure!

Next best choice for a loyal secretary?

Thurber was nothing if not creative, and he simply. . .well, *created*.

Receiving the newshawks, he told them to wait. He then ostentatiously entered Cleveland's executive office, the inner sanctum, and stayed for a few moments.

That done, he re-emerged and briefed the reporters in solemn tones. Yes, the President was sorrowful; yes, the Nation had suffered a great loss, and in fact, he, Thurber, hardly had ever seen the President quite so moved!

All this came out the next day. . .but so did news that Cleveland had just passed through Virginia on his way back to the White House in Washington, where he had NOT been the day before.

Embarrassing.

##  *'Mrs. Presidentress'*

In the anteroom, among those awaiting an audience with the President, was one fellow who was "oval-faced" and "bilious looking." This same specimen seeking some special presidential favor was distinguished by the fact that he "sucked the head of a thick stick, and from time to time took it out of his mouth, to see how it was getting on."

Also in the waiting room were "a Kentucky farmer, six-feet-six in height" and "a tall wiry, muscular old man, from the West." So observed English writer Charles Dickens when visiting the John Tyler White House in 1842, the year before Dickens was to concoct his array of colorful characters—one of them, Scrooge, now a part of the English language—in his legendary *A Christmas Carol*.

Dickens always did tend to see—and concoct—caricatures of people he'd observed, and so it shouldn't be too surprising that he also would seize upon the spitting of the American favor-seekers awaiting their turn in the White House: "Indeed, all these gentlemen were so very persevering and energetic in this latter particular [spitting] and bestowed their favors so abundantly upon the carpet, that I take it for granted the presidential housemaids have high wages."

Dickens returned soon to England, and to deserved literary fame, much of it based upon novels first seen as serialized installments in British periodicals—like today's familiar soap opera. He could have looked to the Tyler White House in America, however, for just such a serial story.

Tyler, a Virginian who had been state lawmaker, U.S. House member, governor and U.S. Senator, was Vice President when Virginia-born William Henry Harrison of the Ohio "frontier" died just a month into his presidency. Tyler, far more experienced in politics, at first was called "His Accidency," and, true, he was the first Vice President to succeed so suddenly—and constitutionally—to office upon the death of a sitting President.

Even so, Tyler insisted upon being a President, rather than an acting title-holder or caretaker. That was in the spring of 1841, and he entered the White House as husband to the gracious Letitia Christian Tyler and as the father of their five living children.

But his wife, a stroke victim, was an invalid, and once settled into the family quarters on the second floor, she came downstairs only rarely. One such occasion was the wedding of daughter Elizabeth ("Lizzie") in the East Room in January of 1842. For the most part, though, daughter-in-law Priscilla Cooper (Mrs. Robert Tyler) acted as Tyler's White House hostess.

All that changed not long after Letitia Tyler's death on September 10, 1842. Priscilla, a stage actress before she married Tyler's son (and secretary), wrote that after her widely loved mother-in-law's death, "Nothing can exceed the loneliness of this large and gloomy mansion."

As months passed, Priscilla continued as acting hostess, a genuine hit with Washington society. She was ably advised by the *grand dame* in her seventies who lived across today's Lafayette Square, Dolley Madison. During this period, Tyler children and slaves from the family homestead in Virginia lived—and ate—at the White House. Tyler was not wealthy, and the presidential salary was only $25,000 a year at the time. The Whigs in Congress, angered by Tyler's political independence, would not provide the public monies needed to touch up the downstairs public rooms of the Executive Mansion, and they became so run-down that the press began calling the White House the "Public Shabby House." Tyler, a brave man politically but until now most conservative personally, struggled on—suddenly so unpopular that the Whig press seized upon a flu outbreak as the "Tyler Grippe."

Enter a plump, rosy-cheeked young woman the age of Tyler's own older children, Julia Gardiner, socially prominent daughter of former New York State Senator David Gardiner.

It was the winter social season of 1843, not long after Mrs. Tyler's death, and suddenly John Tyler, 53, was falling in love with Julia, 23. But. . .no, no, she allegedly said to his earnest entreaties at first, even though she admired "the incomparable grace of his bearing," the elegance of his conversation, the "silvery sweetness" of his voice. No, no, marriage would be unthinkable, despite the mutual attraction and his loneliness.

Even so, the busy social activities continued, and one February night in 1844 she gladly joined many others at a White House ball, all the more titillated by the plans for a Potomac River cruise the next day, a gay champagne outing aboard the U.S. Navy frigate *Princeton.* . . . And when they called down the companionway and said to the President, come on up and see the last shot fired from the frigate's new gun, he said no, he was "better engaged" for the moment because of a song about to be sung. It was a favorite song for Tyler, and Julia Gardiner.

Minutes later, they heard the boom. They noticed smoke wafting down the companionway. And there were shouts, a tumult, on deck above.

Earlier in the day, bright and brisk on the Potomac, all had gone so well! The U.S. Navy's new frigate, the *Princeton* had taken on board the President, Julia, her father, the Secretary of the Navy and members of the Cabinet, along with various military officers and even the redoubtable Dolly Madison. They had boarded at Alexandria, across the Potomac shoreline from the District of Columbia on the morning of February 28, 1844—350 distinguished guests and crew of 178.

The *Princeton* shoved off and shortly after, the 12-inch bow gun, called the Peacemaker, was fired—a success! The ship's iron gun represented a possibly major new development in ordnance.

Near Mount Vernon, where the frigate turned about for the return leg of the day's extravaganza, a second shot thrilled the festive onlookers anew. They then were treated to dinner below decks, followed by singing. At 4 o'clock or so, the guests were told another shot would soon be fired. Julia Gardiner had just told Tyler that *their* favorite song was coming, and so he declined to go above. Her father, though, went topside with others in the party to watch the final shot with the new cannon.

The breech burst, however, and on the new cannon's left side all seven men standing by, including two of the ship's crew, were killed. The slain visitors included Secretary of State Abel Upshur, Navy Secretary Thomas Walker Gilmer. . .and Julia's own father.

Below, with the dull report, they heard the shouts: "The Secretary of State is dead!" Julia was distraught: "Let me go to my father," she cried. And later she wrote: "Someone told me that there had been an accident, the gun had exploded. . .that drove me frantic."

A woman, noting Julia's distress, told her, "My dear child, you can do no good. Your father is in heaven."

Would Dickens have written this sequel to such events? For it wasn't long before Tyler's daughter-in-law Priscilla had to abandon the mansion to a usurper. Julia took over as the first First Lady to be married to a President already in office. *And not everybody quite understood.* John Quincy Adams, by now 77, confided to his diary that Tyler and wife were the laughingstock of official Washington.

Be that as it may, Julia Tyler put on a brave show—so "brave" that she became noted for her queenly reign at social functions, for sitting on a dais in the Blue Room to receive guests while ostentatiously flanked by 12 "maids of honor." She obviously loved her role as queen of the White House and did not at all resent it when Daniel Webster or John C. Calhoun presented toasts to "Mrs. Presidentress." The conservative Mr. President, meanwhile, responded in like manner, seemingly glad now to welcome the waltz at White House soirees, even though he once had condemned the dance as "vulgar."

A realist in gauging his popularity as close to zero, Tyler declined to seek re-election and took his new wife home to Virginia and his Sherwood Forest plantation house.

# ⚓ *Power Dive Underway*

Coming straight at the White House out of the sky one spring day in 1946 was a large, large, LARGER airplane. . .looming bigger and bigger every fractional second. Aboard the ever-*huger* and speedy four engine job, his face pressed against a window, waving, laughing all the while, was the passenger who had ordered the pilot to break all the rules, who had told him to "dive" on the White House. To make "like a jet fighter," because, "I've always wanted to try something like that."

And so. . .first leveling off at 3,000 feet in the forbidden zone above the Capitol and White House. . .and then down to 2,000 feet, throttle up to full power, and then down some more, to 1,500 feet. And here, said the pilot later, "Our angle was still steep and our noise was deafening."

On the roof of the White House, the Truman White House of the 1940s, people were watching warily. . ."stiffly". So goes the story. . . .

At 1,000 feet, "the flat, white target looked big, filling our whole world."

At the cockpit window, a little, middle-aged, bespectacled man. Graying at the temples.

And 1,000 feet was nothing yet for the roaring *Sacred Cow,* name of the big plane. Nothing, that is, to 500 feet instead. Which is where the plane was next, in mini-seconds. "At 500 feet," said pilot (Air Force Colonel) Hank Myers later, "I had the *Cow* leveled and we roared over the White House roof wide open. I caught a split-second glimpse. Everyone there was frozen with fear and wonder."

And the man in command, face pressed against the cockpit window, just carrying on. He knew Margaret and Bess Truman were on that roof.

Nor were the fiends in the airplane through yet!

"We climbed up to 3,000 feet again, swooped, circled, and fell into another dive. Everybody was watching us. But this time Margaret and her mother were jumping and waving. We shot past them, at little below 500 feet and roarded back upstairs once more."

Presidential wife and daughter, of course had recognized the plane by now—the President's own four-engine official aircraft. Which now turned quickly out of the forbidden air space and headed for Independence, Missouri, where the bespectacled man in the cockpit planned to visit his mother that Sunday, May 19, 1946.

Things were a bit looser in those days. Harry Truman, related Seth Kantor's magazine story later, had just buzzed the White House.

## 👑 *Pursuit With Cane*

One has to wonder. Who was the more surprised? The President or his assailant? And, in the long run, who was the more forgiving?

Taking a Potomac River steamer downriver on the way to Fredericksburg, Virginia, to lay a cornerstone for a monument honoring George Washington's mother one day in 1831, Andrew Jackson merely looked up and apologized when a nicely dressed, clean-cut looking young man approached him during the steamer's stop at Alexandria, Virginia.

Jackson thought the young man was there to proffer a friendly greeting. And Jackson was discomfited because he was caught in a chair "wedged" between a berth and a table. "Excuse my rising, sir," said the President.

It then seemed the intruder was taking off his glove to shake hands.

Nearly always polite, Jackson said, "Never mind your glove, sir," and stuck out his own hand.

Looking on, among others, were Jackson's recent Secretary of State, Edward Livingston, his new Secretary of State Louis McLane and the famous writer Washington Irving. *Looking on...* as, totally by surprise, the young man "thrust his fist violently into Jackson's face as if to pull his nose."

Jackson, not known, no matter how polite, to abide by such an affront, reacted violently. "What, sir! What, sir!" he exclaimed as, with a crash, he kicked the table out of his way and jumped to his feet. In seconds, the room was in tumult. "McLane, Livingston and Washington Irving grappled the intruder who threw them off and darted through a door with Jackson after him, cane upraised."

At the door, in fact, friends quickly decided the wisest course at the moment would be to stop the enraged Jackson, his health known to be delicate. While the President's assailant disappeared beyond, they shut the door. Jackson was left to pound on it, to shout that they had better open it up, or he would take steps to break it down.

Eventually, a cooler President was allowed to proceed to the deck. There, he was told the intruder had fled down the landing dock and into the town of Alexandria. He had escaped, but only for the moment, since he had been recognized—"as Robert B. Randolph, a former lieutenant of the Navy dismissed for attempted theft of funds belonging to the late John D. Timberlake, whom he had succeeded as purser of the frigate *Constitution,*" said Jackson biographer Marquis James.

Told all of this, Jackson was sufficiently calm to turn down a Virginia man's offer to chase Randolph and kill him within 15 minutes.

"No sir," said Jackson, "I want no man to stand between me and my assailants, and none to take revenge on my account."

More privately, Jackson was still sputtering in fiercer terms—had he known what Randolph was up to, the young man "never would have moved with life from the tracks he stood in."

After a bit more time, though, Jackson was more willing to forgive. Given a chance to testify against Randolph after leaving the Presidency, Jackson not only declined, but asked that any sentence or fine imposed upon the former Navy officer should be suspended. "I have to this age," explained Old Hickory, "complied with my mother's advice to indict no man for assault or sue him for slander."

# ✹ *High-Toned Ball*

Come one, come all (almost)...to the Chandelier Ball! "I went first when I was a girl of 18," said one ball-goer years after the fact. "The Chandelier Ball was the finest dance in town, and the food was fabulous, though my mother would not let me go up to the dining room because of the wine."

To be invited was high honor and prestige. "Everything was done just like at the White House," added Lillian Rogers Parks, who was a seamstress in the venerable presidential residence and later wrote the book *My Thirty Years Backstairs At the White House.* "The palms were from the greenhouse, the little gilt chairs, I guess the white damask tablecloths and napkins, and even the coat racks from the coatrooms."

Also more or less borrowed for the festive and annual occasion was another White House fixture, the Marine Band.

White House dignitaries were invited—and expected to attend. But *not* the President and his wife.

The hosts were all male and all black—and all employees of the White House. Their ball, probably started around 1910, according to White House historian William Seale, was named for the chandeliers in the East Room—itself the scene of many an entertainment and dance. There, too, many of the black employees spent time primping, serving, cleaning up, and other chores. They, of course, had been an indispensable support at White House social functions for years. And as its day-to-day staff.

So, why not have a ball of their own? It was held annually, if somewhat briefly, at the Oddfellows Hall in Washington, 16th and M Streets—dinner on the second floor (where the wine was) and dancing on the first floor.

According to historian Seale, "The prestige of the Chandelier Ball generated a kind of rivalry among the white employers of the blacks who attended." Mrs. William Howard Taft, for instance, went out of her way to provide maid Annie Anderson a silk gown with train, adorned with silk chiffon roses. And Ellen Wilson's social secretary Belle Hagner gave cook Alice Green an evening dress with pearl beads and a net veil.

Alice Green had had to wait until 1914 before she finally was invited to the exclusive affair, "having been passed over before as not being of sufficient rank." Afterwards, she pronounced it "very high toned."

All too shortlived, however, the Chandelier Ball tradition came to a halt with the advent of World War I during the same Woodrow Wilson tenure.

Alice Green did her dancing just in time!

##  *Locked Out*

For Lady Bird Johnson, one of the "funniest little moments" spent in the White House came the night she found herself—in her robe and slippers—locked out of the family quarters and no one to hear her gentle knocks or calls for help. She just couldn't help thinking the obvious. . . she knew it wasn't a bad dream, so what else to think but "those funny ads." You know, a woman, First Lady or not, caught outside a locked door in less than normal attire for public exposure. And so she indeed did think it. "I thought about all those funny ads—I went to the Opera in my Maidenform Bra—and I thought how awful it would be if I walked through the main entrance hall of the White House at about 1:30, in my dressing gown, and met a dozen or so of the departing guests."

Earlier the same evening, she and husband Lyndon B. Johnson had been entertaining Danish Prime Minister Jens Otto Krag and his wife Helle. It was not uncommon for a President and his lady to retire to the family quarters upstairs before all the guests left the premises. And after the guests, of course, there still were the staff cleaning up from the social affair in question.

Lady Bird late that night thought everyone had left. But about the time she was preparing for bed, she noticed the lights in the upstairs hall outside the bedroom were still on. She went out and started turning out one hall light after another, until she reached "the staircase that leads down to the State floor." At that point, she heard "clattering feet below disappearing in the distance," and she saw "a great blaze of light going down the steps."

To complete her entirely commendable mission of turning off the lights—now a main set of lights—she would have to step "out into the hall only a few feet." But would the door at that end of the hall then swing shut behind her. . .and lock?

It would. It did. Cautious at first, she tried leaning and reaching while holding open the door with one foot. No good. So. . ."Some giddy instinct of daring led me to just let the door close gently and to walk over and turn out the lights. Then I went back and turned the knob—sure enough the door was locked!"

That was when she began gently knocking, "hoping maybe the guests in the Queen's Room would hear me." And thinking about the Maidenform Bra ads.

Below, no more sounds, she soon would be able to write in her diary, but still a few lights on. What to do?

There wasn't any real choice, short of loudly banging on the locked door itself. There was nothing, for it but to be bold, assume "a very assured look" and head on downstairs for the little elevator that would carry her back to the *inside* of the family's second-floor quarters. Girding herself, she demurely walked on down the stairs. She walked through the first-floor hall and met "only" two or three people—departing musicians and staffers. Met them and, what else to do? "Smiled as if the whole thing were a matter of course." And, minutes later, so to bed. . .after a brief recording stint with the diary. No great harm done. No Maidenform Bra.

# Ugly Fellow Encountered

Walking one time between the White House and the War Department building was Abe Lincoln. It was at the time a small park. Along came a crippled soldier cussing and swearing and complaining about the government, President and all. And then he encountered this tall lanky stranger who asked what the problem was. The young private, recently released from the Confederate Libby Prison in Richmond, said he couldn't seem to collect his pay from the War Department, despite his good and faithful service.

Well, said the tall stranger, he once had been a lawyer and if he could look at the soldier's papers, perhaps he could provide friendly advice. They sat down under a tree to go over the documents. Then Lincoln wrote something brief on the back of the papers and told the soldier to see "Mr. Potts," who was the Chief Clerk in the War Department.

They parted, each going his own way, but a pair of unnoticed onlookers, bemused, stopped the young soldier and asked if he knew the identity of the helpful stranger.

The soldier obviously had not been all that impressed. "Some ugly fellow who pretends to be a lawyer," said the crippled soldier, perhaps made a bit bitter by his recent POW experiences.

He agreed to show the two onlookers the place where the stranger had written a line. What the line said was: "Mr. Potts—Attend to this man's case at once and see that he gets his pay."

By the end of that day, the young man who had been heard cussing the President received both his discharge and his pay—in full.

# 🦅 *Chippewa Revenge*

Tshusick was the visitor's name, and Louisa Adams, wife of John Quincy Adams, hung closely upon her words because Tshusick, a Chippewa Indian woman, talked often of Louisa's sister out there on the frontier, Harriet Boyd. Harriet was married to George Boyd, an Indian agent in the Detroit area, Michigan territory.

Tshusick had appeared out of the gloom one winter's night in 1827, to knock on a Georgetown tinsmith's door and ask to warm herself by his forge. Her story was that she walked all the way to Washington to find Mrs. Boyd's sister, "who lived in the White House of the Great Father."

That would be Mrs. Adams, the First Lady of the land, of course, and it wasn't long before helpful hands brought them together.

More of the pretty Indian woman's story was that she began her trek after her husband died, and she persevered in her quest to reach the White House despite snow, rain, ice, sleet—you name it.

But why? Why had she come? It apparently had something to do with her husband's death. Her account was that she made a vow after he died, and that vow was to find Mrs. Boyd's sister, who as the wife of the Great Father, would help her to become a Christian.

Louisa Adams was more than happy to give her blessings, social and otherwise, to the Indian woman who could speak French so well, sew and design dresses so well and just in general comport herself so well. And such a virtuous goal Tshusick had set for herself! With the President's wife as her sponsor, says James D. Horan's book, *The McKenney-Hall Portrait Gallery of American Indians,* "Tshusick was soon one of the most talked about women in Washington."

For Louisa Adams, cut off by the great distance from her sister on the remote frontier, it was just so-o-o-o fascinating to hear the enchanting Indian woman's stories about Harriet Boyd's "life in the wilderness, her husband, their daily chores, the Indians, and how Harriet kept house in a log cabin."

Even the President was taken by the visitor's charms—he gave her a silver medal. And arrangements indeed were made to have Tshusick christened at Christ Church in Georgetown. She took the name Lucy Cornelia Barbour, borrowing the first two names from the appropriately touched wife and daughter of the Secretary of War. The new Ms. Barbour found an attentive escort about the capital city in the person of the U.S. Army's next general-in-chief, Maj. Gen. Alexander Macomb.

Clearly, Washington officialdom was agog over the comely visitor from the West, but Colonel Thomas McKenney, head of the Federal government's Bureau of Indian Affairs, had become just a mite suspicious that all the appearances were too good to be true. He had written for information from the governor of the Michigan Territory, Lewis Cass—another name that Tshusick/Barbour often cited with proprietary abandon.

Informed of McKenney's supposedly casual note to his friend Cass, the Indian woman suddenly announced that she must return to her people back West. As a result, Horan's book reports, "So many presents from disappointed admirers who begged her to stay poured into the White House that President Adams told his wife to buy Tshusick a trunk."

The First Lady and family also loaded her up with gifts for the Boyds in their wilderness cabin, and the White House itself "arranged for the Chippewa to travel to the end of the stagecoach line, then buy a horse to continue her journey to Detroit."

Before she left, her constant escort, General Macomb, personally fastened about her waist a money belt "stuffed with currency." On the way west, Tshusick arranged to stay, free, at Barnum's Hotel in Baltimore for several days as the owner's guest.

Long after the Indian woman had passed from sight, it seems, came the reply to McKenney's letter from Territorial Governor Cass. Its news was somewhat deflating.

In the first place, the woman's husband was alive and well. He happened to be a short, fat Frenchman employed as a "scullion" in Harriet Boyd's kitchen!

Next, Tshusick was known far and wide in the Western territories as "superb confidence woman." She had "duped the great and the near-great" throughout "the whole length of the Canadas, from Montreal to St. Louis and from Quebeck to the Falls of St. Anthony and many times in the interior."

And now she also had conned Washington, the White House included! *Chippewa revenge.*

 *Wedded There*

They were married in the White House. One President and several (unrelated) progeny. . . .

• Like John Quincy Adams' son John Adams II and his brother George's onetime fiancée Mary Catherine in 1828. Who then spent their honeymoon in the White House as well!

• Or Lynda Byrd Johnson and Charles S. Robb in December 1967. Like many another young wife, Lynda Byrd then had to watch her Marine Corps officer-husband go off to war—the Vietnam War that ended her own father's dreams of a second elected term as President. Lynda returned from seeing him off in late March 1968 looking "like a ghost—pale, tall and drooping," said her mother. Robb, once assigned to the White House as a social aide, came back unscathed from Vietnam and acquired a law degree from the University of Virginia, won election as Lieutenant Governor and Governor of Virginia, then as U.S. Senator from Virginia.

• Again in the modern age, Richard Nixon's history-making daughter Tricia and Edward Cox, who set new precedent in June 1971 as the first couple to be married *at* the White House but *outside* the White House—in the Rose Garden. Only 400 guests and onlookers could squeeze into the garden confines, and flamboyant Martha Mitchell's "orange sherbert" garden party dress and parasol were not the only news to come out of the affair, as reported later by UPI's veteran White House reporter Helen Thomas. The big news was the rain, which delayed things for "a few hours." In the end, Tricia Nixon made the decision to brave the elements and proceed, as planned, in the Rose Garden.

She was "petite and exquisite in white lace as she came down the aisle on her father's arm." Wet chairs, but no more rain, it seems.

• Looking on, incidentally, was Alice Roosevelt Longworth, herself one of the few persons ever married in the White House. Was her wedding of 1906 comparable? Not a bit, she exclaimed, "I was married 20 years before Hollywood. This wedding was quite a production."

Actually, hers also was quite a production—it took place in the East Room, the service itself conducted by a bishop, the altar area adorned with gold cloth, and all punctuated by Easter lilies. Looking on, of course, were diplomats and members of her father Teddy Roosevelt's Cabinet, along with the socially prominent, family members and friends. One high point (of sorts) came when the irrepressible

Alice borrowed an officer's dress uniform sword to cut her wedding cake. Which she then did with stroke after stroke from the saber. The groom was Nicholas Longworth, already, in 1906, a member of Congress and later destined to become Speaker of the House.

• Another President's daughter married in the East Room was Ulysses S. Grant's winsome Nellie, united with her Englishman-fiancée Algernon Sartoris in 1874 beneath a huge bell of flowers, set off by orange blossoms imported from the South to decorate the large room. Slices of this wedding cake were "put up in little white boxes about six inches long and three inches wide," recalled White House Doorkeeper Thomas Pendel later. It was his job to pass out the wedding cake to the ladies in the nearby Red Parlor.

• Only one presidential family saw two daughters married within the White House confines—the Woodrow Wilsons, one of their weddings a grand affair with thousands of guests, and the other, just a few months later, more an intimate, family-*cum*-friends wedding. The first Wilson daughter to make White House nuptials history was young Jessie, married the evening of November 25, 1913, to Francis B. Sayre, an assistant district attorney in New York City. Theirs was the big Wilson wedding, with vows exchanged— once more, historically speaking, in the East Room. The throngs of guests were received afterward in the Blue Room and then offered refreshments in the State Dining Room. Next came sister Nell Wilson, who surprised all by falling in love with a widowed member of her father's Cabinet, Treasury Secretary William McAdoo, 26 years older than Nell. And since he had been married before, this was the smaller, more private of the two Wilson weddings. It took place in the Blue Room on May 7, 1914, and during the ceremony, McAdoo's oldest daughter, Nona, became hysterical and had to be led away. Later, Nell and her new husband dodged reporters by leaving from the South Portico in the fifth car to pass through the gates and drive off—by then, the awaiting reporters had all gone after the wrong cars.

As Nell left, she looked back and saw her mother and father standing hand in hand, and, she later said, "I horrified my husband by dissolving into tears in the darkness of the car." The next time she saw her mother, Ellen Wilson, was in late May, after Ellen had taken a fall and become ill. In bed when Nell returned from her honeymoon, "She [Ellen Wilson] had changed—she looked very small and white, and all her lovely color was gone." The daughter's "heart sank" at the sight. And all too soon Ellen Wilson died—in early August of the same year—of tuberculosis of the kidneys.

- As for the one and only President's wedding to take place in the White House, the hour was 7 o'clock in the evening, the day June 2, the year 1886. The groom was Grover Cleveland, the bride, Frances ("Frank") Folsom, his late law partner's daughter, a young woman and recent college graduate he had known since her infancy. Eight marriages had preceded Cleveland's within the White House, but none, of course, featured a President. Cleveland, himself, walked the bride down the grand stair to Mendelssohn's "Wedding March", along the transverse hall on the first floor and into the Blue Parlor of that era. He wore evening clothes of black, with a white lawn necktie and a white rose in his coat lapel. Her wedding gown, with a four-yard train behind, was decorated with orange blossoms.

The ceremony in the Blue Parlor was followed by a wedding supper served in the East Room, where the chief decoration was a "full-rigged ship" composed of flowers—roses, pansies, pinks—and set on a mirror in the center of the main table as the ship's "sea". Guests received their slice of historic wedding cake in small white satin boxes also containing a card autographed by the happy couple the night before.

Since the White House was really theirs, they could have honey-mooned on the spot, like young John Adams in 1828, but they chose not—Grover and new bride "Frank" slipped away that very evening to a special train that sped them off to a hideaway in the Alleghanies.

## 🦅 *Progress Report*

Progress at the White House. . .electrician Ike Hoover was at the venerable mansion in 1891 on behalf of the Edison Company, which had been engaged to install the first electric lights in the grand old structure. He was on the job for four months, installing both the electric-light wiring and an electric call-bell system, it seems. The official White House occupants, the Benjamin Harrisons, were hopelessly inept in dealing with such wonders of modern science, it also seems.

They were afraid to turn a light on or off "for fear of getting a shock," Hoover later recalled.

For a long time, the President's family simply wouldn't use the lights now at their disposal in the upstairs family quarters. And Hoover, himself, had to turn on the lights in the halls and parlors. They would burn all night long, "until I returned the next morning to extinguish them."

110

As for the electric call bells...why, perish the thought! "The family were even timid about pushing the electric bell buttons to call the servants! There was a family conference almost every time this had to be done."

As for Ike Hoover himself, he was so helpful, it seems further, he stayed on...and on, soon joining the ushers' staff and finally becoming a rather famous Chief White House Usher and author of the well-known book *Forty-two Years in The White House.*

Progress, progress...the John Adamses' outdoor privy, Thomas Jefferson's early water closet placed indoors. Iron stoves installed in 1809 (Jefferson also), and Martin Van Buren's rudimentary central heating system added in the 1830s.

Progress, you say...Calvin Coolidge shook 'em up when he shucked the traditional mourning coat in favor of a dark business-man's suit for normal workdays in the Oval Office. Then, too, Teddy Roosevelt it was who built the enclosed West Wing containing the same Oval Office, who did away with the old greenhouses next to the 19th-century White House and accomplished other major restoration.

And Coolidge again, moving *out* to be out of the way while replacing the shaky attic and roof with an entire, fully livable third floor, complete with sky parlor, or sun room, above the South Portico—a quiet retreat ever since for presidential folk, its view of Washington vistas considered magnificent.

Progress...also was Andrew Johnson's barber's chair innovation in the 1860s.

Or the running water initiated under Andrew Jackson, another and earlier Tennessean. And what an intricate job that was! Until Jackson, the White House had relied upon two wells, located between the main structure and, the low wings on either side that Jefferson had added in his day a bit earlier.

Engineer Robert Leckie devised and built the complex system that, with the help of gravity, would supply water to the White House and nearby public buildings such as Treasury, the State Department or War Department. By his plan, water was sent coursing through iron pipes from a spring at Franklin Square to three brick-lined, sand-bottomed reservoirs—holding ponds, really. Here, the piping surfaced to spew out the water as fountains that served to keep the reservoirs properly stirred up. Gravity had carried the water downhill to this point, but when the water moved from the reservoirs into the nearby buildings, it took constant hand-pumping by an attendant at the "ponds" to achieve the pressure necessary to push the water uphill through the internal piping.

The job took about a year to reach completion, but the result was real luxury for that era. Moreover, it wasn't long before Jackson then installed a "bathing room" in the ground level East Wing, with hot and cold baths and a shower (the water heated by coal fire under boilers).

Jackson also installed a fine brick-and-stucco stable southeast of the house to replace a jerry-built arrangement long occupying Jefferson's West Wing.

Progress, progress...there would be other improvements, many, many of them, as history moved on. So much that we take for granted today. Freezers. Cars. Telephones. The latest, always, in communications equipment, even a "hot line" to Moscow. And the items we just might have forgotten...like the underground bomb shelters dug out under the lawn during World War II.

## 👑 Workers All

They worked at the White House...all these, and so many more—
• William Henry Crook came to the Lincoln White House as one of four plainclothes guards assigned to the President...and served through five administrations before he called his career quits. "Colonel" Crook by then, he served in many capacities—as doorman for the U.S. Grants, as executive clerk and disbursing agent for the Rutherford B. Hayeses, as Chief Disbursement officer under Grover Cleveland and William McKinley. He saw, and later said, a lot. He said it was he who brought the news of Andrew Johnson's acquittal from impeachment to the Executive Mansion. He couldn't believe it when William McKinley was fatally wounded by a shooter in Buffalo, New York—"Good God!" he thought. "First Lincoln—then Garfield—and now McKinley!" He later claimed another Lincoln guard, John F. Parker, had left his post outside the Lincoln box at the Ford Theatre to watch the play himself, leaving the way clear for John Wilkes Booth to enter and shoot Lincoln in the back of the head. By the time of McKinley's arrival, meanwhile, Crook had been at the White House longer than anyone, except possibly usher Tommy Pendel, who had been a doorman and guard in the Lincoln era himself. Crook had little hair on his head and a bush growing from his chin instead.
• John Ousley began his stint as a gardener under John Quincy Adams...and stuck for more than 20 years, his home a small cottage on the White House grounds. Always faithful to his job, never

adequately paid, he grew the flowers and the vegetables in oasis-like beds to the sides of the long White House sweeps, placed the shrubbery stands more visibly and used a heavy roller to flatten the grass, often after it was nibbled close to the ground by cattle and sheep. The effect was a clean, closely cropped vista of green—like a golf course tee. He watered with the big wooden vat on wheels that Andrew Jackson provided. Then, in 1852, Millard Fillmore and his advisers wanted something much fancier, creative...symbolic of a strong nationalistic feeling. Ousley, an old man by now, received his walking papers and no thanks ("...your services as gardener or laborer on the President's Square will not be required after the end of the present month."—from the Commissioner of Public Buildings). As White House historian William Seale has put it, "Ousley and his wife passed through the gates...; within two brief years, both vanished from the written record."

• Another Colonel, Arthur Brooks, first joined government service as a War Department janitor, but he quickly saw that the White House offered good opportunity for a determined and ambitious black like himself. He had reached the status of messenger at the War Department by the time he joined the William Howard Taft White House as a valet in title, but soon enough as a domestic confidant and aide to a succession of Presidents, until his death in 1926 as a member of the Calvin Coolidge entourage. In the meantime, the "beloved" Brooks wielded considerable influence within the White House—and he always seemed to know what was happening. He is credited with persuading Woodrow Wilson to loosen up and begin wearing his now well-known straw boater, blazer and white flannel trousers. For many years in charge of the White House silver, he also served his government and country as a lieutenant colonel in the District of Columbia National Guard.

• Husband and wife, steward and housekeeper, under John Quincy Adams were Antoine Michel Giusta and his wife...a romantic little tale. Adams found and hired Antoine Michel as his valet in Belgium in 1814, not long after the latter had deserted Napoleon's French army (but before Waterloo). The new valet then married Mrs. Adams' maid in London—as husband and wife, they stayed with the Adams couple as private family and, in the White House, as First Family. They stayed on in the White House after the Adamses left, but did not care for hot-tempered successor Andrew Jackson and his entourage. They left his employment in about 1834, to open a highly successful oyster bar in the Federal city. In six years, they were able to retire to a farm to live out their lives quite happily.

• A man for all seasons was a White House favorite under Teddy Roosevelt and William Howard Taft—Major Archibald Wilingham Butt, military aide, chief ceremonial and protocol expert, riding companion to Teddy, confidant to wife Edith and...only White House staffer to go down with the *Titanic*. Exhausted by his pace at work and the busy social schedule he and housemate Frank Millet kept up among the city's elite, Butt was sent off for a long-planned vacation in Europe early in 1912, "with gifts and slaps on the back," reported historian Seale later. "Everyone loved Archie Butt." He and fellow bachelor Millet, an artist, decided to return early, however, because they then could sail aboard the fabulous and "unsinkable" new ocean liner, the *Titanic*. And when the ship hit the iceberg, Butt, typically, was attending a small dinner party in the First Class smoking room on A Deck. In the confusion and tumult that soon followed, there were other glimpses—with Millet and two other men, he calmly remained at a table in the smoking deck room for a time; later, a departing wife, Mrs. Walter D. Douglas, begged her husband to "get off with Major Butt and...[another man]," since "they are big, strong fellows and will surely make it." Butt later was seen, still calm, near the Boat Deck rail as others panicked or even fought to get off. How he (and Millet) died is not exactly known. "In the stories told later," wrote Walter Lord in his *A Night to Remember,* "Archie Butt had a dozen different endings—all gallant, none verified." In Washington, President Taft at first was told most passengers survived, but when informed that wasn't true after all, he wired for news of Butt and Millet. It was a full day before he found they were not among the survivors. Taft was distraught. "He was like a member of my family, and I feel as if he had been a younger brother," he wrote afterward.

• She was found through an "exclusive" New York employment agency. She had her own second-floor suite in the White House overlooking the North Portico. One room would be her office, the other (with bath), her bedroom, her living quarters...her private life for the next 17 years. Elizabeth Jaffray, army officer's wife widowed young, came to the William Howard Taft White House as the first housekeeper in decades. Aloof, severe, she joined 25 fulltime servants and was regarded by many as a terror. Some, like Arthur Brooks, were unawed and wise enough to work *with* her, although she, herself, admitted to a revolt when she decreed that the black servants, "regardless of rank or position," must take their meals separately from the whites. The revolt dissipated when she threatened firings for backtalk or resistance. Under the Woodrow Wilsons, she issued another decree. The kitchen workers had been arguing and even resorting to brawls over the new war in Europe. Mrs. Jaffray, surprising one kitchen fray, ordered no more discussion of World War I. She served on through the Warren G. Hardings, but then encountered Calvin Coolidge, who called her "Queenie"...and who replaced her, reasons not totally known. Except that word? *Queenie.*

• Another and slightly later housekeeper was Eleanor Roosevelt's import from Hyde Park, Henrietta Nesbitt, who rather notoriously overturned Mrs. Jeffray's notorious racial edict by firing all the white servants in the household staff and replacing them with blacks. Her reasoning, apparently backed by the Roosevelts, was that "a staff solid in any one color works in better understanding and maintains a smoother-running establishment." Her simplistic menu, meanwhile, soon gave the FDR White House the reputation of having the "worst" food in official Washington, said historian Seale. Indeed, FDR himself insisted upon having *his* meals fixed by his mother's longtime cook, Mary Campbell, in a newly installed diet kitchen on the third floor. Nesbitt's food (and attitude) was still an issue when the Harry Trumans suddenly took over the mansion, daughter Margaret has recorded. "Her taste in food was atrocious and her attitude toward the Trumans was openly condescending," wrote Margaret Truman. Then came The Brussels Sprouts Flap. Margaret's father hated them. So informed by Margaret after serving them one night, Mrs. Nesbitt, wouldn't stop there but served them again for the next two nights. Mrs. Nesbitt was gone a few weeks later. "Retired," was the word, and by the Trumans, not a moment missed.

Through the years, of course, there have been hundreds who have worked at the White House, and every one of them has his or her story to tell, too. If only there were room....

# 🦅 Silver Jubilee

No one who saw it, or shared it, could possibly forget...from the rooftop, kept straight and unfurled by hidden fans, floodlit and spectacular, a huge American flag was extended. And all over the grounds were thousands of electric lights, all colors, some of the strands borrowed from U.S. Navy ships at Norfolk and Annapolis and hurriedly shipped to Washington by freight car.

Not only the White House's own shrubs and trees were displayed in this extravaganza of light, but so were banks upon banks of tropical plants and trees borrowed from florists and greenhouses all over the Washington area. The weather on this June night was just right, described as "balmy," and when the 8 o'clock arrival hour came, it appeared that nearly all 8,000-plus invitees were standing at the gates and ready to rush in. Indeed, thousands of onlookers had gathered also to watch, to ohh and ahh, at the spectacle of President and Mrs. William Howard Taft's silver wedding anniversary party at *their* White House in 1911.

"On the south grounds, night was to be turned into day by means of multicolored electric lights," noted historian William Seale. Taft, himself, was so excited and caught up in the plans that on the day before he "paced the flat platform atop the roof of the White House, issuing orders for more strands, more spotlights, more paper lanterns." By then, electricians had been working for four days to prepare for the gigantic garden party and "illumination."

The guests were given an hour to wander the grounds and take it all in before the Tafts, to the crescendos of the "Star Spangled Banner," made their deliberate way down the grand staircase inside, along the first floor transverse hall, through the Red Room and out onto the South Portico.

Alternating that evening were the Marine Band and the Engineers Band, and it was the Engineers' turn for the presidential couple's appearance.

"A great cheer rose from the several thousand people by then on the lawn, and the cheering spread to the estimated 15,000 outside the fences. The President smiled, took his wife's [Helen's] hand, and nodded to the band; and as the band played the Wedding March, the Tafts walked down the stair to the lawn, Mrs. Taft in white satin embroidered with silver roses and carnations."

They then received guests under the trees for hours. Buffet supper was served at 11 p.m.—in the State Dining Room and East Room and in tents outside, in "groves flanking the south lawn." Mrs. Taft had to retire at midnight, quite exhausted, but her portly husband told the bands to keep playing and stayed with his guests until the music finally stopped at 2 a.m. Even then, he sat in the dark on the South Portico "until the last guest had gone."

It had been a real spectacle; no one could say the party had failed in any way...or ever could be *forgot*. In fact, Taft liked it so well, he ordered that the lights should stay where they were, the bands should again be at their respective stands...and the very next night, the grounds would be re-opened, not merely to his guests this time, but to the general public as well.

# 🦅 *Horses*

Old Hickory loved his horses, and thereby hang a tale or two from his presidential stewardship of 1829-37. In 1832, although about to seek re-election, Andrew Jackson insisted upon keeping race horses in the White House stable. He raced them at nearby tracks under the name of his young ward and secretary Andrew Jackson Donelson (his late wife Rachel's relative), "but it was no secret to whom they actually belonged," noted Jackson biographer Marquis James.

In April of that year, a close Jackson associate, quite well meaning, stopped Jackson's Hermitage overseer from sending three horses and three black jockeys to join the stable entourage at the White House. "With a campaign coming on, further display of the President's sporting proclivities would be inadvisable; and to run the horses under Donelson's name would deceive no one," was the point that this old friend, former Secretary of War John Henry Eaton, earnestly hoped to impress upon the man in the White House.

Old Hickory took it all in stride. . .and again sent for the horses and their handlers anyway. On arrival, they were installed in a "show place carriage house and stable, with stalls for ten horses." And he was indeed elected for a second term.

Not long after, Andrew Jackson could boast of three "promising" fillies in his White House environs, named Emily, Lady Nashville and Bolivia. Indeed, "The stable, with its complement of colored jockeys, was as much a part of the White House establishments as the East Room, and as frequently honored by eminence and fashion."

One spring day in 1834, Jackson, his Vice President, Martin Van Buren, and several other close associates and "devotees of the turf" were at the National Jockey Club, within riding distance for them all, "to watch a trial of the White House horses."

All three fillies were there, plus a brute of a stallion named Busirus, property of a Jackson friend. The stallion was to be ridden by a White House jockey named Jesse. Two stout fellows held the high-spirited animal for the rider, who promptly lost control. . .and the onlookers scattered in a hurry.

As the horse dashed against a fence and others panicked, the Hero of New Orleans was clearly heard to offer protection to his Vice President: "Get behind me, Mr. Van Buren! They will run over you, sir."

Then, when it appeared the onlookers were safe enough, the President admonished the still-clinging jockey: "Hold him, Jesse! Don't let him break down that fence."

And to the stallion's trainer, one Balie Peyton, Jackson said: "Why don't you break him of those tricks? I could do it in an hour."

To which Peyton muttered, out of Jackson's hearing, that "he would like to see any man break Busirus of those tricks in a week."

On the way home that day, Jackson related another race horse tale, although in this case the White House stable was not involved. Years before, it seems, after a race at Jackson's own Clover Bottom track in Tennessee, an angry crowd of disappointed bettors confronted a horseman friend of Jackson's by the stable. Jackson happened along and, seeing the crowd's ugly mood, first offered to have his friend meet any one of them in a duel, then said he would himself meet any such champion in a duel.

When no one accepted but the unruly crowd showed no signs of desisting either, Jackson realized that he was in a dangerous situation... he also realized that the evening dusk was fast thickening.

This was in 1811, and telling the story on the way back to the White House in 1834, Jackson related that he pulled a tin tobacco box from his coat pocket and told the mob, "I will shoot dead the first man who attempts to cross that stile."

And one of the crowd did step forward, as yet undeterred.

And so Jackson played out his bluff.

"I raised my arm and closed the [tobacco] box with a click very like the cocking of a pistol. It was so dark they could not distinguish what I had in my hand—and, sir, they scampered like a flock of deer!"

It might be, added Jackson, that in the crowd there would have been individuals quite willing to "meet" Jackson or any other man "on a one-to-one basis." And now Jackson came to the moral of the story for his Vice President. "But, Mr. Van Buren, no man is willing to take a chance of being killed by an accidental shot in the dark."

It is not recorded if Van Buren ever had occasion to take Jackson's homily to heart.

# 🦅 *Boy With Message*

A good old boy of the old school was Starling of the White House. Secret Service Agent Edmund W. Starling, that is, for many years—and four Presidents—a member of the White House detail. Quite a gentleman... quite an old boy with old fashioned, all-American values and no-nonsense attitude.

Meeting Teddy Roosevelt for the first time, Starling liked the fact that Teddy appeared "a strong man with a good, courageous eye."

Starling tended to look a man in the eye and measure the other fellow that way. And he was very direct at times, even if most of the time he had to be fairly circumspect.

One of those "direct" exceptions came the day that Woodrow Wilson was in the Versailles Palace outside of Paris to sign the famous Versailles Treaty of 1919 officially ending World War I. Great was the excitement throughout the world, and very exacting indeed— circumspect, you might say—was the protocol laid on for the great event among nations.

In the Hall of Mirrors, the French, the British and the Americans, led by Wilson, were ranged at center of a long, long table. At a far, far end, sat the defeated Germans. Starling, of course, was concerned with the security of his own ward, and he wasn't too happy with the deterioration of Wilson's health nor with what he viewed as condescending treatment of his President and entourage by various of the Europeans.

When Starling chose on his own to stand directly behind Wilson, a Frenchman in a cutaway came over and seemed—in French, of course—to be telling Starling to move on. Starling wasn't about to do any such thing. Giving vent to pent-up fury, he told the Frenchman that it was his job to guard the President, and no "snivelling little pipsqueak in a hired suit" was going to interfere with him.

*The direct approach.* The Frenchman, whom Starling knew to be superintendent of the Versailles Palace, did the moving on. Then there was the time Starling, a young railroad detective in those years, helped the Secret Service guard Teddy Roosevelt on a trip in the South in October 1905, including a stop to visit the Fair Grounds at Birmingham, Alabama. The presidential carriage followed a pathway between ropes with Starling and a colleague each walking on a side and two Secret Service agents in the carriage, one of them, Frank Tyree, perched on a high seat in front.

Starling was startled at one point to see a man jump the rope barrier and start running alongside, "crowding close to the carriage."

From his high perch, Agent Tyree yelled: "Get him outside the ropes and keep him out." Starling complied by "hustling" the intruder out of harm's way.

In seconds, however, he was back. Starling again chased him off.

And once more the stranger darted into the roped-off area and crowded too close.

That was enough. "I picked him up and threw him over the rope and into the crowd like a sack of corn meal."

*Direct approach.* That was Starling...that sometimes had to be his job. But there was more. He also was a compassionate, understanding, likeable and sometimes funny man who really loved his Presidents; who taught Calvin Coolidge to hunt and fish; who tried to look the other way—or at least dawdle way behind—when Woodrow Wilson was courting his future second wife; who insisted the doctors immediately get together and sign a death certificate at the time of Warren Harding's sudden death on the West Coast (cerebral hemorrhage, they said); who cried when Wilson was taken ill while promoting the League of Nations across the country; who did his best to comfort Calvin Coolidge when young Calvin Junior died of blood poisoning...who one day saw a boy, sad face pressed against the iron railings outside the White House, and asked him what he wanted. To see the President, was the reply. "I wanted to tell him how sorry I am that his little boy died."

Starling of the White House, *Colonel* Starling by now, brought them together and, since the boy then was overcome with emotion, delivered his message for him. Coolidge also couldn't speak for a moment, but afterward he said: "Colonel, whenever a boy wants to see me always bring him in. Never turn one away or make him wait."

# 🦅 *Alice's 'Majicks'*

Harkening back to Alice Roosevelt Longworth's buried idol in the White House garden, she—seriously or not—wished bad luck on Woodrow Wilson the day he returned to the White House from his long stay in Europe that produced the Versailles Treaty of 1919 officially ending World War I.

Democrat Wilson in 1912 had won his first term as President over incumbent William Howard Taft, the *regular* Republican nominee, and *break-away* Republican Teddy Roosevelt of the shortlived Bull Moose Party. Former President Roosevelt of course was Alice's father—deceased by the year 1919.

Wilson had lost his wife Ellen in his first White House years; he now was married to the former Edith Galt. On his return from Europe he hoped to win Senate approval for his dream of a League of Nations. But the proposal was not all that popular at home, as Wilson soon found out.

He probably never knew Alice Roosevelt's vehement reaction to his return that summer day in 1919. With a friend, she checked out the crowd (very small it seems) awaiting Wilson's train at Union Station. Outside the White House itself, only 200 to 300 onlookers awaited Wilson's arrival. Again Alice was watching. Watching. . . . And more than simply watching!

When the Wilsons approached, Alice stood on her car's running board and resorted to her childhood trick of "magicks," but her incantation calling for a plague on Wilson was not so childish-sounding. "A murrain [plague or disease] on him, a murrain on him," she chanted.

Her companion, afraid of the Secret Service, told her to stop and get back into the car. Alice objected: "Who are you afraid for? Me or Wilson?"

It *must* be entirely coincidental, and it is no secret in any case, that Wilson's plea for Senate ratification was defeated—the United States never did join the League of Nations, soon viewed world-wide as a paper tiger despite its noble aims. And Wilson soon suffered a major stroke ending his political career and leaving him an invalid in the White House.

# 🦅 *Looted, Burned. . . Gone*

The Brits were slow and they were methodical about the job. *Infuriating!* First, with Washington empty now of defenders, the officers marched their 150 seamen down Pennsylvania Avenue from the Capitol, already set afire. Fourteenth day of August 1814 and 7:30 in the evening, it was. Still quite light out.

But a thunderstorm threatened as they wound their way down our historic mile—two by two, it is said.

They rounded up a local citizen, a bookstore proprietor named Roger Weightman, and made him an unwilling witness/participant in the sport to come. *Infuriating!*

They found the home empty, broke in and rumaged through. Others, citizens, already had been inside, rumaging themselves. *Looters!*

Forbidden to steal and pilfer in earnest, the British sailors were allowed to take little things—as an example of sorts, Rear Admiral George Cockburn took an old hat and a chair cushion. And as their men made ready for the burning, the officers appreciated the well-spread dinner table, enjoying themselves below the empty frame that

121

held George Washington's portrait just short while before. (Until Dolley Madison, by most accounts, had ordered it ripped out and hustled out of town for safekeeping during the British sacking of Washington in the War of 1812. . . .)

As the officers enjoyed themselves among the spread dinner plates and decanters holding several kinds of wine, the triumphant Admiral Cockburn forced Citizen Weightman to make mocking toast to the departed President James Madison. The seamen/housewreckers, in the meantime, had been busy—methodically smashing windows throughout and piling up the furniture for their proposed indoor bonfire. They then were assembled—organized, that is—50 men in a ring around the building and each holding an oil-soaked ball of rags on the end of a long pole. The rest of the company—and a few wary citizens—watched from nearby as the rag-balls were fired up until all were lighted, and then, in concert, by a single order, all were hurled through the windows from all sides of the stricken house at once. In an instant, said one onlooker, "The whole building was wrapt in flames and smoke."

The same witness said the spectators looked on in "awful silence," and "the city was light and the heavens redden'd with the blaze." The thunderstorm finally came and went, and by morning, only a shell was left—the outer walls. It looked *better* than it really was, because of those very walls that hid the absolutely complete gutting that had taken place inside the outer shell.

Indeed, the White House of old, the original, was gone. Not only would James and Dolley Madison have to live elsewhere for now (Washington's landmark Octagon House), but when the job of restoration began in 1815, considerable portions of even those outer walls would have to be shored up or totally re-built . . . a fact not immediately and fully revealed to the public, just in case of any impression that the White House had to be rebuilt completely. In fact, except for some foundation and basement walling, it did . . . and it was.

# ♔ *Herbert the Modern*

Efficiency would be the byword in Herbert Hoover's White House. Efficiency and new ways. It would be a thoroughly modern outlook befitting this brilliant mining engineer with unequaled resume as a humanitarian and public servant—he, after all, was the relief organizer who "fed" a prostrate Belgium during the World War I era, who did the same for famine-stricken Russia, Bolshevik Russia at that, in the early 1920s.

The former Secretary of Commerce paraded through Washington on his inauguration day in 1929 with Army bombers and even a dirigible overhead. He drew the largest inaugural visitation in Washington history to date, an estimated 200,000 persons. His was the first inauguration filmed for the "talkie" motion pictures, the first carried by radio nationwide.

The "perfect" President was no robot—he could react emotionally to things. He just *didn't,* usually. Or visibly.

He did tip his top hat that inauguration day when a boy yelled from the onlooking fringes, "Oh you Herbie!"

The day before, though, a Sunday and going to church publicly, he frowned when well-wishers at his church shouted too loudly.

In the White House he soon developed the reputation of being the *workingest* President.

That may be opinion, but he *was* the first President to install a telephone on his desk. Those who came before used the instrument, to be sure, but they repaired to another room for that purpose.

Hoover also installed five fulltime secretaries, to his immediate predecessors' one, and he installed buzzers that would bring them hurrying to his side.

Not interested in play, he retired the presidential yacht of the day and shut down the White House stables. Issues, actions, subjects of all kinds were to be documented. *Organized, all was to be organized.*

At the Hoover campaign headquarters in California on election night the previous fall, reporter Thomas Stokes noticed that even then Hoover "showed no outward emotion."

As President, however, he was not afraid to break the rules. Reporters couldn't quote a President directly? Forget that tradition. Instead, let's have news conferences. But...with categories. One kind will be for direct quotes, one will be for remarks by an unnamed but White House level source, and one will be strictly background information, non-attributable.

Then came The Crash, the 1929 stock market crash. Hoover would not panic. He immediately brought a series of corporate, labor, farm leaders to the White House for conferences, followed by brave and encouraging pronouncements.

Then came the Depression.

For the next round of agonized conferences, he left the White House to see the financial magnates of the country in secret, rather than have the public worry over the sight of them arriving at the White House.

He couldn't persuade them or Congress to take the restorative steps he thought best. He wasn't able to fire up the country with a strong, positive message. He felt, he *knew,* that so much of it simply was a matter of psychology—the nation's psychology.

He called writer Christopher Morley to the White House and asked him to write an uplifting poem. He once asked Rudy Vallee for a brave song. . . . Hoover's own psychology needed the same boost, the same injection of new confidence.

To the world outside, however, it simply seemed the non-smiling Hoover was becoming more and more invisible. Many felt he was simply uncaring, callous.

Even now, by the way, he dressed formally for dinner every night, company or no company—probably the last President to do so.

He didn't like to see the White House servants at all, and little bells would warn them he was on his way to their individual sectors, reported Gene Smith in his book *The Shattered Dream: Herbert Hoover and the Great Depression.* "And so they hid. . .footmen holding trays high in the air as they scurried into hall closets already crowded with maids."

Remote and sad, Hoover only once spoke to his wife's personal maid—to ask where wife Lou was. "By the fall of 1930, Hoover while dining would sit in complete silence, sunk in concentration."

Then came the Bonus Army, World War I veterans desperate for jobs, setting up tent cities in Washington's parks, lobbying and pleading for help. Hoover had to call out the real Army.

In the White House, Lou Hoover unfortunately had developed an uninspiring and severe image all her own. Everything was so precise— butlers and footmen all the same height, meals exactly on time, no talk in the pantry, no clink of silver against china while clearing the table, and for the butlers, tuxedos in the day and tails in the evening. Mrs. Hoover had a system like a baseball-team manager for her servants. "Her hand touching her hair meant dinner should be announced; her hand touching her glasses meant that the table should be cleared."

And always Herbert Hoover worked, totally, foolishly, unbending while hurting inside. "There was never a good morning or even a nod of the head," said head usher Ike Hoover. "Never a Merry Christmas or Happy New Year. All days were alike to him. Sunday was no exception, for he worked just as hard on that day if not harder than on any of the others."

124

In time, Hoover was working 18 hours a day, sleeping three, trying to end the economic crisis gripping his country. "He worked those about him until they could hardly drag one foot after the other," said press secretary Theodore Joslin later. Fresh workers came and soon were burned out. Hoover, his hands trembling, kept up the pace anyway. "My men are dropping around me," he once admitted to Joslin. "Fighting this Depression is becoming more and more like waging a war."

His only exercise was to toss around a medicine ball in the mornings with male aides or friends.

Then came the election of 1932. Hoover versus Roosevelt, Franklin Roosevelt. Hoover re-galvanized himself and plunged into a fresh eruption of work. Mrs. Hoover had reconstructed the furniture and appurtenances of the Lincoln study, and here Hoover relaxed, now sometimes smiling, full of fresh energy; here he received his advisers and wrote his speeches and planned his campaign stumping. For one speech, there was a draft of 71 pages, but 15 rewrites produced a more workable length.

Then came the vote, and Hoover lost to FDR in a landslide.

On FDR's inauguration day, they rode together to the Capitol, the city grim, the crowds subdued, and Hoover unresponsive in the car to FDR's attempts at conversation.

And at the Capitol, when Hoover, ahead of the President-elect, came out on top of the steps, in view of the crowd in the plaza, silence. Just silence. That afternoon, Eleanor Roosevelt said she had been struck by the very solemnity of the onlookers in the Capitol Plaza. That night, her husband, the new President, sat with friend and aide Louis Howe while others in the family attended the Inaugural Ball.

The polio-crippled President sat in the Lincoln study Mrs. Hoover had so painstakingly refurbished for her husband, the most modern President yet.

Thirteen years later, newly installed President Harry Truman called Hoover to the White House one day to ask his services as head of a new program providing food relief for war-devastated Europe, a job somewhat familiar to Hoover. The presidential summons was the first time anyone in the White House had been in touch with Hoover since the day he turned the mansion over to FDR. Truman was startled to see Hoover was in tears, unable for a minute or two to speak.

#  Discovery Corps

Over a two-year period together at the White House, Thomas Jefferson had noticed at times that his young private secretary, Meriwether Lewis, exhibited "sensible depressions of mind." But Jefferson ascribed the younger man's "hypochondriac affections" to an inherited family trait and asserted later, "They had not...been so strong as to give uneasiness to his family."

Later still, Jefferson had to revise his opinion and blame the great explorer's mental state for his mysterious death in Tennessee at the conclusion of the famous Lewis and Clark Expedition. Jefferson wrote that Lewis must have taken his own life, although others have wondered ever since if he were not murdered.

Jefferson had known the future explorer as a child in Albemarle County, Jefferson's own home. And Jefferson long before becoming President had been convinced that Americans—rather than British or French subjects—should explore the American West, find a route to the Rockies, push on to the Pacific. He had British interests to fear on the one hand, and Napoleon's possible designs on the Spanish lands to the south and southwest to fend off on the other hand.

It was imperative to know more about the great unexplored land mass stretching westward from Atlantic to Pacific...but several proposed expeditions fell by the wayside in the years before Jefferson became President. When he did, in 1801, however, he recalled his youthful Albemarle neighbor who, as a boy, had volunteered for one of the abortive expeditions.

And so it was that a fairly untutored Army officer—he couldn't spell or stake any claim to good grammar—found himself installed in the early White House as private secretary to perhaps the most erudite of all American Presidents, before or since. Not only that, Meriwether Lewis spent about two years in the job, working alone with Jefferson most of the time. And much of the time was spent in their discussing and planning the expedition that Lewis (together with fellow Army officer William Clark) would lead into the uncharted West.

Congress appropriated a few thousand dollars for the effort, and in May of 1804, the so-called "Corps of Discovery" set off from St. Louis. In the months ahead, the party of whites, one black, one Indian, one half-breed, would travel to the West Coast and back to St. Louis, mapping, observing and making note of various discoveries and geographic features all the way.

They went so far and were so isolated from all normal channels of communication that an anxious President Jefferson had to content himself with mere rumors of their progress or well being, rumors passed along through Indian tribes and frontiersmen, and often altered or distorted in the process. By summer of 1806, the explorers had been written off by many a wise head as irretrievably lost. *Dead.* But not by Jefferson. He kept faith in their return with the information—as did happen—that could open up the American West to *American* settlement and development.

In retrospect, he might *not* have approved of the leadership style the two explorers adopted for their expedition...but he certainly would have found it interesting. He clearly intended his well-coached and -instructed Meriwether Lewis to command, but the awkward fact was that Clark, younger brother of George Rogers Clark, in an earlier role had been Meriwether's company commander and now officially was only a second lieutenant, while Lewis was an Army captain. They arrived at their own private arrangement to share command, brickbats or laurels equally, even in the land grants that Congress wished to bestow upon them afterward. With Lewis calling Clark "Captain on an expedition for North Western Discovery," the Army soldiers on the trip with them never knew that one really outranked the other.

They returned to St. Louis in September of 1806, then turned to writing up their notes and observations. With a book in the offing three years later, Lewis left St. Louis for a visit to Washington (not for the first time since the expedition ended, however). He stopped, alone, at a house in Tennessee. Before this, a companion thought he showed "some symptoms of a derangement of mind," wrote Jefferson later. And Lewis fretted and worried over the possibility he might lose the papers and expense vouchers he was carrying.

Jefferson related more of the story—"He stopped at the house of a Mr. Grinder, who not being at home, his wife, alarmed at the symptoms of derangement she discovered, gave him up the house and retired to rest herself in an outhouse. At three o'clock in the night, he did the deed which plunged his friends into affliction, and deprived his country of one of her most valued citizens...."

It is known that he died of a gunshot wound. But...murder or, as Jefferson maintained, suicide? That has been a question ever since.

# White Lodge Visited

After visiting raw young America in the early 1820s, an astonished Englishman wrote that in front of the White House he had witnessed Indians dancing a war dance—Indians "in a state of perfect nudity, except a piece of red flannel around the waist and passing between the legs."

The dancers, he also wrote, were "men of large stature, very muscular, having fine countenances, with the real Roman nose, dignified in their manners and peaceful and quiet in their habits."

Actually, they weren't all men—those he saw performing war dances for some 6,000 spectators were men from the Pawnee, Missouri, Omaha and Kansas tribes, true, but their delegation visiting Washington and the White House of President James Monroe also included an 18-year-old wife of an Oto chief. Eagle of Delight by name, she captivated all who encountered her.

Nor was the delegation of 17 native Americans that met with the President and attended his New Year's reception of 1821 at the White House all that unusual, historically speaking. It was one of the first Indian delegations to visit the White House, true again, but not *the* first and certainly not the last, since in the course of the 19th century hundreds of Indians visited the "Great Father" in his White House abode.

Some didn't survive the capital pilgrimages—two Indians visiting George Washington in Philadelphia years before died, their deaths rightly or wrongly blamed on rich food and drink. Later, in Washington, D.C., itself, a chief died in a local hotel from "the croup," and another Indian stepped off a cliff to his death.

One group headed for Washington from the wilds of the West wound up on exhibit in Europe, thanks to an unscrupulous French promoter who told them the cross-Atlantic trip to Europe was the way they had to go to reach Washington.

Years later, divided into two groups, they set sail for home, and one group landed in Norfolk, Virginia, and found shelter in Rachel Anderson's boarding house while city officials sought Federal help in directing the Indians to their next stop. In the meantime, two of the Osage had died of smallpox on board their ship. All were penniless and confused. They were in a pitiful state.

In time, the Indians were brought to Washington, but not until weeks had passed and the boarding house bill had mounted up. And when the Osage did arrive in Washington, it turned out Mrs.

Anderson was holding one of their chiefs back in Norfolk as sort of a hostage, until the bill was paid. The government paid, and the Osages did see the President—Andrew Jackson was in office. He apologized for the treatment they had suffered, but at *French,* not *American* hands, he pointed out. (The second Osage group later turned up marooned at a waterfront den in New York, also stranded without money or friends.)

Still another time, a Mandan chief named Big White visited Thomas Jefferson in Washington and became so enamored of the *white* way of life that he wanted to live among whites. He was unhappy, *so* unhappy, when he returned West, he told a white friend. He was repelled by the insecurity of Indian life, the ferocious manners and the ignorance of his fellow Indians. They, in turn, didn't believe his reports of white society and decided he was under the spell of a white witch.

A very early White House visitor, Big White was present for the dinner that Thomas Jefferson gave in early 1807 for explorers Meriwether Lewis and William Clark in honor of their three-year exploratory expedition in the West. Indeed, the explorers themselves were responsible for sending some Indian visitors on their way east to meet with the Great Father.

The Indians visiting Monroe in the winter of 1820-21 appeared at his day-long New Year's reception fully decked out in colorful native dress. Eagle of Delight was a major focus as the President's other guests crowded close to see, even to reach out and touch these strangers from the western frontier and beyond. Wrote a local reporter: "The music and hilarity of the scene occasionally relaxed the muscles of their stern countenances and in the place of pensive gravity, a heartfelt joy beamed in the eye of the sullen Indian warrior."

As the word *sullen* might suggest, the Indians who visited Washington and its White House over the years were both a stereotype and a curiosity to most onlookers. When it came to sitting next to them at a hotel dinner table, some whites balked. Likewise, some hotels were not anxious to have them as guests.

And, true once more, the Indians often drank too much and broke up hotel furniture and glassware. They didn't always help their own cause, even quite innocently. A newspaper reported in the late 1830s that a Washington "gentleman" looked out the window of his carriage, saw an Indian's painted face in front of him and fainted from the shock. But the Indian only wished to ask for money.

The Indian chiefs were brought to Washington to discuss treaties, to mollify their outrage about the wave of settlement engulfing their ancient lands...to avoid hostilities on the frontier. But another purpose, quite obviously, was to let them see the power of the white establishment that had taken firm root by now on the eastern seaboard. Thus, when Eagle of Delight and her companions visited the White House of James Monroe, the dances and sight-seeing stopped one day for serious business at the White House.

As the local *Intelligencer* reported, someone had persuaded the Indians to doff their usual native dress for "completely Americanized" outfits—military-style clothing presented to them by government agents. Thus: "They were dressed in blue surtouts, red cuffs and capes, blue pantaloons and shiny black boots." They did wear paint on their faces, but "in less fantastic style than usual."

Monroe received them in company with *his* many chiefs—Cabinet members, congressmen, Supreme Court justices and the like. He spoke to his "Red Children" of peace, but also made careful note of the white man's military strength.

In response, the leading Pawnee present, Chief Sharitarish by most accounts, said that, true, the white man could make clothing, guns and furniture and be fed on the flesh of domesticated animals. The red man, on the other hand, had to hunt for his skins and his meat.

But what did such differences matter? After all, "the Great Spirit intended that there should be both white men and red men, and he looks down and regards them as both his children." Unfortunately, some of the *children* have not always looked at it the same way.


# 🦅 Hotel

Rarely has the White House been so stuffed to the rafters as it was during the Roosevelt era. Time, that is, of Franklin, Eleanor, their children, their various relatives, their friends, their aides, their official state visitors, their servants, their mere acquaintances.

The FDR *house,* wrote retired Chief Usher J.B. West, "was like a Grand Hotel." Eleanor Roosevelt found some guests who would stay for months—and some "she'd just picked up on the street." She sometimes forgot who her guests were and it was not unknown for her to go to bed at night not really aware of "who was sleeping down the hall."

The visitors, often left to their own devices, "used the White House like a hotel, meandering in and out at will, sometimes stopping by the Usher's office for help in scheduling their day in Washington."

If visiting themselves, the grown Roosevelt children "were accorded no special privileges," wrote West. He recalled the time one of FDR's sons had to shift to "his third bedroom of the week," to make room for an incoming guest.

In addition to servants such as Housekeeper Henrietta Nesbitt, whose notorious menu FDR himself detested, or Eleanor's personal maid Mabel Webster, the house residents included FDR aide Harry Hopkins, a widower who not only made his own home in the White House, but brought along eight-year-old daughter Diana—he lived in the Lincoln suite on the second or "family" floor, and Diana lived in a room on the third floor. In time (in the Yellow Oval Room, second floor), Hopkins remarried and moved bride Louise Macy Hopkins into his own small apartment, a development that provoked a long letter from Eleanor laying down a few rules for the newcomer: "I hope you will feel entirely free to have anyone there [the Monroe Sitting Room] for tea or cocktails at any time you wish to be alone" was one thought; another was, "I would suggest that you talk to Mrs. Nesbitt about some regular arrangements for your wash, so that you will know on what days it must be sent and when it will be returned to you, and what it costs."

Typically, wrote West further, Eleanor hosted breakfast in the West Sitting Hall, "where she presided over a table of assorted houseguests, business appointments, or just friends." And next came lunch. If not traveling or invited out herself, she always had guests for lunch—a formal sitdown in the Private Dining Room "for at least 12." Dinner, again in the Private Dining Room, would be a black tie affair, often for more people working in the areas of Eleanor's many interests and public causes. And Sunday would be culture night—"authors, artists, actresses, playwrites, sculptors, dancers, world travelers, old friends," plus a mixed grill of diplomats and administration figures. Since Eleanor served scrambled eggs that she cooked at the table in a silver chafing dish, the staff called her Sunday menu "scrambled eggs with brains."

A major feature of the Roosevelt "hotel" of course was its frequent VIP visitor—the kings and queens, the potentates of all stripe and variety who came avisiting over a remarkable 12-year period. Not only the storied Winston Churchill, or the sour-faced Soviet Foreign Minister V.M. Molotov, but, by Private Secretary Grace Tully's account, those "favorite wartime royal visitors in Washington," Norwegian Crown Princess Marthé and her three children, one of them Norway's future King Harald.

And then there was Madame Chiang Kai-shek, the Chinese gener-alissimo's dynamic wife, described by Tully as "one of the most spec-tacular of the Roosevelt guests," described by West as "not so democratic as her publicity had us believe." Tully recalled hearing Madame's peremptory clapping of hands for service one day on the second floor and asked an usher, Wilson Searles, what was going on. He said the "Chinese crowd" had the staff running ragged and complained further, "They think they're in China calling the coolies."

For his part, West recalled "an entourage of 40, many of whom were stashed away on the third floor, the others at the Chinese Embassy." Sheets became a trial, he noted. Madame Chiang insisted her silk sheets had to be laundered by hand every day, then "stitched back inside the heavy quilted sleeping bag she had brought along from China."

Quartered on the second floor with the visiting "Mrs. Generalis-simo" were her maid and her "closest aides," two individuals at first taken for nephews—until the valets sent to help them unpack dis-covered, to everyone's embarrassment, that one nephew really was a niece. Even after that staff discovery, a hospitable FDR at dinner kept calling her "my boy."

During all the comings and goings at the Roosevelt "hotel", West also wrote later, "We never saw Eleanor and Franklin Roosevelt in the same room alone together." They "met" in the evenings and dis-cussed papers, ideas, issues, programs...all sorts of things. Eleanor "was perhaps his [FDR's] most trusted observer." But: "They had the most separate relationship I have ever seen between man and wife. And the most equal."

# 🦅 *More of Progress*

Gas lighting came to the White House in 1848, under James K. Polk, and the story is that Mrs. Polk insisted upon keeping her favorite chandelier unconverted. It was in the Blue Room and she saw that it kept its wax candles. Then, the night of the first gaslight enter-tainment in the White House, the gas company inadvertently cut off the supply at 9 p.m. One light remained—Mrs. Polk's candle-powered chandelier in the Blue Room.

Progress...it never stops. Even at the White House.

Thomas Jefferson it was who provided a 16-foot deep "icehouse" outside in 1801—a wine cellar, in reality.

A primitive central heating system that James Madison had installed went the way of all other things when the British burned out the interior of "his" home, and no real hot air mechanics would replace it until 1840. Until then, the rooms were heated by fireplaces (four in the East Room, but only one in most non-public rooms).

In 1840, as Martin Van Buren's term was drawing to a close, the oval-shaped servants' waiting room in the basement was turned into a furnace room. The coal-eating firebox sent hot air through new plaster ducts up to the first-floor public rooms by the age-old principle that hot air rises.

Van Buren, meanwhile, could thank predecessor Andrew Jackson for the fire engine-like water machine that kept the White House lawns and plants properly dampened. (A vat on wheels, actually.)

And if Jackson also had provided the bathing room in the East Wing with two copper bathtubs, Van Buren added several more, plus screening walls for added privacy. Upstairs, tin tubs in the bedrooms remained the vogue. "There would be no running water upstairs for many years to come," noted White House historian William Seale.

Franklin Pierce brought fairly dramatic change in the 1850s in the areas of heating, bathing and toilet arrangements. Much more modern central heating now improved upon Van Buren's gravity hot air system, upon James K. Polk's two added furnaces and upon Millard Fillmore's extended ducts that reached all over the house with their welcome hot air. The improvement now was a gravity hot-air system in which the coal fires of the three furnaces heated water in copper coils, and the coils heated the air wafting upstairs through the duct system to registers in the rooms above. Less stale air and much greater efficiency, reported Seale.

As for the plumbing advances under Pierce, there now was the first "bathing room" on the second floor, located in the same southwest closet that had housed Thomas Jefferson's water closet all these years. Both hot and cold water reached the new presidential bathroom. No more portable tin tubs here. No more trips to the East Wing shower-bath facility of many years' standing.

On the first floor, installed or improved under Pierce also, was a water closet handily placed near the private dining room. Much better for the White House guests.

The servants of the 1850s, however, still had to make do with the old rather than the modern—they bathed in portable tin tubs, and they still had only privies at their disposal, just outside the big house.

The bearded teetotaler Rutherford B. Hayes, meanwhile, installed speaking tubes for internal communications, plus a typewriter and a telephone for outside communication. He didn't use the telephone very much, since the Washington of the 1880s didn't have many other telephones to call. The mansion's first telegraph room, it perhaps should be noted, too, had been installed much earlier, in 1866, under Andrew Johnson.

It was the ill-fated James Garfield who ordered the first White House elevator—but he was shot and grievously wounded shortly into his term as President, and so the difficult installation of the hydraulic lift had to await his successor, Chester A. Arthur. The job then took two months and resulted in "endless trouble," according to historian Seale. "The hydraulic system included a large water tank on the roof made of wooden staves," he wrote; "being extremely heavy, it caused serious damage to the timber framing in the attic." Its hot-air engine activating a hydraulic pump in the basement "was so undependable that it was eventually replaced by a steam engine," added the historian. A nonetheless pleased Arthur had the interior of the elevator upholstered "in tufted plush."

That was only the beginning of the small elevator's saga, which included the time, in 1902, a Senate aide, Charles Moore, was caught between floors in the uncooperative contraption...until Usher Ike Hoover got it moving again.

The same Teddy Roosevelt era was the last in which the First Family relied upon the foot or horse for local transportation. From there on in, Presidents—like everyone else—used "motorcars" for getting around. The telephone, of course, also became ubiquitous, with the first transcontinental line installed in Woodrow Wilson's Oval Office in 1915.

Soon after, Herbert Hoover, as a most modern and successful engineer, not only added to the number of telephones, but also brought 13 radios to the White House. Even an electrical savant like Ike Hoover (no relation) was astounded. Thirteen!

The indoor swimming pool so famously favored by polio-victim Franklin Delano Roosevelt was built in 1933, thanks largely to a fund-raising campaign launched by the *New York Daily News*. It was built in a thoroughly gutted west wing, its walls containing lunette windows designed by Jefferson, its flooring masking what was once the flooring of James Monroe's stable.

Air conditioning came to the second-floor rooms in 1933 as another FDR era innovation, with electrically controlled central air—and heat—installed in the new sub-basements created by Harry Truman.

And talk about progress! It was Truman who—like the British fire—completely gutted the old White House and "installed" a new one inside the old shell, a complete reconstruction of the White House interior that was finished in 1952, complete with the "Truman Balcony" over the South Portico.

## 🦅 *Visiting Mothers*

As its guests, the White House of 20th-century America has seen a veritable parade of historic, public or celebrity figures come crowding through its doors. A few others, though, may not appear in the standard reference works.

Under Harry Truman, the first weekend guest was his own mother, then 90 years old. And no Lincoln bed for her! "I'll sleep on the floor first," said the elderly Southern belle. She would not sleep in the Queen's Room, either. "Too fancy for me," was her rejection of that one.

She wound up in the adjoining sitting room and placed daughter Mary in the Queen's bedroom.

Then Mrs. Truman went and tripped on some steps left bare by the removal of FDR's wheelchair ramp, but she didn't tell anyone she had hurt herself. A minor injury, but at her age, irksome, to say the least.

In the meantime, Bess Truman's mother, Margaret Gates Wallace, also rather elderly, actually lived in the White House. She stayed in her room most of the time, but daughter Bess spent time with her every day and often read the newspapers to her.

Even under the same roof, she always called her son-in-law "Mr. Truman."

She died in her room at the White House on December 5, 1952, four days after suffering what had appeared to be a mild stroke. It was just a month after Dwight D. Eisenhower's first presidential election victory over Adlai Stevenson. On December 4, the night before Mrs. Wallace's death, the Trumans held a farewell dinner for his Cabinet. Stevenson, Ike's recently vanquished Democratic opponent, spent the night—his only overnight stay at the presidential mansion, ever, even though he would run against Ike again in 1956.

The Eisenhowers, too, had a mother as their White House residential guest—Mamie's mother, Mrs. John S. Doud. She often ate dinner on tray-tables in the West Hall with the Eisenhowers as they all watched the evening news on television. She enjoyed playing her harmonica in her room, and Mamie frequently would accompany her on a small electric organ nearby. Ike for his part, teased her constantly and called her "Min" for a comic-strip character (*Andy Gump* was the strip).

Like daughter Mamie, Mrs. Doud loved to stay in bed late in the morning, propped up against the pillows at the headboard while planning and organizing her day. In fact, they often picked up the telephone in their beds on the opposite sides of the second-floor corridor and talked back and forth, one bed to the other, two women, mother and daughter, so comfy in the 20th-century White House...talking, talking, talking on the telephone.

## 🦅 *Happy Days Afloat*

William Howard Taft's wife Helen took ill on one, Woodrow Wilson did his early courting of Edith Galt on another, Harry Truman enjoyed his poker binges and his swims in the Potomac, Calvin Coolidge enjoyed weekends on the river replete with guests, a string quartet and other Marine Corps musicians. The Wilsons, for that matter, once they were married, enjoyed weekend river outings just as much.

"We both liked studying the charts to see if we could find some little tributary of the river to explore," wrote wife Edith later.

Yachts...presidential yachts were the means and conveyance for such pleasurable, relaxing excursions for many a White House occupant, although that was *not* the case the evening the Tafts embarked upon the U.S. Navy's yacht *Sylph* in May of 1909. They were entertaining friends after a long day for the First Lady, whose son Charles was in the hospital after surgery to remove his adenoids.

Suddenly still, unresponsive to conversation, shortly after the boat slipped its mooring, Helen Taft had suffered a stroke. President Taft was so distraught, said aide Archie Butt, that he "looked like a great stricken animal." And with good reason, since it was more than a year before she recovered her strength. Her face, in the meantime, was partially paralyzed and she hated to be seen in public—so much so that she sometimes "attended" her husband's state dinners sitting alone in a small dining room next to the State Dining Room and, still alone, sharing the dinner viands being served to the President's guests on the other side of the wall.

On happier occasion, the Tafts used the larger yacht at their disposal, the *Mayflower,* for more serious sea-going trips, as did other presidential couples. The Tafts, for instance, would cruise to their summer place in Massachusetts.

Woodrow Wilson and second wife Edith had nothing but pleasant memories of the *Mayflower,* where early in their courting days Wilson often entertained Edith at dinner. This large steam-powered craft offered a private suite and guest compartments, dining room and salon, among its ample spaces, and all the crew, of course, courtesy of the U.S. Navy.

The Calvin Coolidges also enjoyed the *Mayflower*'s facilities, which included a fully equipped office for the President's use. They, too, cruised to Massachusetts for a bit of relaxed summering, while on more limited outings in the Potomac, say for a weekend, they often took along a pianist that string quartet or other members of the Marine Band to help while away the hours for themselves and their guests.

Then came Herbert Hoover. The old steam-powered yacht no longer suited. Hoover decommissioned the venerable *Mayflower,* in use by American Presidents since Teddy Roosevelt's day in 1901. Franklin Roosevelt, occupying the White House during World War II, then had to consign his yacht *Potomac* to combat duty. He often used U.S. Navy warships, both for official travel or for a bit of relaxation. The size of his "yachts," therefore, was on the order of cruiser or even battleship.

In the postwar years, Harry Truman rediscovered the joys his predecessors had found on the Potomac waters, cruising often with his poker cronies and—has any President dared to emulate since?— even swimming *in* the Potomac.

# 🦅 *Telephonitis in the White House*

If Herbert Hoover was the first President to permit a telephone on his office desk in the White House, as historically alleged, Lyndon Johnson must have been the first Chief Executive to treat and deal with modern instrument as very nearly a physical appendage— perhaps as an emotional crutch, too.

Even before he reached the Executive Mansion, the onetime Senate Majority Leader spawned a "telephone story." It seems that Everett Dirksen, as the Senate's Republican Minority Leader, at last rated a government limousine complete with driver—and telephone.

Dirksen couldn't wait to call Democrat Johnson on *his* limo telephone, proudly pointing out that he at last had a telephone in his limousine, too. Just like LBJ!

Without missing a beat, it is alleged, Johnson said, "Just a minute Ev, my other telephone is ringing."

As President, clearly, Johnson had greater need of the instrument than ever. Often engaged with more than one call at a time, he used telephones not only to communicate simple fact or instruction, but also to cajole, scold, commiserate, gossip, persuade, threaten...whatever the occasion and/or mood seemed to demand.

Horace Busby, longtime friend and a special assistant to LBJ in the White House, recalled the time he came up to Johnson at Love Field in Dallas and found Johnson before a bank of public phones. He warned against trying to use them. He was making long distance calls. "Then I noticed that the receivers were off all six hooks and you could hear the voices of the operators trying to complete all six calls."

Others close to Johnson told their telephone tales, too.

"We had all these little white phones leading directly from the White House," explained Cabinet member Robert C. Weaver one time, "and he would call at any hour, any time."

One time, recalled staff assistant Will Sparks, LBJ was in the midst of telling a "funny story" to various members of the staff assembled in the Oval Office "when one of his several telephones buzzed." Johnson picked it up and when he realized who was calling, delivered what Sparks described as "one of the worst tongue-lashings I've ever heard in my life." Said Sparks: "That guy at the other end of the phone must have been on the verge of a heart attack to be talked to like that by the President of the United States."

As for Johnson, totally unperturbed, he "slammed" the phone down and pushed it out of sight in a desk drawer. He turned back to his listeners. "Well, now, as I was saying..."

More often, it was LBJ doing the calling. "He was an inveterate user of Alexander Graham Bell's instrument," recalled Senate staffer William Jorden, "and it didn't take very much to prompt him to pick it up; so if he read something in the paper, or if he read something in the briefing memos or staff papers, etc., that interested him he'd get on the telephone and call the guy involved and say, 'What the hell are they doing to us here?' and 'What does this mean, etcetera,' and he didn't just *pick* up the telephone; he *grabbed* the telephone."

In fact, Jorden added: "Secretaries say that he just grabbed the phone away from them while they were talking, cut off their conversation and dialed *his* number. And they would just be in tears."

He loved to call folks early in the morning, said speechwriter Erv Duggan. Awakening them and pointing out he was up and at 'em "was a way of being in control."

White House staffers, of course, always had to be available at the end of that long wire from the Johnsonian Oval Office—whether in or out.

You had to leave word at all times with the White House operator, said special counsel Larry Temple, "if you went to the bathroom, or decided to scratch your nose or something..."

Or a nice lunch out, added Peace Corps official Coates Redmon one time: "If you were having lunch—no matter what restaurant it was—the waiter would come with a message there was a telephone call. It would always be the President wanting to know what you were doing, what you were eating—'Now, have you salted and peppered it?, etcetera?'"

LBJ's little game at such moments was to pretend his listener was eating in one of the fanciest Georgetown restaurants going, although the White House operator knew the actual eating place and had dialed the number for him.

Was there something pathetic here? By Redmon's account, LBJ's often aimless chit-chat with a staffer reached at some restaurant would end with: "Well, you enjoy your lunch—but hurry back—I need you."

And Jorden later would opine on this compulsive telephone business—on this compulsiveness, period: "I think it was the thing that almost did him in, trying to look at three television stations at once and trying to talk over two or three telephones at the same time."

## ⚜ *Rose Garden Created*

You've heard of it...the Rose Garden, created for JFK by Mrs. Paul ("Bunny") Mellon after his trip to Paris and Vienna for the Khrushchev summit in 1961. "The President had noted that the White House had no garden equal in quality or attractiveness to the gardens he had seen and in which he had been entertained in Europe," wrote Bunny Mellon.

So...at a picnic on Cape Cod later, he asked her to design a nice garden in "the area near his office at the west end of the White House, already known as the Rose Garden...."

Visiting soon after, she was struck by the *dis*proportions that must have been bothering him. "The White House proper seemed exceptionally tall where it joined the long, low colonnade that linked it to the Oval Office and Cabinet Room," she recalled. Worse, no trees—none by the wing holding the Oval Office nor any at the corner formed with the west end of the White House. Only Andrew Jackson's "tall, dark *Magnolia grandiflora* near the South Portico."

The garden then greeting her had four rows of privet hedges interspersed with Tom Thumb roses "and occasional standard roses."

What was needed, she could see, was some "harmonious and uncomplicated" way to unite "the tall central block of the White House in one corner and the West Wing, with its two low colonnades forming boundaries west and north...." But...what harmonious way?

Further, JFK wanted a center lawn of 50 by 100 feet that could hold 1,000 persons and/or a festive tent.

Part of the answer came to Mellon when she visited New York that fall and noticed that the three magnolia trees in front of the Frick Museum looked especially attractive even without their summer foliage—"Their pale silvery branches with heavy twigs seemed to retain the light of summer," she thought. "I knew their pattern of growth would continue to give form in winter and would catch raindrops as well as tufts of falling snow." There was the *way!* "I felt I could now design the President's garden!"

And so...she had found the anchors to her overall scheme. *Almost,* since she still had to find the trees of the right size to plant right away, and preferably from public land. And she did—four magnolias taken from unkempt ground behind old Navy "tempos" near the Tidal Basin that later were torn down.

Planted in the four "bare" corners of the Rose Garden, they "changed the entire character of this empty space." They were joined over the spring and summer of 1962 by borders of Katherine crab apple trees in sectioned flower beds...by roses, boxwood, perennials, annuals, herbs, and yet more roses.

"A large diamond-shaped outline of santolina would surround each crab-apple tree. Each diamond would be set in a larger outline: a small clipped English boxwood hedge and, next to the lawn, a low growing hybrid boxwood called Greenpillow, developed by Henry Hohman in Kingsville, Maryland."

In the process of developing the garden, designer Mellon "discovered" Irvin Williams, head horticulturist at the Kenilworth Aquatic Gardens in Washington, and was so taken with his knowledge and interest that she suggested he move to the White House. As a result, he did...he became the head White House gardener and could claim credit for "much of the beauty of the White House landscape" for years after, as well as the quality of the Rose Garden and the Jacqueline Kennedy Garden that greets visitors beginning their tour of the public rooms of the White House as they enter at the eastern end of the building.

The areas in which the Mellon-Williams team dug out and replaced topsoil to a depth of four feet for the new garden had its own historic background. It once held the original White House stable yard, it yielded even in 1962 "Civil War horseshoes." It had held U.S. Grant's vegetable garden and the huge greenhouses that had housed plantings as large as fruit trees and palms in the Victorian era. Teddy Roosevelt's wife Edith then planted a "Colonial Garden" on the same site after she and her husband removed the greenhouses (thus making way for the West Wing). In the colonnade flanking the garden, noted Bunny Mellon, there had been "a milk house, icehouse, workshops, servants' dwelling rooms, and numbers of other small, thick-walled chambers called, in the earliest times, household 'offices.'"

One minor problem in the 1962 digging. . ."we cut into a mysterious cable buried in the corner of the garden." Somewhat "hastily installed" during World War II, "It turned out to be the hot line that set off the Nation's military alert." The future garden space suddenly was "alive" with security personnel.

Another time that the revamped Rose Garden was "alive" with visitors was during a Boys' Nation appearance by select young men from each State of the Union. Shaking JFK's hand in the Rose Garden was a bright young lad from Arkansas—Bill Clinton by name.

# 🦅 *Unofficial Annex*

"This hotel, in fact, may be much more justly called the center of Washington and the Union than either the Capitol, the White House, or the State Department." So said, in harsh Civil War times, that politically attuned literary lion, Nathaniel Hawthorne. And the unofficial annex, you might really say, of the White House, that he was talking about still is a hostelry of note today—not necessarily the center of the universe, no, but certainly a key landmark just two blocks from the White House, a major, a bustling modern-day attraction for lodger, diner and tourist alike. . .and a symbol of haunting historical memories. And ah, yes, the stories, the stories the Willard could tell if hotels, and not mere walls, could only speak. . . .

Of the time, for instance, that delegates from 21 states (there were only 34 at the time) convened here in desperate Peace Convention as last-ditch effort to avert seccession and Civil War. Right in the Willard. February 4 to February 27, 1861. And arriving secretly one dawn even before they left town, spirited during the night past rebelliously seething Baltimore, one Abraham Lincoln...who then stayed on until his first inauguration on March 4. "Lincoln held staff meetings in the lobby and borrowed slippers belonging to the Willard family during his stay," says a Willard-produced history. And on inaugural day itself, he returned from events and ceremony at the Capitol to watch the traditional parade from the Willard, which fronted, as it does now, on Pennsylvania Avenue just before it runs up against the U.S. Treasury Building. A little later, "When Lincoln received his first paycheck as President, he paid his Willard bill of $773.75," adds the Willard account.

Stories, stories...more of the Civil War era. The famous and the infamous, in and out all the time. Troops once quartered here—Union of course. In 1861 also, Julia Ward Howe, visiting town, wrote her "Battle Hymn of the Republic."

But not all the Willard's remarkable history is Civil War history...not by any means. Take U.S. Grant. And no, not the Civil War Grant we all know so well, but the one in later metamorphasis as *President* Grant.

He liked the Willard. He liked the lobby. He enjoyed getting away from the White House, just on the far side of the Treasury. And so he would walk over and spend some time relaxing in the Willard lobby. He enjoyed his cigar and brandy here. In time, of course, people noticed...in time people hoping for presidential favor began to seek him out in the Willard lobby. Says the Willard history: "He called these people 'lobbyists.'"

Less happily, this is where a departing President's wife, Abigail Fillmore, wife of Millard, died in her bed from pneumonia just a month after they left the *antebellum* White House to Franklin Pierce—who also had been a Willard guest while awaiting his turn in the presidential mansion.

Here, too, in the wartime year of 1916, Woodrow Wilson addressed the League to Enforce Peace, a progenitor of the League of Nations that was born after the end of World War I.

More happily than wartime tidings, and much earlier in history, the Willard played host in 1860, James Buchanan's term, to the first Japanese delegation ever to reach Washington for an official visit—three ambassadors with entourage of 74. Supposedly, they were the first "group of Japanese ever to leave their island kingdom."

Less weighty but a gem as trivia is the fact that a U.S. Vice President (Woodrow Wilson's Thomas Marshall) was so annoyed with the price of the cigars at the Willard newsstand that he uttered those immortal words: "What this country needs is a good five-cent cigar."

The grand old structure now seen at 1401 Pennsylvania Avenue was built in the period 1901-1904, and don't be surprised if it seems reminiscent of the Plaza in New York City. Same architect—Henry Janeway Hardenbergh. The ground underneath has been the site of one hostelry or another since 1816; it passed into Henry Willard's hands in 1850 and it would be almost 100 years—in 1946, specifically—before the family sold its interest in the hotel. It shut down in 1968, but sprang back to life in 1986 after a painstaking restoration job, new funding and construction of an adjoining office building and retail shop complex. The hotel has been operated as the Willard Inter-Continental (Inter-Continental Hotels Corporation) ever since.

A magnet for today's visiting statesmen, jet-setters, politicos, beautiful people, moviemakers (the re-makers of *Born Yesterday,* for instance), even an occasional corn-ripened tourist, the Willard is still the Willard...that place where Henry Clay allegedly mixed his first mint julep in Washington; where visited such luminaries of the not-so-distant past as Mark Twain, Walt Whitman, Houdini, the Duke of Windsor, Jenney Lind and even Tom Thumb; where one President made his official residence for nearly a month. For here it was also that Calvin Coolidge, hastily sworn in as the newly deceased Warren G. Harding's successor in 1923, patiently waited for Mrs. Harding's departure from the official residence *down the street,* as it were, at 1600 Pennsylvania Avenue.

Secret Service Agent Edmund Starling later recalled the first time he reported for duty at the new President's side. He arrived outside the door of the third-floor Coolidge suite at 5:45 a.m. and had to wait half an hour for his first glimpse of Coolidge. When it came, at 6:15 a.m., "he stepped out, dressed to go for a walk."

After that walk and another one in the afternoon, a third one the next morning, and then a few more, Coolidge one day paused in front of the Willard and said: "You ought to move in here. It's a good place."

Starling did exactly that, he later noted in his book, *Starling of the White House.* He stayed at the Willard even after the Coolidges finally moved into the nearby White House. As Starling related, he remained throughout Coolidge's two terms, "eventually getting a private telephone wire installed between my room and the White House."

## ❧ *Honest Man at Gettysburg*

When Lincoln delivered his now famous Gettysburg Address, there was a totally honest man among his listeners, the real thing for any Diogenes.

Actually, he was there, at the dedication ceremony for the battlefield and its cemetery, as the main speaker of the day. Actually, he had already spoken for two hours himself, while Lincoln waited. And actually, he had kept Lincoln and a crowd of 15,000 attendees waiting for half an hour for his own arrival.

The President, in the meantime, had taken a train to Gettysburg the night before, a ride from Washington of one hour, ten minutes.

The featured speaker, a former president of Harvard, had been invited six weeks ahead of the dedication planned for November 19, 1863, just months after the battle that took place in early July. Lincoln was invited—an afterthought—on November 2.

But he said yes.

*Four score and seven years ago our fathers brought forth on this continent a new nation....*

He wrote a draft in ink on White House stationery, headed, in the style of the day, *Executive Mansion.* Not a mistake, not a single correction or change in the first, mighty paragraph.

*...conceived in liberty, and dedicated to the proposition that all men are created equal.*

It isn't until the beginning of the third paragraph that one finds new wording written in, over a phrase crossed out by a single slash.

The draft converts to pencil near the end of the first page and continues in pencil through the second and last page. It is thought that Lincoln began writing it at the White House, put it aside for the train trip—no jiggled words or letters are evident—then finished it at the Gettysburg home of David Willis, the local citizen who had taken the lead in establishment of the memorial grounds under official Pennsylvania aegis.

The morning of the 19th, a Thursday, Lincoln took part in the parade that proceeded along Baltimore Street in Gettysburg to the cemetery and battlefield grounds.

Then, together with the onlookers, he settled down to await the arrival of the "real" orator of the day, former Harvard President Edward Everett.

At last appearing, Everett waxed long and dramatic with his silver tongue, and then came Lincoln at last—his two minutes of speech-making come and gone so quick, many in the crowd did not realize he had even begun.

Everybody by now knows the fame of Lincoln's Gettysburg Address, and just about everybody is familiar with the added impression: that it was not immediately appreciated for what it really was...that its full beauty and value were not immediately grasped by those initially exposed.

Well, largely true, of course, but there were *some* who quickly recognized the short speech for its grandeur. Henry Wadsworth Longfellow, no slouch with words himself, that same day told the editor of *Harper's Weekly* that it was "admirable." Others also were quick to praise, and before two years were out, the great savant of the Northeast, Ralph Waldo Emerson, was willing to say it "will not easily be surpassed by words on any recorded occasion."

Lincoln himself, though, is said to have considered his Second Inaugural Address as his best effort in the speech department.

The "honest" man present, who put his own thoughts in writing the very next day, was the ceremony's featured speaker, Everett. Writing to Lincoln with generous words, Everett said, "I should be glad, if I could flatter myself that I came as near the central idea of the occasion, in two hours, as you did in two minutes."

## 'Only a Poor Indian'

Like any President, Grover Cleveland usually had plenty to do, but one time he stopped his normal work to look—minutely—into the case of an American Indian facing a hanging for killing another Indian in a drunken brawl. It wasn't the usual fare for a President, or even the lawyer-politician from Buffalo, New York, which is what Cleveland was when he wasn't serving two separated terms as President.

The presidential examination of the facts in the case took some doing, too. "The record was an elaborate one," recalled White House aide Alexander Boteler later, "even as we had prepared [i.e., summarized] it, but it was still insufficient to satisfy the President and his scruples."

With little time to investigate further, Cleveland ordered a stay in the execution date and "called for the full shorthand report of the trial."

But even that didn't satisfy him. He also ordered up letters from the district attorney (the killing took place on Federal Indian territory), from the judges in the case, even the jurors! "When these were submitted, he went all over them with the most elaborate and painstaking care. . . ."

Having digested the entire record assembled for the most unusual, self-instigated perusal in the White House, Cleveland finally ended the legal matter with a short presidential memo. He ordered the death penalty commuted—the Indian would *not* be executed.

And what was Grover Cleveland's burning interest in the case? He told Boteler that he couldn't have slept nights if the defendant had been hanged simply because he, Cleveland, failed to take an interest and look into the man's case. Said Cleveland: "He is only a poor Indian, but I cannot forget that he had nobody else in the world to look after him and see that his rights are fully preserved."

## Dolley's Black Benefactor

"When Mr. Madison was chosen President, we came on and moved into the White House; the east room was not finished, and Pennsylvania Avenue was not paved, but was always in awful condition from either mud or dust. The city was a dreary place."

So wrote Paul Jennings, born a slave at James Madison's Montpelier estate outside Orange, Virginia; later the very man who prepared the White House dinner consumed by the British interlopers who fired the presidential mansion in the War of 1812. . . still later a free man working for Daniel Webster as a "body servant."

We whites either forget or don't know. . .that the Federal city awaiting Madison and Jennings in 1809 was a major slave trading center. . .that it was located between two slave states, Maryland and Virginia. . .that coastal vessels brought in slaves, to be held in slave pens like the one just off Lafayette Square in front of the White House. . .that both public and private construction work here often was done by hired slave labor.

And yet, the city also was a Mecca for free blacks—123 in 1800; 1,796 by 1820; 3,129 by 1830; 8,158 by 1850, and some 9,200 by 1860, the year before the Civil War broke out.

To be free as black, however, was not quite the same as to be free, period.

By law in early Washington (1808), no black, free or slave, could walk around alone after 10 o'clock at night. Four years later, free blacks had to register with the city government and always carry a "freedom certificate" showing they were not runaway slaves.

Later still, free black families had to post $500 bonds backed by two whites (men, that is). And Congress went so far as to ban blacks from the Capitol and its grounds unless they could show that some legitimate "business" took them there.

Even so, blacks from 1800 to the time of the Civil War made up one-fourth to one-third of the city's population, (60,000 in 1860), with the number of free blacks overtaking the number of slaves as early as 1830.

Some of the free blacks were homeowners, a few were professionals or business owners, but most blacks were laborers or servants, and by and large blacks and whites tended to live in their own residential concentrations—black and white neighborhoods.

But not always without tension....Virginia's Nat Turner Rebellion of 1831 resulted in new limits on the freedom of the Federal city's black population, and ugly vigilantism appeared after a slave allegedly attacked a prominent white woman. White mobs attacked schools, churches, and tenement houses, their actions known as the "Snow Riot" because they broke into the black-owned Beverly Snow restaurant and destroyed its furnishings. A spate of new laws forbade black ownership of restaurants, but these eased shortly afterward...another black entrepreneur reopened the smashed-up Snow establishment and ran it for 20 more years.

President Madison's "body servant"/slave Jennings, meanwhile, stayed with Madison long past their White House years, until Madison's death at Montpelier in 1836. It apparently was a happy association. "Mr. Madison, I think, was one of the best men that ever lived," wrote Jennings later. "I never saw him in a passion, and never knew him to strike a slave, although he had over one hundred...."

After Madison's death, Jennings remained with an ever-more poor Dolley Madison when she moved back to Washington to live on Lafayette Square. He was still a slave then, but arrangements were made to have an insurance man *buy* him for $200, and later *sell* him to Daniel Webster for $120. Webster then freed Jennings on the understanding that Jennings would work for him and pay off the $120 at the rate of $8 a month.

With Dolley "in a state of absolute poverty," wrote Jennings, he often took her a market basket of provision at Webster's instigation, and he sometimes gave her "small sums of money from my own pocket."

The freed black Jennings later was one of the chief plotters organizing a mass escape of slaves from 41 owners in Washington, Georgetown and Alexandria by means of the Potomac River and schooner *Pearl*. Unfortunately, the *Pearl* was becalmed downriver at Point Lookout the next morning, even as the shocked slaveowners gathered a posse back in Washington.

The posse gave chase in a steamer after a black informer told them where the missing slaves had gone. The recaptured fugitives (and some free blacks with them) were so severely punished that Northerners were shocked and Harriet Beecher Stowe began her serialized novel *Uncle Tom's Cabin*. In 1850, meanwhile, slave trading finally was abolished in Washington by law.

Jennings almost was a victim of the *Pearl* fiasco himself. He was planning to go with the schooner and its escaping passengers, it is said, and he had left his benefactor Daniel Webster a note apologizing for leaving "with so little ceremony"—in secret, that is. But he felt so badly that he returned to Webster's house before the *Pearl* sailed—without him—and took back his note before Webster ever saw it.

Jennings, incidentally, is credited with writing the first inside memoir to come out of the White House. Incidentally, too, he says it wasn't Dolley Madison who rescued the Gilbert Stuart portrait of George Washington from the British come to burn down the White House in 1814, but rather it was the White House gardener and doorkeeper who did the rescuing.

*Ends*

*Leavetakings, Leavetakings*

Leavetakings, leavetakings. Always so hard for almost anyone. Sentimental at the least. Ronald Reagan left a note for George Bush in the top desk drawer in the Oval Office. Prayers and thoughts. Then went back the morning of Inauguration Day 1989 for a last look. He placed both hands on the desk and bowed his head, then he walked out the door leading to the Rose Garden.

At the door, pause, a last look back.

Gerald Ford, giving way to Jimmy Carter, heard the latter's inaugural speech and then flew to California, where he was hitting golf balls before day's end. He played in the Bing Crosby Pro-Am Tournament at Pebble Beach the very next day. Arnie Palmer was his partner.

Didn't matter all that much?

Well...before leaving Washington, he directed his helicopter pilot "to make one last swing over the White House and the Capitol," reported Henry F. Rosenthal for the Associated Press in 1989.

Harry Truman, the same story recalled, took the train home to Independence, Missouri, and began the chores of carrying the luggage or fetching the newspaper from his front yard himself. A concession to Secret Service concerns with protection was the addition of a fence in front of the unpretentious Truman home on North Delaware.

Dwight Eisenhower was chauffeur-driven to the farm in Gettysburg and "a couple of days later" was off shooting quail in Georgia.

Jimmy Carter, when his turn came, had to deal with Iran's release—at last!—of the American hostages it had held so long in the latter half of Carter's one-term presidency. Iran acted five minutes into Ronald Reagan's presidency, and presumably Carter didn't have to do anything at all now. No longer his problem.

But he flew off to Germany to greet the newly released hostages anyway, despite exhaustion and the needed sleep it cost him.

In an earlier day, an ever-so courteous Martin Van Buren walked along Pennsylvania Avenue to the Capitol in 1841 to attend successor William Henry Harrison's inauguration, and a bitter, cold day it was, too. Among the first to shake his triumphant opponent's hand, Van Buren then watched the exultant crowds from a friend's house and, later, took a train home, back to New York state.

Harrison had planned to run again, but in a month the new President died of pneumonia. It was blamed on the weather Inauguration Day. John Tyler moved up to president, but the Democrats next time nominated neither him nor Van Buren, but rather James K. Polk.

After *his* four years in office, he and Mrs. Polk spent the night before Zachary Taylor's 1849 inauguration at the nearby Willard Hotel (Willard's Hotel then). Busy until last minute signing papers and legislative bills, Polk strolled through the empty White House the day before Taylor's advent, happy at the thought of being "free from all public cares."

After Taylor died in office, Millard Fillmore took over, and in short order he gladly attended the fetes honoring his successor, Franklin Pierce, on the latter's Inauguration day in 1853. In another *antebellum* leavetaking, Pierce gave way to James Buchanan and with fond nostalgia said goodbye inaugural morning to a cabinet that included Pierce's good friend—and future president of the Confederacy—Jefferson Davis. When Buchanan, laid low by illness, didn't appear at the White House, Pierce hopped into his own carriage, proceeded to Buchanan's National Hotel lodgings, and conveyed Buchanan to the Capitol for his inauguration.

It was Buchanan, of course, who then turned over the White House in 1861 to one of its most towering occupants ever, Abraham Lincoln. And Buchanan did the amenities to the end, even with civil war brewing...he stood by as Lincoln delivered his first inaugural speech at the Capitol, in a cold wind, and he returned to the White House with the newly sworn President afterward. Just inside the door, before they reached the public rooms and the waiting crowds, Buchanan halted. He said his goodbye to Lincoln and left the gaunt, black-suited figure to his—and the nation's—destiny.

Much earlier, the nation's father-and-son Presidents each managed, not entirely by accident, to skip the inaugural events attending the ascension of a successor. John Adams, who had complained to Thomas Jefferson, "You have put me out!", rose early in the morning blackness of Jefferson's Inauguration Day in 1801 in order to leave the White House and the still primitive capital city. Traveling by horse-drawn coach, it took him 12 days to reach home in Quincy, Massachusetts. Later, his son John Quincy Adams moved out of the White House the night before Andrew Jackson's inauguration in 1829 to a private home on Meridian Hill. He went horseback riding the next day, while exultant mobs trampled the White House grounds, even its interior rooms, in celebration of Old Hickory's ascent to power.

More than a century later, Richard M. Nixon would be the first President to resign from office, a bitter pill that no predecessor had experienced.

As he spent his last night in the White House, family, staff and the American public all were fully aware of his announced resignation in the wake of the Watergate scandal which had left him under threat of impeachment. The next day, before Vice President Gerald Ford's mid-day swearing-in as the new President, Nixon had to say his good-byes to tearful staff and Administration figures. He and Pat Nixon would leave the White House to Jerry Ford's oath-taking. The Fords would not actually move in, though, until David Eisenhower and wife Julie Nixon Eisenhower, grandson and daughter of Presidents, could finish packing up the Nixon belongings and memorabilia. For now, August 9, 1974, Jerry and Betty Ford walked to the White House helicopter pad with the downhearted Nixons, the two wives behind the men, arm in arm, and Pat Nixon said: "My heavens, they've even rolled out the red carpet for us, isn't that something?"

But then she thought and said to her successor as First Lady: "Well, Betty, you'll see many of these red carpets, and you'll get so you'll hate 'em."

The Nixon chopper took off from the White House grounds at 11 o'clock that Friday morning.

Five minutes later, as determined by the protocol experts orchestrating the unprecedented scenario, Nixon's formal, written resignation was presented to Secretary of State Henry Kissinger. And at noon, Ford, accompanied by his wife Betty, followed Chief Justice Warren Burger into the East Room of the White House to be sworn in as America's 38th President.

# ⚜ *Ford Theatre Aftermath*

What would happen, say you, the moment *after* Abraham Lincoln was shot by his assassin? The chronicler in this case is Walt Whitman, and he first makes note that it was in a momentary stop of the stage business that the muffled shot was heard. First, that pause on stage at Ford's Theatre. A sort of hush. "At this period came the murder of Abraham Lincoln. Great as that was, with all its manifold train, circling around it, and stretching into the future for many a century, in the politics, history, art, of the New World, in point of fact the main thing, the actual murder, transpired with the quiet and simplicity of any commonest occurrence—the bursting of a bud or pod in the growth of vegetation, for instance. Through the general hum following the stage pause, with the change of positions [on stage], came the muffled sound of a pistol shot, which not one hundredth part of the audience heard at the time—and yet a moment's hush—somehow, surely a vague startled thrill—and then, through the ornamented, draperied, starred and striped space-way of the President's box . . . ."

*Appeared and leaped to the stage,* 15 feet below while also spraining his ankle, John Wilkes Booth, of course. And he then faced the audience and mouthed his words justifying the insane intent for himself and of himself. *Sic Semper tyrannis.* And then, he is gone, into history. . . .

But in the theatre, among those left behind, stunned, uncomprehending, what of them? What then? With Lincoln slumped over from his not-yet fatal wound?

Well, by Walt Whitman's account, there was the startling appearance of Booth and still another moment's hush . . . perhaps even the same one now twice punctuated—the shot and Booth's leaping flight. And now came the reaction! Mrs. Lincoln's piercing cry—"Murder!" And, "He has killed the President!" Her cry and her leaning from the box and pointing to the departing Booth.

And next, well, confusion . . . pandemonium in Ford's Theatre. A storm of noise—"the people burst through chairs and railings, and break them up." In the turmoil also, women faint, the feeble are trampled underfoot. And there is a rush to the stage, quickly filled, many of the actors and actresses mixed with the howling mob and terrified, while some do press water up from the stage to the stricken man's box and others try to climb up there, too.

A crowd of soldiers—Whitman calls them the President's guard—now burst and storm into the theatre, 200 strong and in absolute fury—"literally charged the audience with fixed bayonets, muskets and pistols, shouting *Clear out! Clear out! You sons of . . . ."*

And outside, while the chase began in earnest for Booth and his co-conspirators, the infuriated crowds were looking, too, on their own and ready to punish on the spot. They "come near to committing murder several times on innocent individuals," wrote Whitman. In one case, police rescued a man being dragged to his own hanging from a nearby lamppost. They kept him in custody all night long at a station house for his own protection.

# ❦ *'You Yellow Rat!'*

Warren G. Harding may have "looked like a President," as his own Attorney General once said, but as President this 20th-century occupant of the White House ran up a remarkable scorecard of scandals, albeit not all of his own doing.

He alone, of course, would be the one responsible for his affair with Nan Britton, but most if not all the monetary conniving was done by other members of his administration. One such case, the Teapot Dome scandal, is probably better known today than is Harding himself. It's just that Harding, generally described as genial (and unthinking) in the extreme, was not very astute in his choice of associates—such as Cabinet members.

He picked a one-time Army deserter to be head of the Veterans Bureau, while for Secretary of the Interior, he chose an oil man and land speculator. The same supposed protector, Albert Fall, was the very man who secretly leased government lands to oil speculators in the Teapot Dome scandal.

Naive, gullible or whatever he might have been about his associates, Harding himself contributed to a certain White House and administration "atmosphere." About twice a week an early dinner at the White House was followed by a lively poker game.

And while poker itself may not seem so very terrible, it often means gambling, and in the Harding White House it was gambling indeed, no holds barred.

One time, Harding told visiting newspaperman Louis Seibold that the very fine pearl tie-pin adorning the Harding tie was won at a poker game the previous Wednesday night. Seibold, who himself was sporting a pearl pin, could see that Harding's was worth $4,000 or more. Harding explained that he had won it with a four of spades in a side bet with one of his poker pals, against a $100 stake. As Seibold also knew, in that same poker game had been a cabinet official and other VIPs.

In his own bumbling way, it often is suggested, Warren Harding *tried.* He did reach out and name Charles Evans Hughes, Herbert Hoover and Andrew Mellon to his Cabinet . . . as the stars of his

Cabinet. But then, as counterbalance better remembered today, there were the hacks—his Attorney General, the one who said Harding's *best* qualification was *looking* like a President, was Harry Daugherty, a big business lobbyist.

Apparently sleep-walking through his White House years, Harding later would protest: "Some day the people will understand what some of my erstwhile friends have done to me in these critical times when I depended so much upon them."

But that was late in his administration. At first, Harding was not so troubled by the failings of his friends. From the outset, he was simply a genial fellow from Ohio who welcomed public contact. He had the Marine Band play on the White House lawn and at 12:30 most days he shook hands with unscreened visitors. To staff protests that such hospitality was too time-consuming, he simply said: "I *love* to meet people. It is the most pleasant thing I do; it is really the only fun I have. It does not tax me and it seems to be a very great pleasure to them."

One time, finding Harding spending valuable time answering trivial letters, Columbia University President Nicholas Murray Butler said it was silly for a president to devote himself to such minor things. "I suppose so," Harding allegedly said, "but I am not fit for this office and should never have been here."

But he was...and when one scandal, then another, began to come to his attention, Harding at first refused to believe the allegations against his poker pals. When one of them, Attorney General Daugherty, finally revealed the indiscretions of Veterans Bureau Chief Charlie Forbes, the worm turned.

Angry at first, Harding wouldn't communicate with Daugherty for two days. But investigation of Forbes showed that the charges against him were true. Harding was, in his own word, "heartsick."

How much so was revealed a day later, when a White House visitor climbing the stairs to the second floor was startled to hear Harding's voice raised in anger and, in a nearby room, to see the President, himself, throttling a man. Harding shouted: "You yellow rat! You double-crossing bastard! If you ever...."

Harding then spotted the intruding visitor and curtly directed him to an adjacent room. The other man stumbled off. On the way out later, the visitor was told the man with Harding earlier had been "Colonel Forbes of the Veterans Bureau."

Forbes then went to Europe, and after Congress began to mount an investigation of his activities resigned while still in Paris.

Meanwhile, history may never know the substance of a coded message Harding received while traveling by ship off the West Coast in 1923. Was it about more of the still-brewing scandals? Whatever it was, Harding "suffered something of a collapse" after reading the message, wrote biographer Samuel Hopkins Adams. "For the rest of the day he seemed half stunned, muttering to himself and breaking off to ask whoever was with him what a President should do when his friends were false."

Several days later, after he made "listless" public appearances, Harding refused to go on deck when his vessel, the *Henderson,* collided with a U.S. Navy destroyer in Puget Sound. Lying in bed, hands covering his face, he said, "I hope the boat sinks."

His Secretary of Commerce (and later President), Herbert Hoover, later recalled frantic, endless bridge games—Harding would play with any and all willing to sit at the game table with him, around the clock. Hoover never could play bridge again.

Arriving in Seattle, Harding stumbled through two speeches. On Sunday, July 29, he was in San Francisco, visibly ill after suffering violent stomach trouble, possibly ptomaine poisoning. On Friday, August 3, he died in his hotel room of an apparent stroke. No autopsy.

# ⚜ *Mid-Century Melodrama*

For a decades-long period between the War of 1812 and the Civil War, the White House and its occupants went through more improbable real-life dramas than a soap opera would ever dare to emulate. At the same time the personages who stepped in and out of the picture were "names" we now look back upon as towering, strangely unreal giants of history.

It is difficult for us today to imagine how small America once was in population, how young it was, too. In the political leadership that either resided in or passed through Washington in the first half of the 19th century there were many who had known George Washington personally. Their generation was just giving way to another that would know Abraham Lincoln, Robert E. Lee or Jefferson Davis personally. Some would have brushed elbows with them all!

Nor do we always remember how very human these legendary figures once were, the fact they were people who, like us, ate their three squares a day and enjoyed their creature comforts, even if there wasn't always running hot water.

We must assume that Henry Clay, Daniel Webster and John C. Calhoun fell into that same category, along with the Presidents, their families and their political retinues. But...during those *antebellum* years, such intrigue, such entanglements, such real tragedy! And often, such recuperation. And...sadly, sometimes not. Jefferson Davis, for example. Both son-in-law and confidant to Presidents, Cabinet member...here was a real study!

After graduating from West Point in 1828, he had married a young woman against her father's wishes. So adamant had been the father that they were married in an aunt's home instead of hers. Three months later, in a development typical of the day, the young bride was dead. Typhoid.

The bereaved husband and the father-in-law met years later on a battlefield of the Mexican War, by one account falling in one another's arms and weeping.

Soon after, the father-in-law, Zachary Taylor, was President and onetime son-in-law Jefferson Davis was a U.S. Senator from Mississippi. By this time, too, Jefferson Davis had remarried. Taylor, on the other hand, had long been married to aging, aristocratic Margaret Mackall Smith of Maryland, an invalid who had opposed his presidential bid, who at first did not join her 64-year-old husband at the White House and who, when she did, was such a recluse socially that all kinds of rumors sprang up to "explain" her absence from public view. One was that she smoked a pipe!

It was Jefferson Davis' second wife, Varina, who often visited Mrs. Taylor and spoke up publicly in her defense, to say she was absolutely charming and just fine.

This was at mid-century exactly, and Taylor's famous Mexican War mount, "Old Whitey," busily chomped the grass of the White House lawn. Six Osage Indians had appeared for Taylor's first reception in a refurbished East Room. Up on Capitol Hill, Clay, Calhoun and Webster were debating the slavery issue almost daily—or nightly—and Millard Fillmore was presiding over the Senate as Vice President. One Franklin Pierce of New Hampshire, once a congressman, was not yet back in sight.

Washington still had not forgotten Taylor's immediate predecessor, James K. Polk, who, by all accounts, had been a workaholic. He signed bills until the last possible moment. Then, on his way home in the spring of 1849, he endured one smalltown parade or visiting delegation after another, until, facing a huge fish dinner at New Orleans, he begged a servant to slip him some ham and cornbread.

He cancelled all other public displays—and went home, only to die shortly after. Age: 53.

Another who died later that same summer, was the impoverished presidential widow and Washington social doyen Dolley Madison.

Ironically, the deceased Polk, on the day of his replacement by Taylor, had called his successor "a well-meaning old man," not to the newcomer's face, but in a diary. Ironic, in view of Polk's fate, but hold the phone. . . .

In Washington over the next year, "old man" Taylor enjoyed the summer concerts by the Marine Band on the South Grounds of the White House. He walked among the onlookers and shook just about anyone's hand. On July 4, 1850, he took part in ceremonies at the site of the future Washington Monument, its cornerstone laid by Polk two years before. A newspaper reporter noted Taylor's "listless attitude."

Afterward, Taylor returned to the White House and enjoyed a quantity of cherries and iced milk. In five days, he was dead—generally, history says he was a victim, not of a bowl of cherries *exactly,* but of *cholera morbus,* which means, in effect, gastric disaster. (An exhumation in 1991 failed to prove the theory he had been poisoned with arsenic.)

His reclusive wife, who had prayed Henry Clay would defeat her own husband in the presidential race of 1848, underwent agony during the state funeral. Said Varina Davis later: "[She] trembled silently from head to foot as one band after another blared the funeral march of the different organizations, and the heavy guns boomed in quick succession to announce the final parting."

Taking over the presidency next, Millard Fillmore also had to wait a short while before his wife joined him.

She had stayed home all during his vice presidency, but in the meantime, they wrote each other letters every day. His wife, Abigail Powers of Buffalo, New York, once had been his teacher.

Nor did Fillmore himself move right into the White House. One newspaper said his inaction was due to malaria wafting up from the Potomac River. Fillmore himself later blamed the Taylor mourning period for delays in entertaining at the White House.

Fillmore's wife, began a library at the White House, but she was herself in ill health and mourning a recently departed sister. Their daughter, Mary Abigail, was acting hostess at age 18.

The couple finished their White House term seemingly unscathed, to be succeeded by the Franklin Pierces. With English author William Makepeace Thackery and American author Washington Irving in attendance, the Fillmores wined and dined the incoming President, then moved from the White House to the very suite Pierce had been occupying at nearby Willard's Hotel.

There they laid plans to travel abroad, but Mrs. Fillmore died a month later in her hotel bed, perhaps due to catching cold on Pierce's inaugural day while standing next to authors Thackery and Irving in the winds blowing at the Capitol.

Pierce also arrived alone at the White House, since his family, too, had just weathered a tragedy—the third of three, actually. After losing their two young sons to disease, the couple just two months before the inauguration of 1853 had seen their third and last son, 11-year-old Benjamin, horribly injured and killed in a train wreck that left the two parents untouched.

Even before that, Jane Means Appleton Pierce had fainted upon hearing the news that her husband was elected President and must go to Washington. Now, she would only go as far as Baltimore until after the inauguration; Pierce had to go there to visit her.

When Jane Pierce finally took up residence in the White House, it was as another recluse. But that situation—with the encouragement once more of Varina Davis—gradually changed, and Jane Pierce eventually was able to serve as hostess at major White House social occasions. Jefferson Davis, meanwhile, was Pierce's Secretary of War—and one of the New Englander's closest friends.

Not even Vice Presidents were exempt from the grim reaper's work during this period. Elected with Franklin Pierce, Vice President William R. King went to Cuba to recover from an illness. He took his oath of office there, missing the Pierce inauguration. The Alabama Senator then journeyed home. And died.

Pierce, meanwhile, was an alcoholic, history tells us. One story recounts the time, years before, when as a congressman he spent a convivial evening with a local newspaper editor, only to see his companion fall into a creek at night's end. Unable to pull him out, the drunken Pierce jumped in with him!

As President Pierce made way for *his* successor in 1857, neither he nor Davis, despite the latter's fierce pro-slavery views, could have foreseen that less than 10 years later Davis would himself be a president—of the secessionist Confederacy.

Pierce was succeeded by a bachelor, James Buchanan, whose young, vibrant niece, Harriet Lane, served as his hostess. No tragedy or melodrama here. . .except that a congressional friend of the President shot and killed his wife's lover in Lafayette Square, fronting the

White House. The victim was Francis Scott Key's son...and the city's Federal prosecutor.

Except that, in another grim instance, bachelor President Buchanan thought he had rid himself of a pesky newspaper critic—a woman—when he ordered her husband—a general—to Central America to deal with problems there. The newspaper woman dutifully left town with her husband. And both drowned when their ship sank in a storm.

Buchanan, of course, is best remembered today as the President who handed over the reins of government—in a most fateful exchange—to Abraham Lincoln. Then came tragedy and drama on really massive scale!

#  Wilson Abroad

When Woodrow Wilson left the White House for the great Peace Conference in Paris less than a month after the World War I Armistice of November 11, 1918, he seemingly was well-coddled, protected and equipped for any and all emergency.

Aboard his ship the *George Washington* as she steamed out of her Hoboken, New Jersey, slip that December 4 was a Secret Service detail of eight sturdy men. He had along also his valet, his Secretary of State, his chief White House usher, and two stenographers. His wife, also making the historic trip, carried along her secretary and a maid. The entourage also included Wilson's doctor, U.S. Navy Captain Cary Grayson; historians; economists and, of course, lesser diplomats.

Wilson's suite on board ship was sensibly appointed—bedroom, bath and an office. There were two telephones, one a wireless.

Forging ahead of the transport as both escort and unofficial "minesweeper" was a mighty battleship that served as the flagship of the U.S. Navy's Atlantic Fleet—the *Pennsylvania*. Additionally, a covey of 10 destroyers ran alongside.

The American President, armed with his idealistic peace proposals, his Fourteen Points, was the war-weary world's man of the hour...and at first, no one would let him forget it. When the *George Washington*—the interned German ship *Kaiser Wilhelm,* actually—reached the Azores, two additional destroyers joined the party. Two days later, the European landmass coming into view, nine U.S. battleships approached, and, one-by-one, passed with a 21-gun salute. Next it was more destroyers—12 of them. Next, two French cruisers and nine more destroyers. Overhead, airplanes, and on shore, more guns firing in welcome.

When Woodrow Wilson stepped ashore December 13, 1918, ecstatic crowds cheered and cheered. He took a train to Paris, another train arrowing ahead of his Special as protection.

In Paris, more of the same happy, happy crowds—masses! The Wilsons stayed at the Palace of Prince Murat, safe behind high walls and guarded entranceways.

Six months in all (with a brief shipbound return to the United States), Wilson's visit was to be the longest stay abroad by any American President at any time. And while negotiations he expected to go quickly instead dragged on and on, his free time initially was spent in ceremony and state visits.

In England, the Wilsons stayed at Buckingham Palace. Everywhere they went the crowds were clamorous and happy, and all ceremony was carefully arranged, protocol flawlessly followed. In England, one joy for Wilson was attending the Presbyterian Church his grandfather Woodrow had served as pastor. Wilson spoke from its pulpit, obviously touched to be there.

In Italy, it was more of the same. Staying with royalty, feted by the country's other leaders, a visit to the Pope and, if possible, crowds that were even more enthused than those already seen in France and England.

However coddled from human gaffes as he apparently was, and protected as he was, loved as he was at first, Wilson the Just—as the Europeans initially called him—could not forever remain immune from human fickleness or his own human frailty.

With the victorious European powers determined from the outset to punish and weaken Germany, Wilson's idealistic goals and manner simply didn't suit. The negotiations wore him down. Political opposition to the League of Nations at home wore him even further. Indeed, much of his program may have been unworkable in a rivalry-ridden Europe so fresh from such awesome bloodletting as World War I.

Secret Service Agent Edmund Starling, after watching Wilson arrive in Paris before Christmas "in fine fettle," soon was noticing an ominous decline.

In mid-February, the American party headed back across the Atlantic for a two-week interim. By then, wrote Starling later, they were leaving behind in Europe, "a quagmire of misunderstanding, doubt, fear, suspicion, jealousy and greed."

Wilson reached America in late February, first going ashore at Boston. He then spent a week in Washington, where the Republicans in Congress were in revolt over the proposed League of Nations. He reboarded the *George Washington* for the trip back to Europe the evening of March 5, and on Friday the 13th, the ship dropped anchor at Brest again. Wilson's previous arrival also had been on the 13th—December 13, 1918. He was delighted both times, since he considered 13 to be his lucky number.

Not so, really. That very evening, after an argument with his long-time confidant and aide, Colonel Edward M. House, Wilson seemed to be all in. He looked at Starling without recognition, "his arms hanging loosely at his side." He was pale, drawn, and obviously tired.

And yet they had just arrived in France again after a sea voyage that Wilson seemed to enjoy.

As the negotiations leading to the Versailles Treaty of 1919 continued, Wilson deteriorated steadily. He went to bed with a cold or flu (perhaps even a mild stroke) on April 3, and Mrs. Wilson for the next few nights sometimes asked Starling to move his bed or raise a window. "He did not stir as the bed moved or the windows rattled, sleeping deeply and peacefully, but looking more like a dead man than the living hope of the world."

Wilson's Allied counterparts by now were more like adversaries, as they tried to enforce their interests upon the peace treaty—almost overnight, Italian popular opinion had turned against "Wilson the Just." His political opposites from France and Britain continued to pick at the treaty terms.

Wilson left his sick bed, but in Starling's opinion, the President still was weak and exhausted. "He never did regain his physical strength, and his weakness of body naturally reacted upon his mind. He lacked his old quickness of grasp and tired easily."

One day, Wilson twice left behind an important briefcase full of confidential papers as he gathered his belongings after a negotiating session. Britain's Prime Minister Lloyd-George noticed Starling rescue the briefcase both times—"It was a telltale sign that the President was no longer at his peak, and was tiring fast, and since it was Lloyd-George's task to wear him down he must have felt a twinge of triumph at this indication of success."

The Briton had reacted visibly by giving Agent Starling "something between a knowing look and a wink."

In the meantime, Wilson was giving up—compromising—on positions he had taken prior to and early in the Peace Conference. The pressure from the French and British was taking its toll, especially since Wilson for the most part did his own negotiating as the American spokesman, even his own typing of memoranda, when the others quite sensibly used their staffs for such purposes.

Wilson often played solitaire for hours at a time, erupted into fits of temper, and once asked to rearrange the furniture in his suite, because, "I don't like the way the colors of this furniture fight each other." His hair turned whiter and he developed a nervous twitch of the eye.

With the treaty finally signed in June, the Americans rejoined their ship for the cruise back to Hoboken. Taking a few turns about the deck with the Wilsons the day after sailing, Agent Starling was startled to see Wilson stumble three times in a row against a lifeboat ring embedded in the deck. As they approached a fourth time, Starling stepped in the way and with Mrs. Wilson's help steered their weakening charge in a safer direction.

The party arrived in the United States on July 8. For two months Wilson fought for ratification of his beloved League of Nations from the U.S. Senate, then left for his famous whistle-stop railroad tour of the West intended to drum up public support.

His physician Grayson, by now a Navy admiral, warned that Wilson might not even survive the demanding trip. He almost didn't— one day, Starling nearly had to lift him up to the podium for a speech. Wilson rambled weakly and even wept.

That night, Wilson suffered a stroke, and the train turned back to Washington. Starling, going on furlough for a long-planned visit to his mother, said good-bye and left the Wilsons at St. Louis.

By his own written account, he sat and watched as the presidential train slid on out of the railyards, a "little red light" after a time that was fading from sight. He felt a friend's hand on his shoulder, and his friend asked, "What's the matter?"

"What do you mean what's the matter?" demanded Agent Starling.

"You're crying, you damn fool!"

## ☙ *Sickroom Cooled*

The house on Pennsylvania Avenue was ever so still. Silent, absolutely silent "Quiet as death," wrote a reporter staying overnight on the same floor as the President's offices and private living quarters. "I listen for every sound," added Franklin Trusdell of the National Associated Press to his wife Genie. "A dog barking in the distance is heard. A fountain splashes on the lawn. Not a step is heard in the mansion."

And true, silent it was that dread summer of 1881. And hot, so hot!

The main floor was a mess. Some of the furniture had been taken upstairs for the convenience of visitors, aides and others concerned with the immobilized President. Summer covers stayed on the furniture left behind while empty spaces spoke of the pieces hastily carried upstairs and the blinds remained closed against sun and heat.

Oddly, too, out of place in appearance, up the great space of the grand staircase from a newly created ice chamber in the basement and along the second-floor corridor ran a series of tubes of canvas stretched over wire—ducts for cold air blown by fan through the makeshift system to the bedroom where the President lay suffering.

Silent was the house, and silent were the crowds that stood outside in vigil for the stricken man within.

James A. Garfield had been president for less than six months when a disturbed and disappointed job-seeker shot him twice at the Baltimore & Potomac rail station on July 2 as he was about to embark upon a July Fourth stay at a New Jersey beach. He sustained a relatively harmless wound in one arm, but the real difficulty was the second bullet—now festering deep in his back. The doctors attending him in the White House could not find the spent slug. Even the famous inventor Alexander Graham Bell could not find its deadly site with an electric detector gadget he carried up to the bed in the hot, hot White House.

With no helpful medical procedure immediately in evidence, all the doctors, family and onlooking public could do was to wait...wait, watch, hope and pray for their President lying on a bamboo frame bed in great pain.

But the heat! One of his greatest discomforts was the heat that drove previous Presidents out of the mansion during Washington's summer heat waves. What could be done to at least relieve him of the heat on the second floor, without risking a dangerous move to cooler quarters? This was before air conditioning, of course...and the answer was an early and rudimentary form of that very item. *Air conditioning.*

The public had responded with all kinds of gifts for the stricken President, and among the helpful devices sent by inventors were two cooling contraptions. One, reported White House historian William Seale, "consisted of a large closed-up vat of ice, from which tin pipes ran from the President's office in a downward slope to the President's bedroom on the opposite end of the house."

Still, the freshly cooled air at the ice end didn't get to the bedroom end quickly enough to do much good.

The second *machine,* for lack of a better word, incorporated a fan that blew air through a six-foot box holding a series of cheesecloth screens that were wetted down with ice-cold water. The result here was better...but still far from perfect. Cool air reached the uncomfortable patient at the end of the tin-pipe system, but the cool air was also humid air.

Enter now, a U.S. Navy scientist called to the scene by Garfield's doctors, one Simon Newcomb.

Intrigued by inventor R.S. Jennings' fan-powered blower apparatus, Newcomb calculated how much ice would be needed to replace the heat units that must be taken out of the sickroom. He also realized that putting ice between the cheesecloth box and the pipes would soak up the unwanted moisture.

Jennings was called in to help build a much larger and modified cooling system, as was John Wesley Powell, head of the U.S. Geological Survey and a first-rate scientific mind. "The three worked around the clock with a contingent of navy engineers for three days....On Monday morning, July 12, the machine was turned on. Newcomb wrote that the air that passed from the office to the sickroom was 'cool, dry and ample in supply.'"

When Garfield protested the noise of the fan motor echoing through the tin pipes, the experts conceived of canvas-over-wire ducts to absorb the disturbing decibels. The final step was to expand the coolant capacity by using a more powerful fan engine, installing a larger ice container in the basement and running the canvas ducts upstairs to the President's room.

For all the success achieved, however, Garfield finally died, even though a transfer to the Jersey shore in September seemed at first to benefit him up mentally and physically. Before Garfield was carried out of the White House for the futile trip to his beach cottage, newsman Trusdell had spent many nights in a makeshift press center established down the hall in the waiting room to the President's office. He at first had been, "almost sure he [Garfield] will recover."

The act of assassination was an outrage and a shock; the outcome after moments of hope and small victories was sad...all true. While not a matter to be weighed upon the same scales, it also is true, as historian Seale pointed out in his watershed history *The President's House* that the coolant system developed for Garfield's relief really had given him *some* peace. The makeshift effort was even "a great advance in technology," for at the White House that grim summer "had been discovered the basic principle of air-conditioning."

# ⚜ *1:00 P.M. in Dallas*

Dallas on the 22nd. Atop the Texas School Book Depository Building, the clock within Secret Service Agent Rufus W. Youngblood's view from the approaching motorcade said 12:30. The motorcade turned southwest onto Elm Street. The open area known as Dealey Plaza was on one side, the Depository Building on the other.

The President waved to a crowd standing at the foot of the building.

One onlooker, Howard L. Brennan, across Elm and facing the Depository, noticed a slender man about 5 feet, 10 inches, tall, probably in his early thirties, in the sixth-floor corner window. That was a few minutes before the motorcade turned the corner and approached.

Now, there were shots heard, probably three in all, and "in rapid succession," according to the scenario presented in the Warren Commission report on the assassination.

Brennan actually saw the mysterious figure in the southwest corner window take aim with a rifle and fire.

It wasn't quite 12:34 p.m. in Dallas, Texas, November 22, 1963.

In the rear of his open car, the President grabbed at his neck. "He appeared to stiffen momentarily and lurch slightly forward in his seat." It later was determined that this bullet had struck him at the base of the back of his neck, right of the spine, coursed downward and out the front of his neck, tearing a "nick" in the knot of his tie.

Several cars behind in the motorcade, Dallas motorcycle policeman Marrion L. Baker heard a shot. Just returned from a deer-hunting trip, he was sure it came from a high-powered rifle. Looking up, he saw pigeons bolting in the air from perches on the Depository Building. Gunning his motorcycle, he rushed to the front entrance and dismounted quickly.

In the Presidential limousine, meanwhile, the Governor of Texas, John Connally, had been struck a stunning blow in the back. This from a round that passed through the right upper torso, after its entry below his right armpit, exited below his right nipple then passed through his right wrist, just then resting on his lap, and also wounded him in the left thigh. He was caused to spin to his right, and his wife pulled him down into her lap.

Shots were still coming. "Several eyewitnesses in front of the building" would report seeing a rifle being fired from the same southeast corner window on the sixth floor.

In the limo, the President was struck for a second time after John Connally's wounding...all in seconds or even less. This bullet brought about "a massive and fatal wound" to the rear of the President's head. He fell leftward into his wife's lap.

One car behind in the motorcade, Secret Service Agent Clinton J. Hill heard a "firecracker" noise and saw the President's lurch to the left. Leaping from his running-board post in the slow-moving motorcade (about 11 miles-per-hour), he ran to catch up with the all-important limousine before him.

Accompanying Vice President Lyndon B. Johnson, a car behind Hill's "follow-up" vehicle, Agent Youngblood had heard an explosion and seen "unusual movements in the crowd." He also reacted quickly. "He vaulted into the rear seat and sat on the Vice President in order to protect him."

Up front, two cars ahead, Secret Service Agent Roy Kellerman turned from his front right seat post just in time to see that his ward, the President, had been hit. "Let's get out of here; we are hit," he barked at the driver. He also radioed terse instruction to the motorcade's lead car: "Get us to the hospital immediately."

Secret Service Agent William R. Greer, driver of the Presidential limo, "immediately accelerated." To the vehicle's rear, Agent Hill sprinted forward and climbed the back of the open car. He pushed forward the President's wife, who in her shock and confusion, had climbed out onto the back of the car from the rear seat. He pushed her, then shielded her and her inert husband with his body as the motorcade sped away from Dealey Plaza.

Eyewitness Brennan promptly told a policeman about his sighting of the gunman in the sixth-floor corner window. At 12:34 p.m., the Dallas Police radio named the Depository Building as "a possible source of the shots, and at 12:45 p.m. the police broadcast a description of the suspected assassin based primarily on Brennan's observations."

Long before, relatively speaking, police "motorman" Baker had dismounted his bike and charged through the front door. He and the building superintendent, Roy Truly, first tried two elevators in the rear of the ground floor, but both lifts were somewhere above, at some upper floor. Not waiting, the two men raced up the nearby stairs. "Not more than two minutes had elapsed since the shooting."

At the second-floor landing, Baker glimpsed someone through the glass window of the door in the stairway hall. Inside was a lunchroom. Gun drawn, Baker went in, followed by Truly. They encountered a lone, empty-handed young man whom Truly recognized and identified as a Depository employee. Baker and Truly then resumed their dash up the stairs to the sixth floor, leaving behind, in the second-floor lunchroom, Lee Harvey Oswald.

A minute later, holding a full soft drink bottle in his hand, (purchased from a lunchroom vending machine), "Oswald was seen passing through the second-floor offices."

At 12:35 p.m., the Presidential limousine and other motorcade vehicles arrived at Parkland Memorial Hospital, four miles from the shooting scene. Previously alerted by the police, the emergency room staff began all-out emergency procedures to revive the stricken President, who was unconscious and barely alive...motor responses only.

At the Depository, meanwhile, Oswald at last sight had been walking toward the front of the second-floor level; at the front, both an elevator and stairs allowed access to the first floor and its entranceway below.

Seven minutes later, or at 12:40 p.m., he was seen boarding an Elm Street bus seven blocks away. Since he was then east of the Depository and the bus was traveling west, it quickly ran into a traffic jam in the vicinity of the shooting scene. Having been aboard for only three or four minutes, Oswald left the bus. He had been seen by a former landlady, Mrs. Mary Bledsoe.

Minutes later, he found a taxi four blocks away and took it to the neighborhood of his roominghouse quarters. He would arrive there about 1:00 p.m.

At Parkland, doctors performed a tracheotomy, used cardiac message and intravenous cut-ins in heroic medical measures to save the President...but to no avail. After receiving Last Rites, John F. Kennedy was declared dead. Official time: 1:00 p.m.

In the Oak Cliff area of Dallas, meanwhile, Patrolman J.D. Tippit, an 11-year veteran of the police force, was following instructions that had been radioed to his patrol car at 12:45 p.m.—to be on the lookout for the suspect last seen at the Depository window with a rifle (by Brennan's description).

At 12:54, Tippit radioed in that he was in the area, "as directed and would be available for any emergency."

At his roominghouse not far away, Oswald obviously was in a hurry. Housekeeper Marlene Roberts remarked at his haste when he rushed in, but he didn't even reply. He was gone in just a few minutes.

Shortly thereafter, a man was walking eastward on East 10th Street near its intersection with Patton. Cruising the same street and approaching from behind was Tippit in his patrol car.

He pulled alongside at about 1:15 p.m. Tippit and the man talked for a moment by way of the police car's right front window, then Tippit got out of the car and started to walk around the front to approach his quarry on the sidewalk. The man drew a revolver and fired four shots at Tippit, killing him on the spot. As the assailant fled on foot, a passing witness, Domingo Benavides, used the slain policeman's patrol car radio to notify Dallas police. "The message was received shortly after 1:16 p.m."

At 1:20 p.m., Vice President Lyndon B. Johnson, waiting in a heavily protected anteroom at Parkland, was told the President was dead. Johnson now would be President, but there were fears of a possible conspiracy to kill him, too.

Shortly before 2:00 p.m., Tippit's as-yet-unnamed killer was apprehended in a movie theater, still armed with a pistol.

Back at the Depository, three empty cartridge cases had been found on the floor just inside the suspicious window. Then, near the sixth-floor staircase, a bolt-action rifle with a telescopic sight was found. Soon to be identified as the murder weapon, it belonged to one Lee Harvey Oswald, further investigation revealed.

Building superintendent Truly, in the meantime, had told police that he noticed Oswald was missing from the Depository's normal daily work force of 15 men.

At 2:00 p.m., Dallas Homicide Chief Will Fritz returned to his headquarters with this information and was telling one of his detectives to pick up Oswald for questioning. "Standing nearby were the police officers who had just arrived with the man arrested in the Texas [Movie] Theatre. When Fritz mentioned the name of the missing employee, he learned that the man was already in the interrogation room. The missing School Book Depository employee and the suspect who had been apprehended in the Texas Theatre were one and the same—Lee Harvey Oswald."

At 2:38 p.m., on board Air Force One at Dallas's Love Field, Lyndon Johnson was sworn in as President by Federal District Court Judge Sarah T. Hughes. Oswald remained in custody as Air Force One then took off for Washington with both the new President and the former, the *slain,* President's body aboard. Two days later, Oswald was fatally shot while being transferred from the Dallas city jail to the Dallas County jail. In full view of millions of television viewers, nightclub owner Jack Ruby stepped out of an onlooking crowd of reporters with a .38 revolver in his right hand and fired one shot that crumpled Oswald quickly to the ground, unconscious.

That was shortly after 11:20 a.m., November 24, two days after the first shooting. In seven minutes, the shooter, Oswald, also arrived at Parkland. Never regaining consciousness, he was officially pronounced dead at 1:07 p.m.

# 🦅 *Travels With Wilson*

Blinds drawn, the presidential train passed through the rail yards of Wichita, Kansas, without making its scheduled stop for still another speech by Woodrow Wilson. Instead, it sped on toward Washington, hurrying the stricken President back to his White House quarters as rapidly as possible.

They had tried to stop him, hadn't they? His doctor. His wife. His private secretary. Admiral Cary Grayson, the presidential physician, had hinted to Joseph Tumulty, Wilson's secretary, that the speaking tour might cost Wilson his very life. And Mrs. Wilson dismissed both the League of Nations and the presidency as absolute imperatives. Her only interest, she said, was "my husband and his health."

Wilson himself admitted, "I am at the end of my tether," but he was adamant—he *had* to lobby the American people for their approval, over Senate objection, of his pet, the League of Nations that was decided upon at the recent Versailles conference formally ending World War I. To stir up a public in favor of Senate ratification, Wilson decided after his months in Europe, he must rally the country, "swing around the circle," plunge into a nationwide speaking tour.

Launching a rail journey from Washington, D.C., to Washington State and back, Wilson set off to make 40 or more speeches plugging the peace-keeping League and his conviction it must be ratified by the U.S. Senate.

As if that itinerary alone were not enough strain upon the obviously exhausted Wilson, the so-called "swing" was more like a race. For behind Wilson came a squad of anti-League Senate members addressing audiences at the same stops, drawing larger and larger crowds, some greater than his own.

For 22 days Wilson pressed on—and in one speech could be notably forgetful of things said in another, and often was notably bitter, even depressed as well. Much of his imagery had to do with death. Came a day—September 25, 1919—in Pueblo, Colorado, and tears coursed down his cheeks. That afternoon, he and Mrs. Wilson left

171

the stopped train for a short walk on a country road. But he was running a fever when they returned.

Tumulty, with Wilson ever since he had served as Governor of New Jersey a decade before, had asked Wilson to put off the speech-making trip before they had left Washington. Even then, Tumulty had thought his longtime boss and friend was "plainly on the verge of a nervous breakdown." And now, before dawn the day after the crying incident, Tumulty heard the tapping on his sleeping compartment door.

It was Grayson knocking at 4 in the morning. The President! Come quick, the President is sick.

And of course he was—pale, unable to speak clearly, one side of his face frozen, an arm and leg also not functioning properly. And again tears! "My dear boy," he told Tumulty, "this has never happened to me before. I do not know what to do."

When Tumulty quite logically said the rest of the trip was to be cancelled, Wilson still objected. "Don't you see," he said, "that if you cancel this trip, Senator Henry Lodge and his friends will say that I am a quitter and that the Western trip was a failure and the [Versailles] Treaty will be lost?"

Unswayed by Wilson's plea, more concerned for his health and well-being, Tumulty and others in the Wilson entourage of course ordered their train to speed on back to Washington. But they also did their best to disguise Wilson's illness, to play it down. Tumulty issued a press statement saying Wilson "so spent himself without reserve on this trip that it brought on a nervous reaction in his digestive organs."

Upon arrival in Washington, Wilson somehow summoned the strength to walk from the train. Barely a week later, he suffered a more severe and disabling stroke, also kept secret, never to recover fully from the two attacks of fall 1919. And the Senate never did ratify the proposal that the United States should join the League of Nations.


# ❦ *Died There*

They died at the White House. In the building itself—

• A relative. Ulysses S. Grant's father-in-law, Judge Frederick Lincoln Dent, an unreconstructed Confederate sympathizer despite his middle name or his daughter Julia's marriage to the famous Union general Grant. In 1873. Old age, essentially.

- A slave child. Infant born in the White House 1806, deceased by the end of 1808. Record kept of small coffin ordered.
- A President. The first of them to die in office. William Henry Harrison in April 1841, only a month after taking office. Caught cold and fever, it is thought, at his chilly inauguration in March.
- A President's wife. John Tyler's first wife, Letitia, in 1842, hardly more than a year after her husband succeeded the ill-fated William Henry Harrison. Young by today's standards, she was 52 and had been in ill health since moving into the White House the year before.
- Another Harrison. Same family, a later generation. Caroline, that is, wife to President Benjamin Harrison, who was William Henry Harrison's grandson. In her late 50s. TB. In 1892. And then, misery on misery, her father, late the same year.
- Another presidential wife. Woodrow Wilson's dear Ellen. TB of the kidneys. In her mid-50s, and the year was 1914. The day, August 6. In Europe, World War I had just erupted.
- A President, the second to die in the presidential home. Zachary Taylor in 1850. His stomach upset after drinking ice water and eating cherries and milk on July 4, he died five days later.
- A President's son. Young Willie Lincoln, 12, who together with younger brother Tad caught fever in the winter of 1862. Tad recovered, but Willie did not.
- Aftermaths and other details. After Willie's death, Abe Lincoln went to his secretary John Nicolay's office, sobbed and wept. Mary Todd Lincoln went to bed and screamed until she fell asleep. During the funeral five days later, said an onlooker, the sky was black and a fierce wind rolled up tin roofs in Washington and toppled chimneys and church steeples.
- Aftermaths...Woodrow Wilson was so affected by wife Ellen's death, he wouldn't allow her remains to be placed in a coffin. He had her laid out on a sofa in the presidential bedroom, curtains pulled shut and lights low. He stayed there with her for two nights. After her funeral service in the East Room, he rode the special train to her hometown of Rome, Georgia, in the compartment with her casket.
- Aftermaths...Caroline Harrison's death came in the last weeks of a presidential campaign, but neither her husband nor his Democratic opponent Grover Cleveland had done much campaigning. Cleveland had made only one public appearance after learning of Mrs. Harrison's serious illness in 1892, and incumbent Harrison had stayed close to his dying wife all along. When it was announced that Cleveland had won the election—as the first and only President ever returned to office after *leaving* the White House—Harrison was

visibly relieved. "For me there is no sting in it," he said. "Indeed, after the heavy blow the death of my wife dealt me, I do not think I could have stood the strain that a re-election would have brought."

•Aftermaths...visibly ill for several days, Zachary Taylor was treated by a doctor, Thomas Miller, often accused of having "bled" the dying William Henry Harrison a bit too much back in 1841, when *he* died in the White House. Taylor, in any case, was tormented by a restless delirium in which he spoke self-debasing nonsense. Congress and the public awaited the frequent White House bulletin. Senator Jefferson Davis and wife Varina were repeated visitors. At the very last, for the final hours of July 9, 1850, members of the Cabinet and other officials waited in an upstairs room down the hall from the President's own bedchamber.

In the bedroom itself were Taylor family members and Jefferson Davis and wife Varina again. By now, Taylor was still. Alive barely, but still. And the remarkable thing...the remarkable moment was when he suddenly spoke and said: "I am about to die. I expect my summons very soon. I have tried to discharge my duties faithfully; I regret nothing, but I am sorry I am about to leave my friends."

He said this, turning to look at his wife Margaret...and died a half hour later, still turned in her direction.

## 🦅 *Outlaw of Falahill*

"I am accustomed," said this White House occupant, "to hearing malicious falsehoods about myself, but I think I have a right to object to libelous statements about my dog." And furthermore, said "The Boss," just forget the malicious rumor that he sent to a United States Navy destroyer scampering back to the Aleutian Islands in the middle of a war to fetch an AWOL White House dog, even this very famous and popular White House dog, "at a cost to the taxpayer of two or three or twenty million dollars."

No sir, added FDR in a 1944 campaign speech before the Teamsters union, the "Republican-concocted story" did not sit well with his dog Fala. Not well at all. "His Scotch soul was furious."

Fala ("my little dog," FDR called him), of course was a Scottie. He arrived at the White House, already housebroken, in 1940 as a present to Franklin Delano Roosevelt from his cousin Margaret Suckley, and FDR apparently fell in love with the spiky-earred pet immediately.

"He was a shaggy Scotsman, known in the books as Murray, the Outlaw of Falahill, wrote FDR's secretary Grace Tully. He slept in the Master's bedroom, he shared FDR's breakfast tray in the mornings, and during the presidential workday he "raced himself dizzy" in an outdoor pen within view of the Oval Office.

He then was seen "accompanying his master triumphantly back to the big house at the end of each day."

Among various talents, he was good at chewing the presidential trouser cuffs, just a gnaw or two, to get attention. More formally, he did tricks—roll-overs, hindleg stands, or hurdles over upraised human legs.

The Boss usually handed him his dinner, presented in the presidential study in a bowl. Fala, as another trick, had to learn to beg with some decorum—too eager, and he'd have to wait for a moment.

Quite naturally, he traveled with the President—to the family home at Hyde Park, New York; to the "Little White House" at Warm Springs, Georgia; even to the ships down at the sea, when FDR traveled by shipboard.

In that regard, though, Fala could be a major problem—a real security risk. So often pictured in the press, so well known as he was, Fala, by appearing in public anywhere, would reveal the fact that FDR was not far away. In wartime, that could be a problem, and Tully recalled, "the secrecy would break down whenever a train stop enabled the young ruffian to persuade Arthur Prettyman, the valet, to take him out for a trackside walk."

One of FDR's Secret Service entourage went so far as to call Fala, "The Informer."

At the same time, Fala had a will of his own—sometimes he was where FDR *wasn't,* you might say.

Like the day he turned up on the loose in the downtown Washington streets near the White House. Or the other time he was noticed "sniffing around" at the Treasury Building next door.

In the latter incident, noting that it came on the 15th of the month, frequently a payday, FDR quipped: "He had probably run out of spending money—almost everybody else does on that day."

For such and other winsome ways, Fala was not only well known but loved by the general public. "Hundreds of letters came to the White House addressed to him, some signed by paw prints and many from the very old or very young lovers of dogs," said Tully also.

She once found herself in hot water when she unthinkably agreed to enroll him in the Tailwaggers Club of California, only to find out there was a chapter right in Washington, D.C.—a chapter of outraged hometown Tailwaggers!

The daily visitors to the White House, in the meantime, included people more interested in seeing Fala than the President himself.

From 1940 until the end, *FDR*'s end in April of 1945, Fala was a part of the White House family. Of the family, period.

He only occasionally had been left behind—assuredly sulking too—when FDR traveled, and so he was present when FDR suddenly died at the Little White House in Warm Springs that fateful April day. The possibly apocryphal story, told by writer John Gunther for one, is that Fala quite suddenly sprang to life, barking in anguish, "crashed" through the screen door, ran outside and took up a "vigil" on a nearby hilltop.

He later found some consolation as Eleanor's dog Fala and living at Hyde Park...but, no disrespect intended, there of course could be no replacing FDR in Scotsman Fala's life.

##  *Wretched Little Sofa*

They had loved the White House, but now it was time. Go they must. The farewells would be difficult—so difficult even for others! The intellectual Henry Adams, who lived right on Lafayette Square, would not, could not, bring himself to walk over and say goodbye. He wrote instead: Of all earthly trials, farewells are the worst." He wrote that it would be depressing to look out the window and see the White House without its mistress of the past eight years, Edith Kermit Roosevelt, wife of Teddy the President.

And at a farewell stag luncheon for Teddy, the sheriff of Deadwood, South Dakota, Seth Bullock, was supposed to speak on behalf of the 31 guests—old friends from all walks of life—but the lawman from the Badlands could only choke, wordlessly, when his moment came.

Edith ordered chipped White House chinaware to be smashed up and thrown away, rather than "cheapen" the August home by giving it away or selling it. Teddy went through his study in search of mementoes for friends and family, the personal things.

And there was one fairly "personal" item that the First Lady wanted to take with her when they turned over the White House to the William Howard Tafts on March 4, 1909. That was an antique mahogany sofe she had bought for 400 in 1901 for the Red Room downstairs. After the Teddy-and-Edith Roosevelt refurbishments of 1902, the same small piece would up in the Upper Hall, upstairs with the family. And she loved it. She loved it so much that her adoring husband took it upon himself to write the Speaker of the House, Rep. Joe Cannon, to ask permission to take the sofa and replace it with another.

But he balked, so did an official in charge of public grounds, and then the request made the newspapers, replete with implications that the "retiring" First lady was trying to take away White House furnishings that didn't belong to her.

It seemed obvious that Democrat Cannon had "leaked" the story, and Edith Roosevelt told White House military aide Archie Butt that she wouldn't leave Washington without telling the Speaker what she thought of his "little and petty" action.

"It is the first time since I have been in the White House," she declared angrily, "that I have been dragged into publicity of this kind."

As for the small piece of furniture, once so alluring, it now was that "wretched little sofa." How could she possibly want it now, "now that all the associations with it are of a most disagreeable character?"

And so, on such a sour note, the story might have ended . . . except for an unexpected assist from a key onlooker two years later.

At first, Teddy Roosevelt had been delighted to see William Howard Taft selected as their Republican party's nominee in 1868 and then to greet him as President-elect. Their relationshp later cooled, as Taft developed an agenda of his own in the presidency, but that fact did not stop the kind and thoughtful letter that one day emanated from the Taft White House.

It was to Edith from William Howard, and it concerned "a mahogany settee which you had purchased for the White House about which clustered many pleasant associations . . ." Taft made no bones of his opinion as to the steps taken before he entered the settee picture. One disapproving official he accused of "density," and House Speaker Cannon had merely *assumed* the authority "to speak" in respect to Edith Roosevelt's wish to keep the small sofa.

Taft took note of the custom by which Cabinet officers could take their Cabinet chairs into retirement with them, if they only would replace them. "Why the real head of the White House, the wife of the President, should be denied the same privilege, and especially in respect to a chair or settee that she herself bought for the White House and which has not therefore acquired value by long years of use in the White House I cannot see," Taft wrote also.

Neither the disapproving official nor the House Speaker "had anything to say about it," said Taft.

The final point was, he had replaced the "Roosevelt settee" at his own expense and was sending it by express as a New Year's gift. "I hope," wrote Taft on New Year's Eve, 1910, "the settee will bring back to you the pleasantest hours at the White House."

# 🦅 Life After the White House

Picture this. Father and mother in their bed one night, still awake, and teenaged daughter comes in to protest the family's proposed move from the big city to a little town in Georgia—middle-of-nowhere Georgia at that.

Could be nearly any two parents and their child, anywhere . . . and typical American home, couldn't it? Except that the stereotypical scene in this case was in the White House, and the time was late 1980, the night after Ronald Reagan was elected to succeeed Jimmy Carter. And in the bed this particular night, still stunned by their very-much shared election loss, were Jimmy and Rosalynn.

"Amy came to our bedroom the night after the election and leaned over our high canopied bed with her head on her arms," wrote Rosalynn Carter later. "I'm sad about this election," she told her parents.

Her mother said they were sad, too, but they had tried their best to                                                                                        win.

In Amy's case there was another aspect to the pain. She had no desire to go back to tiny Plains, Georgia, the family's real home.

"You may be from the country," she exclaimed, "but I'm not! I've been raised in the city!"

And . . . true. First Jimmy Carter had served as governor of Georgia. Headquarters, Atlanta. Then, after only a brief hiatus, it was on to Washington . . . and the White House. As Rosalynn Carter later wrote: "She was right. We had moved to the governor's mansion when she was just three years old."

Naturally, Amy was not the only family member hurting. Jimmy Carter later acknowledged that his disappointment was "great", but he "kept it bottled up for a long time." And Rosalynn, more visibly upset, just couldn't understand the rejection. "It just didn't seem fair," she felt. In her view, "We had done all we could, and somehow it had not been enough."

They would eventually develop a new life, aggressively search out new challenges—even write a book together about the traumatic experience, *Everything to Gain: Making the Most of the Rest of Your Life.* But those first days, weeks, even months, were difficult, and the readjustment took deep, personal reappraisals. Leaving the White

House, a relief to some presidential couples, was not a welcome activity to the Carters.

There was the feeling of so much else to do before the next occupants—the Reagans—moved in. There was the feeling that life back in the small town of Plains could be pretty dull "after the exciting life of the White House and the long years of political battles," they wrote together in their book. Amy had a point!

And what readjustments when they did return! Their bungalow in an oak and hickory grove had not really been a fulltime home for 10 years—outside, both topsoil and lawn had washed away. And after the White House, it offered terribly cramped quarters. Now, they wished they had put a floor in the attic so it could be more fully utilized for storage. As it was, boxes and crates returning to Plains with the Carters "were stacked to the ceiling in the house and garage." Now, too, there were no servants to help in the unpacking or physical maintenance of their home.

Worse, after the election, the Carters discovered they were in serious financial difficulty back home—the family peanut business was in jeopardy. As the Carters explain in their book, they placed their financial affairs in a blind trust before going to the White House in 1977, and it was only after the Reagan election that they found out "what had happened to our estate during the four years we had been in the White House."

What had happened was the farm lands had been rented, while the family peanut warehouse had gone through various management changes, and Georgia, meanwhile, had suffered three years of unremitting drought. The Carters were "deeply in debt."

To salvage the situation, they would have to sell the warehouse operation, then find something to replace it as a financial base. "Just as almost two decades of political life were about to end," they wrote, "we found that the results of the preceding 23 years of hard work, scrimping and saving, and plowing everything back into the business, were now also gone. No one could accuse us of becoming rich in the White House. We had not expected to, but we had hoped at least to be able to leave with what we had had when we came in. That, too, was not to be."

In the meantime, the final weeks in the White House meant, in addition to affairs of state, a last sentimental Christmas at the venerable Executive Mansion—and then all the farewells. As one phenomenon, the old house seemed to have *so many visitors* suddenly. "Many close friends and relatives wanted to spend just one night in the White House while we were still there." Then, too, "Night after night we had farewell parties, along with luncheons and receptions during the day."

There were so many people to thank, but sometimes the pace and the emotion could be wearing. Well-meant assurances that they were about to begin an exciting new life simply weren't true (". . .and we'd rather not hear people say it"). And, no, they would *not* be happy to go home and avoid the slings and arrows of politics (". . .we'd thrived even with the criticisms and we loved politics").

As one welcome parting gesture, though, the Carter Cabinet and its staff gave him "a complete set of tools and machinery for a wood-working shop," and if there were anything Jimmy Carter liked to do, all his own, private, relaxed self, it was to fuss around making furniture.

While there had been many issues, many political triumphs and losses, the *burning* issue of the Carter presidency had been the American hostages held in Iran. And now, on Inauguration Day for Ronald Reagan, they were freed—Jimmy Carter flew to Wiesbaden, Germany, to welcome them back and help to celebrate their new freedom. "Although I had not been to bed for three days during the final negotiations about the hostages, I didn't even feel the fatigue during our long trip to Germany," wrote Carter in the joint book. His return, though, was not to the White House, but to Plains, where, exhausted, he slept for almost 24 hours, "and then awoke to an altogether new, unwanted and potentially empty life."

Jimmy Carter at the time was 56, Rosalynn, 53, and Amy 13 . . . and all now had to put their lives back together again. Jimmy and Rosalynn soon began on book projects—contracts with needed monetary benefit. He soon embarked upon a teaching career at Emory University in Atlanta and made plans for the Jimmy Carter Library. In time, they became more and more involved in peace and health care organizations and projects, plus the Christian Habitat for Humanity, the voluntary housing project that provides housing for the needy.

Amy Carter at first attended school near Plains, but there were few children her own age in town, and she missed out on many activities because no one knew what to do with her Secret Service detail ("those policemen") if she went on a weekend camping trip or an overnight "with the girls." Her parents then placed her in a boarding school in Atlanta with more girls her own age—they knew her readjustment was coming along just fine when she said that if her father hadn't lost the 1980 election, she wouldn't have made those new friends at the school in Atlanta. In time Jimmy and Rosalynn could say in their shared book, "There is life after the White House!" Exclamation point theirs.

 # *Lincoln and Stanton*

Abe Lincoln and his Secretary of War Edwin Stanton did not start out close friends—the outspoken Stanton once said he found "no token of any intelligent understanding by Lincoln, or the crew that govern him." As time went on, however, Lincoln worked more closely with Stanton than any other of his Cabinet members, and Stanton's esteem for his President steadily improved.

If there were any doubt as to their eventual closeness, a scene at the White House after the Battle of Gettysburg would serve to dispel it. For here, late that night of July 3, 1863, last day of the three-day battle, came a breathless Stanton pounding up the White House stairs, dispatch in hand, and then to knock on Lincoln's door.

"Who's there?" asked Lincoln, half asleep, and the simple reply was all Lincoln needed to know. "Stanton" was that reply.

Lincoln, with a light in hand, appeared as the door partially opened. He appeared, said the account in the *New York Tribune* of January 23, 1887, in his nightclothes—"in the shortest nightgown and the longest legs," said Stanton later, that *he* had ever witnessed on a human being.

And Lincoln knew just what Stanton wished to impart—once his War Secretary caught his breath. He knew it had to have been a victory. Such a crucial victory, too! Lincoln "gave a shout of exultation, grabbed him [Stanton] with both arms around the waist and danced him around the chamber until they both were exhausted."

The pair then sat on a nearby trunk, Lincoln still in his sleepware, read the War Department telegram again and again and stayed there until dawn as they talked over "the probabilities of the future and the results of the victory."

In the future, of course, was Lincoln's assassination, two years later, a prospect that Stanton had feared and guarded against for some time. It was the War Secretary who indefatigably—even ruthlessly—pressed the prosecution of anyone involved in the assassination conspiracy.

Stanton may *not* really have said of Lincoln's death, "Now he belongs to the ages," as often averred. But he certainly mourned his friend and colleague of the Civil War era. Said Lincoln's son Robert Todd: "For more than ten days after my father's death in Washington, he [Stanton] called on me in my room, and spent the first few minutes of his visits weeping without saying a word."

#  Piece of Paper Misplaced

To quit the presidency or not to quit? The answer, it seemed, was on a piece of paper. And as he neared the end of his State of the Union address to a joint session of the U.S. Congress, with the Supreme Court justices, the diplomatic corps and just about all the other leading lights of Washington officialdom also looking on, Lyndon Baines Johnson reached into his pocket for the piece of paper.

A draft of a statement saying that he would *not* run for reelection, it wasn't there.

There is no guarantee that Johnson would have cast the die then and there, that early in 1968, but the paper's absence was nearly a guarantee that Johnson—complex, often vacillating, often blustering, often firm and yet often impulsive—would not make his final decision then and there, in front of the country; before the world, really.

The Vietnam War, really *raging* by now half a world away, was one factor, yes. But not nearly quite the deciding factor that many suppose. It had blown up in his face, like a mine, since he assumed office upon the assassination of John F. Kennedy in 1963, true.

He hated it, and it was tearing him apart, also true.

But there also was his health to consider. Fears of death. A desire for time with his family. . .a yearning for peace and quiet.

In 1955, still a member of the U.S. Senate from Texas, he had suffered a nearly fatal heart attack. In 1967, as President, he underwent surgery for removal of his gall bladder and a kidney stone. By one informed account, he at first bounced back, "but then he relapsed." The same source, ABC-TV newsman William Lawrence, said: "His staff, including press secretary Bill Moyers, openly admitted his pain, his fatigue, his need for a long rest and rehabilitation."

According to longtime friend Willard Deason, a college classmate, Lyndon Johnson always had a premonition of dying young. "I believe both his father and grandfather died in their early sixties [not true, actually], and he thought that would happen to him, which of course, it did."

The thing is "He didn't want anything like that to happen while he was President."

Johnson himself later said his mind "always" was on his 1955 heart attack. And, further, whenever he saw Woodrow Wilson's portrait in the Red Room of the White House he recalled Wilson's last months as President—a President incapacitated by a stroke. He never looked at Wilson's face "that I didn't think that it might happen to me, that I would end another term in bed with a stroke and that the decisions of government would be taken care of by other people and that was wrong. I didn't want that to happen."

Johnson often debated the issue of running for a second term in 1968 or stepping down voluntarily. He talked it over with all kinds of advisers, official and personal...again and again, often appearing to have decided against seeking re-election. In fact, that's what he told his Vice President, Hubert Humphrey, the day after their landslide victory in 1964. Humphrey didn't take Johnson too seriously way back then. "And I don't doubt that he ran it in and out of his mind a hundred, maybe a thousand times."

No doubt, as Lady Bird Johnson could attest. "We must have discussed it hundreds of times, and the discussions began at the very beginning [of his presidency]," she said.

By early 1968, the year Johnson would be up for a second full term, daughter Luci had married and produced a grandson, Lyn...and Johnson loved spending time with this first grandchild. "He could play with the baby and lose himself in this," said his personal physician, Dr. James Cain. In another family development, daughter Lynda Bird had married Charles S. Robb, a U.S. Marine Corps captain due to serve in Vietnam as of March 1968.

Wrestling with his decision, Johnson early in 1968 seemed to feel that he should step down. He apparently agreed with Press Secretary George Christian's view that he "had become a lightning rod for everything people in the country wanted to jump on." Especially, of course, as target of the Vietnam War protest movement.

Johnson had his health to consider, his desire for a few quiet years with a burgeoning family, an escape from the pressures of office... but he also was afraid the troops he had sent to Vietnam would feel betrayed if their commander-in-chief suddenly left the field.

What to do? The morning of January 17, 1968, the day fixed for his State of the Union address, he had studied the withdrawal statement drafted for him by George Christian. Still a big "if," it would *not* be something he would incorporate in the State of the Union itself. "If Lyndon decided to make it," said Lady Bird later, "the statement would come at the end, beginning with a line something like this: 'And now I want to speak about a personal matter...'"

As late as 6:30 that evening, now rushing to keep his State of the Union appointment on Capitol Hill, he paused and said to his wife Lady Bird: "Well, what do you think? What shall I do?"

And she? "I looked at him with that hopeless feeling and said: 'Luci hopes you won't run. She wants you for herself and for Lyn and all of us. She does not want to give you up. Lynda hopes you *will* run. She told me so this afternoon with a sort of terrible earnestness, because her husband is going to war and she thinks there will be a better chance of getting him back alive and the war settled if you are President. Me—I don't know. I have said it all before. I can't tell you what to do.'"

And so, it might have depended upon the piece of paper that Lyndon Baines Johnson sought in his pocket as he reached the very last page of his State of the Union address the evening of January 17, 1968.

What would he have done then? We'll never know, because the draft statement wasn't there.

We'll never *know,* but we can guess from his own explanation. He reached for it in his pocket, he later said. "I don't think I would have used it, but just to see if it was there. I don't know what I would have done if it had been there. I don't think I would have done it then, but it wasn't there, and I didn't have to confront the problem."

Later, of course, he did confront "the problem" and he did withdraw. The rest is history. . . .and the night of January 17, 1968, a President of the United States *did* return to his White House quarters and ask his wife, "Why'd you have to keep that announcement?" And she apparently *did* say, "I gave it back to you." And he? "No, you didn't." And then? "We both looked through my pockets and then went on, and there it was by the telephone table."

## Funeral Train

"I shall never forget that journey," wrote Secret Service Agent Edmund W. Starling. And indeed, mournfully rolling and scraping its way east on iron tracks came the funeral train. Indeed, "Sometimes it was the middle of the night when we crept slowly into a station, the bell of our locomotive clanging dolefully."

And in that doleful night, at that small station, he would see in the darkness on either side "the flicker of white garments," and he would hear "the low rolling tones of thousands of men softly singing 'Lead Kindly Light,' or 'Nearer My God To Thee.'"

They had left the West Coast—San Francisco, specifically—late on August 3 and they now would pass all the way east, practically ocean to ocean, across a nation that was obviously, clearly, "grief-stricken," exactly as Agent Starling said. Every city, every town encountered, "was in mourning."

By the long iron tracks stood the people and singing hymns.

"Masons in full dress uniforms, with helmets and plumage, waited at each stopping place on the long 3,000-mile journey."

Across the continent they came, and "there seemed to be no sound but the beating of our bell and the voices, rising up and washing over our train like a tide."

And in Washington, merely more of the same. He lay in state at the White House first. Then a caisson carried the casket to the Capitol. "Never have I traveled that mile of Pennsylvania Avenue so slowly or with such an ache in my heart," wrote Starling, a White House veteran, many years later.

"Onward Christian Soldiers," played the Marine Band. "Nearer My God To Thee," enjoined "hundreds and hundreds" of school children along the route, the street strewn with their flowers. And then, after the Capitol rituals, another train, headed west to Ohio, his home. All over again, the funeral train and its reception. "All through the night, time after time, the locomotive slowed down and we heard the people singing."

He was on view at his father's house on Center Street. Marion, Ohio, it was. The final rites and burial came on August 10, a procession winding through the hometown streets, past the newspaper where he once worked and his widow was his assistant, and on to the cemetery. More voices. More singing. More hymns. More throngs of mourners.

They don't say much or write much about Warren G. Harding today. . .but there was a time, fairly obviously, when he was both mourned and loved.

## ✷ *First to Come—And Go*

When President John Adams came to see the future city of Washington in June of 1800, hardly 150 Federal employees and only 500 or so households were there to greet him. The future Capitol was far from complete. The future White House had not yet even been granted a privy.

Both the privy and a back stairs were added shortly after he moved into the shell of the presidential home that November, but Abigail Adams found only six rooms of the future mansion to be "comfortable."

Outside, in addition to the unsightly debris of construction, was a stable for seven horses, said to be somewhat advanced in years, together with a chariot, a coach, a market wagon.

For all their travels and exposure to upper-class *Culture* in Europe, the Adams couple tended to be almost simple in taste and lifestyle. Certainly they were not extravagant or socially pretentious. A salvaged inventory list of their furnishings at the White House, for instance, mentions the presidential bedroom had white dimity curtains and his parlor was "in tolerable order." The couple could boast three complete "Setable setts" of china and teaspoons to go with ladles and two fine "urns" of silver. In generally good condition, but perhaps an extraordinary number for householders of today to consider, were their 33 pairs of sheets.

They established their normal life on the second floor—upstairs. Here, a corner room on the west end of the southern side and the room next to it became their bedrooms. The great, unfinished shell was so cold and drafty in the winter that the sun in those rooms was a warm friend. Adams made his office in the room adjoining his bedroom on its eastern side. The next room along the eastward prospect was a parlor and sitting room filled with crimson-hued pieces that once adorned the presidential drawing room in Philadelphia.

Joining the Adamses in their new home as its chief servants were John Briesler and his wife Esther, long-term retainers who now served as the mansion's first steward and housekeeper. Normally, a grand home on the scale of the future White House would have boasted a staff of perhaps 30 servants, but the Adamses made do with the Brieslers and four added helpers, all paid from the couple's own pockets rather than from public funds. Settling in with the President and his wife Abigail for the winter of 1800-01 were their son Thomas and their granddaughter Susannah.

The child's father was not Thomas, but rather son Charles, who died in New York in December. Only 29, a heavy drinker, he had suffered cirrhosis of the liver. His death, the first among all presidential progeny, hit the First Family hard. And on top of that sad news, John Adams lost his re-election bid of 1800 to Thomas Jefferson. And so, more bitterness during a bleak winter, with next a divisive Electoral College tie between Jefferson and Aaron Burr to be settled by the House of Representatives.

Inside the "castle," as Abigail Adams called it, the construction work had continued. The back stairway was finished in January, but only a huge space was evident at the west end of the transverse hall, to be filled during another administration by a magnificent grand stairway. The Adamses used the future Red Room, on the main floor, as a breakfast room. The kitchen was located at basement level, beneath the north entrance hall.

For the convenience of the home's first residents, architect James Hoban quickly built a wooden stairs from the balcony at the southern bow to the edge of a newly installed driveway leading southeast to Pennsylvania Avenue. Temporarily serving as an entrance hall, then, was the future Blue Room, known in its earliest days as the "oval saloon."

Probably the first major social functions held at the White House were the President's receptions for his legislators—House and Senate members. For the first one, the Adamses tried to make a Philadelphia-like procession of the official visitations, but Pennsylvania Avenue was a sea of mud from steady rains—few of the lawmakers could or would walk, as they had done in Philadelphia. Horse-drawn conveyances from as far away as Baltimore were pressed into service for the visitors from the Capitol. "They [then] piled out of rough, muddy vehicles, rushed across the wooden bridge in the rain into the entrance hall, where they stripped off their rain gear," wrote William Seale in his two-volume history, *The President's House*. "With their short-clothes, coats, shirts, hair powder and wigs, hose and shoes relatively dry, they were joined at once by a number of ladies."

After an exchange of remarks, greetings and the like with the body assembled, Adams guided his visitors to the refreshments awaiting them in the west end of the main floor, the "State Room" of the early White House.

It was possibly here, too, in the White House, that one difficult moment of the Adams denouement took place—a sharp conversation between Adams and Jefferson in which the rejected Adams allegedly told his old ally and colleague—"You have put me out! You have put me out!"

While they apparently smoothed over this troublesome moment later, the fact remained that an aging Adams was not to stay, while Jefferson was, and they had continuing political differences now that their young Republic was on its feet and beginning to make its mark upon the world.

Abigail Adams by early in 1801 had left Washington for home, while her husband, who had moved into the White House without her, was again alone for his leavetaking. He thus was the first President to use the White House as a residence and the first to give it up to a successor.

His time *in residence,* for that matter, had been very brief—four months it would be. Busying himself in his upstairs office in the final weeks, making appointments of Federalist allies that would infuriate Jefferson before the latter's inauguration on March 4, 1801, Adams was gone without a discernible ripple when Washington awoke that morning. Wagonloads of his belongings were packed and ready when Adams mounted his coach about 4:00 a.m., long before light, noted historian Seale. "The procession moved eastward unnoticed, leaving the White House to Jefferson."

#  *For The Record*

Already a deeply disturbed woman, Mary Todd Lincoln was so devastated by her husband's assassination that she would not attend his funeral—nor even leave the Executive Mansion for six weeks.

By then, the "funeral", a series of dramatic events, actually, was over—16 days in the unfolding. She had been a voice in some of its planning. It was her decision, for instance, that he should be buried in their last hometown of Springfield, Illinois. And it was by her wish also that little Willie Lincoln's coffin was disinterred from Oak Hill Cemetery in the Georgetown area. . .that little Willie would accompany his father on the long train trip back to Sprngfield and there lie beside him.

By chance, Abraham the very afternoon of his last day had noted the end of the rending Civil War and suggested that between that burden and "the loss of our darling Willie," they both had been "very miserable."

And true, since Willie's death on February 20, 1862, she had been so distraught she never again would enter the rooms in which he died and was embalmed—both in the White House. And now, her husband's body was embalmed on the premises, as well—in the Prince of Wales Room, second floor, west hall, the very room where Willie had died.

Nine doctors gathered in there for the official autopsy first. The spent bullet that killed him was recovered, dropping from one doctor's hands into a china basin below with a clatter. Then came the embalming process. . .in the same room. Lincoln's Secretary of War, Edwin Stanton, personally dressed the body for public viewing before the burial. He rejected an offer to mask a bruise showing on the face. "No," he said, "this is part of the history of the event."

They moved the body that next night down to the East Room, the bearers shuffling along in their socks to avoid upsetting Mrs. Lincoln with the sound of shoes carrying out the unhappy task. Earlier, she had heard the hammering on the elaborate catafalque being built to hold the casket and thought she was hearing gunshots.

It was Tuesday, April 18, 1865, that Lincoln, clad in the suit of his second inauguration, went on view to the silent public filing through the East Room in two lines. He had been shot the night of April 14 and had died at 7:22 the next morning in a boardinghouse across the street from Ford's Theatre.

At noon on April 19 came the first real funeral service, the Rev. Phineas D. Gurley officiating and Lincoln's son Robert Todd in attendance...but not Mrs. Lincoln. That afternoon, the Lincoln coffin was taken to the Capitol, where it remained—on view— through the next day, a Thursday. On Friday morning began the train trip, arranged by Stanton to nearly duplicate the route Lincoln had taken on his way *to* Washington from Springfield back in 1861 to become President.

So it was that this train made its major stops at Baltimore; Harrisburg, Pennsylvania; Philadelphia; New York City; Garrison's Landing near West Point; Albany; Buffalo; Cleveland; Columbus, Ohio; Indianapolis; Chicago, and, finally, Springfield. All along the route, small town or large, crowds and dignitaries marked Lincoln's passing among them, night or day. At Richmond, Indiana, just after three in the morning, some 12,000 persons turned out—a number exceeding the local population census. Funeral arches greeted the train in many towns, tolling bells, saluting guns, and two ex-Presidents saw the funeral train trudge by at its five-mile-per-hour pace for viewing—James Buchanan and Millard Fillmore.

In New York, local officials thought to bar representative blacks from taking part in the official procession from train to City Hall and back, but Stanton quickly put his foot down and quashed the unwholesome thought.

At last, on May 4, Lincoln was buried—temporarily—at Oak Ridge Cemetery in Springfield, with the Right Rev. Matthew Simpson, a Methodist bishop, giving the funeral oration. (Lincoln's remains later would be placed in a permanent tomb at the National Lincoln Monument in the same cemetery in 1882...but not before exposure of a plot to "steal" his remains and hold them hostage for the release of a counterfeiter from an Illinois prison at Joliet.)

In all, the Lincoln funeral events took 16 days. He was buried 20 days after his death. The funeral train, statisticians might wish to know, traveled exactly 1,662 miles and was only 1 hour late arriving in Springfield. A small fact, just for the record.

# ⚓ *Long, Long Wait*

The waiting for him to come home is long and tedious. In the interim, there is an invitation list to consider—four secretaries typing up hundreds of names and then, in a room full of aides, staff members, friends, a brother-in-law in charge, the names are read out loud for approval or disapproval.

Decisions, tough decisions...sometimes ruthless but all necessary. Speed is absolutely mandatory. Telegrams must go out right away. Now!

Barney Ross? Old shipmate. From his Navy days. Yes.

Billy Graham the evangelist? The really respected evangelist....

Silence.

Well?

"Billy considers himself a close friend of the President," says aide Lloyd Wright.

Somewhere in the night outside, headlights will be piercing the dark shroud over Washington. A particular vehicle will be struggling across the vale from air base to White House. A quiet and careful caravan of vehicles, actually, tires softly hissing on pavement. On his way home.

Inside, again a silence.

"By now," wrote an onlooking David Pearson years later, "there is real embarrassment in the air." And someone says they occasionally played golf together.

Finally, a voice of authority.

"No."

Next on the list?

And again the names. Yes, no. No, no, no...yes.

With Pearson, a high-ranking Peace Corps official called in to help, the group headed by his boss, the brother-in-law, eventually has to move on...down the corridors, through darkened historic rooms, into the big room at the far east end of the main floor. The East Room.

By now it is 1:00 a.m.

They are busy studying the old Lincoln pictures. They move out the grand piano. People are draping the mirror frames, the chandeliers above.

The decision is against *exactly* re-creating the Lincoln tableau. Too much. The great room would be "too morose and too dark." But *mostly* Lincolnesque, yes.

Word now comes to expect him at about 2:30 a.m.

What about a crucifix, says Pearson. They send for one, but..."it turns out to be pretty awful, with a bloody corpus."

The brother-in-law, Peace Corps Director Sergeant Shriver, says: "That's terrible. Go get the one in my bedroom."

Soon done. Danish, modern looking, and much more suitable.

New tension suddenly in the air. Air Force One has landed at the air base, at Andrews. He'll be here soon.

But, no, past 4:00 a.m., it turns out...past 4:30 a.m.

"Now, in the blackest part of the night, just before dawn, head-lights begin to cut through the gloom in front of the White House. Most of us, embarrassed and feeling out of place, retreat to a corner of the East Room."

Ready. Ready as can be....

Two candelabra and urns holding magnolia leaves from Andrew Jackson's tree on the South Lawn now stand in the center of the large room, flanking the one really dominating item—the catafalque.

It is really pretty terrible.

He is in the house, after brief detour to Bethesda Naval Hospital for the necessary preparations.

Pearson would never forget. "I hear the routine sound of doors opening and closing, low voices," he wrote in the *Miami Herald* in 1967; "then come sounds that make me shiver. A military voice snaps a 'march' command; there is the clipped staccato sound of boots hitting the hard floors."

In moments, in the doorway, the strained young men, stern-faced but obviously awed by their task. They carry in the casket and set it down. And now a priest and two altar boys have materialized.

Kneeling in prayer....

He is here at last.

"The pallbearers step back from the casket. There is a short pause; no one quite knows what to do first. There has been no rehearsal. No one has had any experience. What do you do when you bring a dead President into the East Room of the White House at 4:30 in the morning?"

Prayers from the priest...and suddenly, in the doorway, *she* stands, his brother Bobby on one side and Defense Secretary Robert McNamara on the other.

An altar boy is lighting candles at each corner of the casket, and she stands there, "feet apart, the slight lean forward," eyes wide with disbelief, clothing stained still by blood...Jackie is back, too.

In an age, in a few minutes, the very private scene has transpired, is over. One long moment she is at the casket kneeling, laying her forehead on it. "There is dead silence. Absolutely no sound of any kind." Then, she kisses the edge of the flag draped atop. She begins to stand, and then it happens. She slumps back down sobbing, sobbing, "rocked by sobs." Bobby helps, holds her...lets her cry. In the days ahead, noted Pearson later, she would present a regal, strong, "almost inhumanly stoic" image to the world...people might even wonder if she mourned, really mourned.

"But those of us in the East Room tonight know she did."

And as she is led away after her storm of grief, taken upstairs to rest and compose herself for the difficult hours and days ahead, this long night's wait is over. "They have brought John Kennedy home."

#  Wartime White House

With the advent of World War II, the Federal city changed, the country changed...our world changed. And not far behind any of them was the White House. Before Pearl Harbor, recalled ABC-TV's David Brinkley in his book *Washington Goes To War,* a person could "walk through the White House gate and into the grounds without showing a pass or answering any questions, since the White House was not yet considered much different from any other public building in the city."

With war came security, unsurprisingly—more guards, underground bomb shelters, a war map room, unusual visitors from distant combat zones and great *secretivity....*

That first December of war, wrote presidential son Elliott Roosevelt later, albeit in a fictional murder mystery (*The White House Pantry Murder*), the windows were given blackout curtains, anti-aircraft guns appeared on the roof. And, "Gas masks in khaki canvas bags hung from their straps on the furniture everywhere in the house."

Winston Churchill arrived in great secrecy after crossing the Atlantic aboard a Royal Navy warship, a dangerous errand to be sure. His presence only was made known once he passed through those gates that Brinkley mentioned, just in time to help light the National Christmas Tree of 1941. Carefully kept secret for much longer was the fact that he suffered a slight cardiac episode trying to open a stubborn White House window one night (the central heating having been a bit too much for his mostly English blood). He carried right on in his planned conferences with Franklin Roosevelt, delighted of course to have America in the war at last as beleaguered England's ally against the Axis powers.

Churchill being Churchill, of course too, his visit gave rise to a number of colorful stories.

'Tis true, by retired Chief Usher J.B. West's later account, that Churchill constantly wore a one-piece jumpsuit, that he expected a bracing shot of Scotch at breakfast time rather than a bracing orange juice, and that "the butlers wore a path in the carpet carrying trays laden with brandy to his suite."

And where in the White House did he actually stay? Well, the future *Sir* Winston settled that matter for himself, it seems. "Mrs. Roosevelt had arranged for him to stay in the Lincoln Bedroom, then located off the West Hall, the favorite of most male guests," wrote West. "However, he didn't like the bed, so he tried out all the beds and finally selected the Rose Suite at the east end of the second floor."

The added story is that when FDR one day was wheeled into the Rose Suite, there stood the famous British bulldog in all his altogether. . .and nothing more. Churchill didn't mind a bit, it further seems, but FDR quickly backed off. "In his room," explained West later, "Mr. Churchill wore no clothes at all most of the time during the day."

Also noted by Brinkley in his book on the war's impact, why meanwhile, was the secrecy that attended various government activities, often necessary of course, but sometimes unbridled secrecy. . . such as the time FDR set off by train in September 1942 to visit U.S. war plants.

Only three reporters were allowed to board the rail special on a hidden spur beneath the Bureau of Engraving and Printing, with the President riding along in his private car, called the *Ferdinand Magellan*—"It was equipped with two elevators to lift his wheelchair on and off, an office, lounge, a bedroom and galley. Beneath the floor were 12 inches of steel-reinforced concrete to protect him if a bomb were planted in the roadbed. The windows were bulletproof. The sides were of armor plate heavy enough to resist an artillery shell. There were three underwater escape hatches. . .to allow him to get out if the train derailed on a bridge and sank to the bottom of a river."

The reporters at first were enjoined from reporting the trip, even though—in wild contradiction to such secrecy—FDR appeared before thousands of factory workers to give them encouraging pep talks.

At a ship launching in Portland, Oregon, he told 14,000 of them: "You know, I am not supposed to be here today. So you are the possessors of a secret that even the newspapers of the United States don't know. I hope you will keep the secret because I am under military and naval orders, and like the ship we have just seen launched today, my motions and movements are supposed to be a secret."

When FDR returned to Washington, the White House reporters who had been left behind were so angry that they pounded on his office door when he was late starting an explanatory press conference. Roosevelt may not have agreed, but usually the press corps treated him with a deference remarkable by today's standards—rarely photographing his leg braces, as one example. Sherwood Anderson, that artist with words who served as an FDR speechwriter, once explained that Roosevelt liked to "irritate" the press, "which so often had irritated him." Further, he had a small boy's fascination with mystery and he enjoyed wearing "the mantle of military security."

Such security often was needed, of course—in war, the President had to be protected. If he flew to a wartime Big Three conference in Teheran, Casablanca or Yalta, his movements had to be clothed in secrecy and he had to be heavily guarded. All quite understandable. . .but FDR also had his visits to the hospital, using more than 30 aliases. He was a sick man before war's end, his clock winding down. At his unprecedented fourth inauguration, early in 1945, he informed eldest son James that he had left instructions for his funeral in a certain safe. He also told James, "Among other things, I want you to have the family ring I wear." And it was just a few weeks later, in April, that a hastily summoned Vice President Harry Truman rode the small elevator to the second floor of the White House, stepped into Eleanor Roosevelt's family sitting room and felt her hand on his shoulder as she told him: "Harry, the President is dead."

# Struggle With The Phone

Leaving the White House after years and years of coddling by staff upon staff was, for Dwight D. Eisenhower, a bit like abandoning a prettified domestic cat in the wildest of jungle. Only, *he* was the cat!

Here, for instance, was the man who led the World War II crusade in Europe (title of his own book about the experience), and he literally in 1961 didn't know how to pick up the telephone in his home at Gettysburg, and make a simple long-distance call! Quite true, according to biographer Stephen E. Ambrose (*Eisenhower The President*).

On January 20, 1961, nighttime, just hours after leaving the White House to John F. Kennedy, "Ike" was back in Gettysburg, a private citizen now, and he wanted to call his son John. But it was an unexpected and frustrating problem for the retired general, the former president of Columbia University, the now-former President. "For the past 20 years, whenever he wanted to make a call, he told a secretary to put it through for him."

In fact, he last had made a call all on his own back in 1941. And back then, all he had to do was tell the operator what number he wanted, and Presto! the call went through.

Now, with a new President settling into the White House, it was fortunate for Ike that JFK had authorized an extra two weeks of duty for Ike's personal Secret Service "bodyguard," Special Agent Richard Flohr.

That night at Gettysburg, Ike tried to make his call by himself, but "[he] heard only a buzzing at the other end, shouted for the operator, clicked the receiver button a dozen times, tried dialing it like a safe, shouted again and slammed the phone down."

Enter Agent Flohr, who quickly showed the red-faced Eisenhower how the contraption worked—one small but essential lesson for the old housecat thrown back into the wild.

As Ambrose also points out, there were many other small details of everyday living that Ike had not had to deal with, things that most of us take for granted. He had never mixed frozen orange juice or paid at an automatic toll booth. Laundromats or barbershops were totally foreign to him. He hardly had ever been to a retail store, it seems. He wasn't in the habit of carrying money or credit cards on his person.

One time, Ambrose reports, Ike, while still President, took grandson David to a sporting goods store in Gettysburg and bought him an assortment of fishing gear. Then, to the owner's discomfort, he turned and walked out, "a Secret Service Agent carrying the packages." No attempt at payment!

Fortunately for all concerned, UPI's veteran White House reporter Merrimam Smith saw what happened and told the store owner simply to send a bill to the White House. Presumably, he did.

# 🦅 *Roaring Crowd*

A pariah to his President and members of that official's inner circle, this was another Vice President who would take his oath of office in the dead of night, in a distant city, before a small group of sleepy-eyed observers rather than the roaring crowd.

A former beneficiary of the spoils system at its 19th-century worst, this onetime Collector of Customs for the City of New York surprised all as President by supporting the Civil Service Reform Bill passed by Congress. Originally named to his party's presidential ticket as a mere sop to those disappointed by the choice for President, this man never was supposed to be President himself.

And when the new President was fatally wounded by a proclaimed follower of the Republican Stalwarts, there was suspicion that the Vice President was somehow connected with the terrible deed.

As James A. Garfield then lay dying over the summer of 1881, Chester A. Arthur was greeted with little warmth by Garfield's grieving associates. He did his best to show compassion...and, rather than serve as all-too bleak a reminder of the vice presidency's central purpose, to stay away.

After Garfield's death, Arthur kept his office in a Senator's rowhouse quarters near the Capitol for another three to four months while directing a refurbishment of the rundown White House interior. In time, Arthur even concocted a scheme to tear down the entire White House and replace it with two structures—one an office building, the other an elegant residence. His notion, thankfully, died for lack of funding—and any further unrealistic thinking. But Arthur nonetheless "redid" the East Room and other interior spaces with the help of Louis Tiffany...and in the process etched himself forever in history as the man who willfully sold off 24 wagonloads of earlier White House appurtenances. The preservationists have been hunting for most of those irreplaceable items ever since.

The greater surprise to the Washington insiders of his day, to the Nation at large really, was his emergence as more of a real President than a political hack. Like John Tyler, Arthur refused to be a caretaker President—he not only endorsed early civil service reform, he generated a small tax cut, he helped to reduce postage rates (from 3¢ to 2¢ for letters), he presided over a tariff reduction and he refused to halt Chinese immigration. During his stewardship also, the Brooklyn Bridge soared over the East River and the Washington Monument, started under James K. Polk years before, finally came to its lasting point.

The public saw an active, energetic President...perhaps a bit of a New York dandy, but a man making an effort, getting along as a widower whose wife had died young (42) of pneumonia, relying upon a sister, May McElroy, to serve as White House hostess....

196

Few were there to see when he awoke one morning at Savannah, Georgia, bent over by abdominal pain and relieved only by a doctor's opiate. Few knew that for some years he had had kidney "trouble." Few knew that all the time he dashed—and he did—around the country and about the White House in the role of President that he was, in fact, dying.

He left the White House on March 4, 1885, to Grover Cleveland, returned to his home in New York—where he had been sworn in nearly four years earlier at 2:15 one September morning—and he died just a year later, age 56, of Bright's disease of the kidneys. He never had really—openly at any rate—aspired to the presidency or considered a real election bid.

The day of his leavetaking, typically of this quite decent man, he returned to the White House as *ex-President* after Grover Cleveland's inaugural ceremony to inspect the State Dining Room, set for a ceremonial luncheon, and bid the staff goodbye, one by one and in person.

When he himself had been officially installed in 1881, the crowd that heard his inaugural address had been hostile, silent. And so, it was nice that as Chester A. Arthur rose from Grover Cleveland's luncheon table at the White House and departed not quite four years later, a watching crowd outside bade him fond, loud, and even *roaring* farewell.

# First Ladies in Review

# First Ladies In Review

## *By Ingrid Smyer*

Some, such as Martha, Edith and Eleanor, came strictly from the aristocracy. Some—Rosalynn, Dolley, Eliza—were of humble beginnings. Rich, poor...some formally educated, most not.

Some were beautiful, some plain. Some were social leaders and trendsetters. Others were demure or even reclusive. Some were vigorous, others frail and sickly. A few were outright invalids.

And still one thread binds together all these disparate women in the tapestry of the Stars and Stripes. All, every one...were First Ladies.

Today, it often is the husbands, the men, who are remembered. And yet "marrying up" frequently was the pattern for those very same men, whose wives later became the Nation's First Ladies.

The women often saw the potential in young men that others just as frequently failed to perceive. Martha Custis, first of them all, chose to marry a man who had been turned down by others, her wealth a continuing bone of contention for them both. Even after he became President, the "Father of His Country" once was told to his face, "What would you have been if you hadn't married the rich widow Custis?"

But with all the power and pomp, all the fame and glory, for the most part these women fell in love with their life partners. And their stories are love stories.

**MARTHA WASHINGTON,** wife of George—

Martha Dandridge Custis, at 25, a widow with two small children, was managing her vast estate when she met the tall and elegant George Washington. It was May and apparently it was love at first sight, for by July he felt free to write to her: "...I embrace the Opportunity to send a few words to one whose life is now inseparable from mine."

Accustomed to the easy life of her childhood on a plantation in Tidewater Virginia, "Patsy", as the future general and President called his bride, was a spunky young woman who once rode her horse up and down the stairs of her uncle's house. But her aristocratic *noblesse* stood her well when the general led the Continental Army, and she joined him whenever she could, both to comfort his soldiers and to bolster the spirit of her "Old Man", as she fondly called him.

And when Washington became the first President of the United States after the Revolutionary War, "Lady Washington" was as diligent in her new position as she had been in every challenge. Americans, and indeed a curious world, were watching as she set a style for the new Nation. She entertained formally yet set her guests at ease. Abigail Adams quickly became an admirer and friend. "A most becoming pleasantness sits upon her countenance and an unaffected deportment which renders her the object of veneration and respect...." Abigail even compared Martha to royalty: "I found myself much more deeply impressed than I ever did before their Majesties of Britain." And who should come next after Martha the trendsetter...but Abigail herself, a First Lady in her own right.

**ABIGAIL ADAMS,** wife of John—

The very first "Presidentress" to live in the "cold and damp" President's House (for all of four months), she is the only woman to have been wife to one President and mother to another.

"Remember the ladies" was the plea Abigail Smith Adams wrote to her husband when he was in Philadelphia to help write the Declaration of Independence. In many ways surprisingly modern in outlook, she insisted that women were the intellectual equal of men. Though she became one of the best-read women in the country, she bemoaned the lack of formal education and the ridicule aimed at "Female learning." If men were trained to become "Heroes, Statesmen and Philosophers," then the other half of the population should become "Learned Women."

Neither her views nor her deportment was surprising for the daughter of a prominent Congregational minister and descendant, on her mother's side, of the Massachusette Quincys. She was a conscientious hostess in the future White House who gave lively levees (receptions), true, but she also was a champion of the President's policies, quite comfortable in discussing the issues of the day. She was his "Lordess" (his pet name for Abigail) and helpmate throughout their long and loving life together.

**DOLLEY MADISON,** wife of James—

Arriving in the President's House after the widower Thomas Jefferson's departure were the thoroughly compatible "survivors" of a once unlikely match. She raised in Philadelphia as a Quaker, widowed with a son, disowned for marrying outside the faith. He an aristocrat from Virginia, puny in stature and dour to some, described by his future wife as the "great little Madison." And they blossomed together.

Beautiful, vivacious and full of fun, the former Dolley Payne Todd quickly became the "Queen of Washington City" whose reign lasted throughout a long life. She was a part-time hostess for the widowed Jefferson as wife of his Secretary of State, and she then presided over the Nation's first inaugural ball when her husband became President in 1809. After their White House tenure, she continued to play hostess to a parade of visitors, domestic and foreign, both at their Montpelier estate in Virginia and later, after Madison's death in 1836, at her townhouse on Lafayette Square in sight of the White House. President Zachary Taylor on the occasion of Dolley's death said: "She will never be forgotten because she was truly our First Lady for a half-century."

**ELIZABETH MONROE,** wife of James—

Elegant, composed, charming and beautiful, even regal, Elizabeth Kortright Monroe was also a bit mysterious. She came from New York City; her father had been a privateer for the British in the French and Indian War of the 1750s, but he was strangely *invisible* during the Revolutionary War. Monroe himself once said that his 17-year-old bride's father was "injured in his fortunes" during that recent rebellion.

In any case, Elizabeth's friends teased her when she chose the young lawyer from Virginia for her life partner, suggesting that she should have done better. But love won out and her husband's rising diplomatic career soon found them in the courts of Europe. The French were impressed with the stately U.S. Minister's wife, referring to her as *"la belle Americaine."* She then stunned one and all by going alone by carriage through the riotous streets of Paris to visit Madame Lafayette in her prison confines. This show of interest by the wife of the American Minister often is credited with persuading leaders of the revolutionary French government to drop any thoughts of sending Lafayette's wife to the guillotine and to release her instead.

Taking up residence in the White House in 1817, the Monroes startled Washington by refusing to pay social calls, but they also instituted weekly receptions open to the public as a democratic gesture all their own. Elizabeth Monroe often suffered from poor health during her White House years, one reason given for her avoidance of the traditional social calls paid on homes scattered across a city of rough, muddy roads. In the White House, she created a formal, almost European atmosphere—oddly, some critics considered her a snob, others complained she was hostess at the receptions to common riff-raff.

**LOUISA ADAMS,** wife of John Quincy—

Only First Lady to be born outside the United States, the former Louisa Catherine Johnson came to this country for the first time four years after she married John Quincy Adams. Born in England, pampered and adored as a child, she seemed as a young woman to be easily drawn to the young New Englander, but in her own words, "had to be coaxed into an affection." Theirs was not quite the unabashed love story of his parents, but their differences eased in their later years.

As they travelled extensively throughout Europe in the course of her husband's diplomatic assignments, her salon became a Mecca for dignitaries of all kinds. She preferred Washington society to the Yankee farm life of Quincy, Massachusetts, and was most happy to spend her allotted years in the presidential mansion (packed with family) and later to live in Washington again after the former President returned to serve as a House member for 17 years. She managed to die in the Federal city as well—and Congress adjourned in her honor.

**LETITIA TYLER,** wife of John—

Shocked to find herself First Lady after the sudden death of William Henry Harrison in 1841, Letitia Tyler was the first First Lady to occupy the White House since the departure of Louisa Adams in 1829. Both Andrew Jackson and his successor, Martin Van Buren, were widower Presidents, and Harrison died before his wife Anna could move into the White House with him.

Nor was Letitia Tyler anxious to fulfill her new role—a near invalid, she really couldn't do so very actively. Even in better health, she would have preferred to stay in her native Virginia tending to the plantation, the children, the neighbors, the quiet and demure life of a very gentle, genteel and self-effacing woman. At the White House later, her frail health kept her out of sight in the family quarters—her only appearance at a White House social function was for the wedding of daughter Elizabeth in early 1842. She then, later in 1842, became the first President's wife to die in the White House (and during a President's term in office).

**JULIA TYLER,** wife of John—

Born into wealth and privilege, Julia Gardiner, "The Rose of Long Island," was in the bloom of youth and fresh from the traditional Grand Tour of Europe when she arrived in Washington for its 1843-44 social season. Here she met a grieving President Tyler...and soon, she also was grieving, over the sudden death of her father in a freak accident aboard the U.S. Navy frigate *Princeton*.

They married the following summer, in 1844, a shock to Tyler's children by his late first wife, Letitia (mother of seven, but two died in infancy). The marriage was socially controversial as well and often ridiculed by critics. But the charming Julia had her defenders. "Under her short reign," wrote a Virginia gentleman, "society was charmed by the splendor and propriety of affairs at the White House." The ladies could be less charitable, complaining that she put on airs by receiving her White House guests on a raised platform—queen-like. Newspapers and sometimes admiring friends called her "Lady Presidentress."

Despite the great disparity in their respective ages (two decades), she stayed by Tyler's side until his death in 1862 (bearing him another seven children in the interim). And nobody ever argued with the Julia Tyler legacy calling for a rendition of "Hail to the Chief" whenever a President appears in public.

**SARAH POLK,** wife of James—

Better educated than most of her female contemporaries, Sarah Childress hailed from Murfreesboro, Tennessee, the child of well-to-do parents who provided formal tutoring at home and further schooling at the Moravian "Female Academy" at Salem, North Carolina. Like Abigail Adams, she became an avid reader and later was a well-informed helpmate—if not the driving force—behind her husband, James K. Polk. With no children to take up her time and energies, she could act as his secretary, his staunch campaigner and close advisor.

She worked hard for his election victories all the way up the political ladder—from Tennessee state house to governor's mansion to the White House. She loved Washington, their last such stop together, and thrived on its combination of political and social life. She impressed widely with her striking "Spanish" looks, her intelligence and her charm.

By all accounts, one of the most popular First Ladies ever.


## MARGARET TAYLOR, wife of Zachary—

Margaret Mackall Smith Taylor did not want her husband to run for President in 1848. In fact, she bewailed the idea as a plot to deprive her of her husband's company and "shorten his life by unnecessary care and responsibilities." Could she have had a crystal ball? Just 15 months later, Zachary Taylor would be dead.

"Peggy" Smith was born into a prominent family in Maryland with connections to the leading families of Virginia, but she had no desire to reign over Washington society. She had given many uncomplaining years to Army life, moving from one rustic post to another, and now she preferred to settle down with "Old Zack" in a quiet little cottage in Louisiana. When she did finally arrive at the White House, she remained in the background and delegated First Lady social duties to her 22-year-old daughter, Betty Knox Bliss, acting hostess at the White House.


## ABIGAIL FILLMORE, wife of Millard—

Another minister's daughter, avid reader, book-lover and teacher. When her Baptist minister father, Lemuel Powers, died, her mother moved westward to a frontier-like village in New York State and it was here, at only 16, that this Abigail began to teach in a country schoolhouse. It was here as well that a determined and ambitious farm boy appeared in her classroom. Over books they fell in love and became engaged, despite objections from her family that he was beneath her socially. But love prevailed and after a long engagement they were married at the home of her brother in 1826.

The first of all the President's wives to hold a job outside the home, Abigail continued to teach until her first child was born, but she never stopped learning. Her husband valued her intellect and often asked her opinions on political matters. She is best remembered for a lasting contribution to the White House—not finding so much as a dictionary in the mansion, she began a crusade to start a White House library. She pursued her goal with such gusto that she secured an appropriation from Congress and established the nucleus of the library still filling the executive bookshelves today.

**JANE PIERCE,** wife of Franklin—

"The shadow in the White House," as she came to be called, Jane Means Appleton Pierce did seem to have a gloom cloud about her. She had lost two sons earlier and just after her husband was elected to the presidency, the Pierces and their third son were on a train that derailed. They witnessed the tragic death of their 11-year-old son Benny, while they themselves were left unscathed.

As daughter of the president of Bowdoin College, the Reverend Jesse Appleton, Jane in happier days had met a Bowdoin graduate, a young lawyer with political ambitions, Franklin Pierce. They were an unlikely pair—he an outgoing and hearty suitor who loved mingling with the rowdy politicians (and his toddy) and she, shy, melancholy and often in poor health. They married some years later, even though her family opposed the match. When she heard that her former congressman husband had been nominated by the Democratic Party to head the presidential ticket in 1852, she fainted. She then hoped he would not be elected, but when that, too, came to pass, she reluctantly and with considerable delay moved to the White House, where she found little pleasure.

She was a devout churchgoer, it seems. She was not easy to know— or to fathom—and Nathaniel Hawthorne, a family friend, perhaps summed up Jane Pierce best when, on the day of her funeral, he said that she never seemed to have anything to do with "things present."

**MISS HARRIET "HAL" LANE,** niece of James Buchanan—

After the gloom of the Pierce White House and two somewhat reclusive First Ladies before, Washington society welcomed the bright and cheerful young "Democratic Queen" Harriet ("Hal") Lane, bachelor President James Buchanan's favorite niece—also a ward whom he treated like a daughter.

Afraid she would be "spoiled outright", Buchanan was reluctant to allow her to join him in London when he was minister to the Court of St. James, but join she did, and soon she was dancing at Buckingham Palace. In letters to her sister, she airily wrote that "Her Majesty was very gracious to me as also was the Prince."

With such happy memories in mind, Harriet returned to a United States rent with sectional controversy. In 1857, as official hostess at the White House, "Harriett Lane glided on the tightrope of faultless social etiquette," wrote Bess Furman in her book *White House Profile,* "balancing with the parasol of discretion."

She left her art collection to the Smithsonian Institution and a generous sum to Johns Hopkins Hospital.

**MARY LINCOLN,** wife of Abraham—

Mary Todd Lincoln came to the White House under the cloud of a Nation in crisis—its worst ever. Several states had seceded...the Union was in jeopardy. The country stood on the brink of war. Her husband had been elected President by a narrow margin—certainly no mandate—and across the Nation, he was a controversial figure at best. As further discomfort for the new mistress of the White House, a largely pro-Southern Washington society was in no mood to welcome the outsiders from the Middle West.

Mary Todd's impetuous ways, along with her extravagant taste in clothes and entertainment, didn't help and soon provoked ridicule in some circles. Then, she exceeded the funds appropriated by Congress for White House renovations. The press had a field day with that one, and Abraham Lincoln was both embarrassed and displeased. Little did he know in the aftermath that she still was running up personal bills that would be difficult to meet.

Mary's critics faulted her supposed influence over the President, a concern that was neither new nor destined to fade away with the appearance of future First Ladies. The same thing was said of Abigail Adams and Sarah Polk in the past, and it again would be said of more recent First Ladies—especially Edith Wilson, Eleanor Roosevelt, Nancy Reagan, Rosalynn Carter. But, few, if any, of the Nation's First Ladies ever were so vilified as Mary Todd Lincoln. Among other charges, this unhappy woman was even accused of treason! Hardly bearing up after the untimely deaths of two young sons, easily overwrought in any case, she found herself "surrounded on every side by people who were ready to exaggerate her shortcomings," wrote 19th-century author and social commentator Laura C. Holloway.

Born in Lexington, Kentucky, to Eliza and Robert Smith Todd, she had all the advantages that a fairly wealthy and well-connected father could offer, including education at Madame Mentelle's finishing school. Later she went to Springfield, Illinois, to live with her older sister and husband. Here she met the man who would be her husband—Mary Todd and Abraham Lincoln were married in 1842. Four years later, she responded to a friend's favorable comment about Lincoln. "Yes, he is a great favorite everywhere," said Mary. "He is to be President of the United States some day; If I had not thought so I never would have married him, for you can see he is not pretty."

The Lincolns had four sons—young Eddie died before they reached Washington; then, the loss of little Willie at the White House in 1862 from typhoid fever (and brother Tad's own near death at the same time) was almost more than Mary could stand. She began to have dreams of Willie visiting her; to assuage her grief she began attending spiritualistic seances. Her excessive mourning was criticized by those whose sons were dying on the battlefields of the Civil War. There are tales, too, of her excessive jealousy—one time, she created an ugly scene over a general's wife riding horseback next to Lincoln and ahead of Mary's carriage.

There were some bright moments in Mary's tenure in Washington, among them husband Abe's second election in November of 1864 and the collapse of the Confederacy in April of 1865. To celebrate the latter, Mary and Abe went for a carriage ride on the afternoon of Friday, April 14. "Dear Husband," she said, "you almost startle me by your cheerfulness." But his joy was to be shortlived. Lincoln was fatally shot that very night.

Through all their life together, Abe Lincoln's devotion to Mary was apparently undying. At one of their White House receptions (the one area in which her "press" was positive), a guest was complimenting Lincoln on Mary's social graces. "My wife is as handsome as when she was a girl," he replied. "I fell in love with her; and what is more, I have never fallen out."

Sad to say, Mary had impossible, crushing burdens heaped on her already weak shoulders—even young Tad would die within a few years of their leaving the White House in 1865. Robert Todd Lincoln, her only surviving child (or immediate family member, for that matter), later in life would serve as Secretary of War under Presidents James Garfield (also assassinated) and Chester Arthur. Mary Todd Lincoln, clearly unhinged by her many trials, briefly was committed to an insane asylum (at son Robert's instigation) and died in 1882, still in her mid-60s.


**ELIZA JOHNSON,** wife of Andrew—

Wife of the first and only President to be impeached by the House of Representatives. Eliza McCardle Johnson's faith in her husband never wavered. When a White House employee brought her news of the Senate's vote of acquittal, she cried, "I knew he'd be acquitted; I knew it."

Her parents, Sarah Phillips and John McCardle, a shoemaker, were simple folk, but they encouraged Eliza in her education. She was delighted she could use her basic education and help her "beau", as she called the young Andrew Johnson, with his writing and arithmetic.

209

The White House years were not happy ones for Eliza, who was ill and had to excuse herself from social duties because, "I am an invalid." Her capable daughter Martha, who as a schoolgirl had been in and out of the mansion when the Polks lived there, took over the running of the White House. This she did impeccably, including supervision of extensive renovations.

Eliza made only one appearance at a social function in her years at the White House, a party for her grandchildren. She preferred to stay in the small room on the second floor that she had chosen for herself.

## JULIA GRANT, wife of Ulysses—

At last a First Lady was having a rollicking good time in the old mansion. After the gloom and doom of the last three presidencies—the country split asunder, the Civil War, the assassination of a President, then the impeachment trial of another—the Gilded Age (as Mark Twain called it) arrived and the Grants were right for the times.

Theirs was a story of life-long devotion between two unlikely candidates—Julia Dent, favorite daughter of Frederick Dent, a Missouri planter and slaveowner, friendly, outgoing and full of fun, was popular in her St. Louis society. He was the shy West Point cadet from Illinois, who had shone at the Academy only in horsemanship. And he was a classmate of her brother Frederick. Julia and Grant met for the first time when he came to visit during a spring holiday.

Her father didn't think a soldier's life would be good enough for his daughter, but with cross-eyed (yes, cross-eyed) Julia and "Ulys," as she came to call him, it was love and that was that.

They were married four years later—after the Mexican War. Grant then resigned his commission and tried his hand at various business ventures, only to meet with consistent defeat. When they were apart for any length of time, he drank heavily. Through good times and bad, Julia was there for him.

His salvation may have been the Civil War. Proud of her now-victorious general, she often visited him at his headquarters. An aide-de-camp said that they would sit quietly in some corner of his tent holding hands, and if anyone happened by they would blush as "two young lovers."

When the General became the President, Julia entered the "happiest period" of her life. She loved hobnobbing with the great, the near great, even the nobodies. At her White House parties "there were ladies from Paris in elegant attire and ladies from the interior in calico," noted social commentator Ben Poore, "ladies whose cheeks were tinged with rouge, and others whose faces were weather-bronzed by outdoor work; chambermaids elbowed countesses, and all enjoyed themselves.''

Fun-loving Julia, showed her serious side at times and wasn't afraid to speak her mind. Grant was known to tease about having to keep his Cabinet choices secret to keep her from interfering.

After they left the White House they went on a grand tour of the world. They were popular in the courts of Europe, where they were known as America's first cheerful family to inhabit the White House in almost 2½ decades. Sadly, Grant the private citizen lost in bad business gambles. He recouped his finances with the proceeds of his autobiography, completed just before he died of cancer.


**LUCY HAYES,** wife of Rutherford—

Madonna-like, praised for her quiet dignity and hailed by the press for simplifying the era's code of dress was Lucy Ware Webb Hayes. She also brought morning worship to the White House, and her Sunday evening ''hymn-sing'', drawing Cabinet members and congressmen, became famous.

When the teetotaler Hayeses were making up the menu in preparation for a dinner honoring two Russian grand dukes in August 1877, Secretary of State William Evarts pleaded with them to serve wine. A table was set with six wine glasses at each place, but these were the last to be seen at the Hayeses' White House.

Thanks to her liquor ban, Lucy became the darling of the Women's Christian Temperance Union (WCTU), but her detractors dubbed her ''Lemonade Lucy.''

Born the daughter of Dr. James and Maria Webb, Lucy was interested in the feminist movement. She wrote that women are not ''the slave of man but his equal in all things, and his superior in some.'' But she never took an active role in the ''new woman'' movement nor in any way supported the WCTU, even though the leaders of both groups had solicited her endorsement. One critic, Emily Briggs, wrote to her wanting to know if the President's wife approved of ''the progress of women in the high road of civilization or whether you are content because destiny lifted you to an exalted position...so you cannot hear the groans of the countless of our sex....''

She remained aloof from all such causes, yet it was the WCTU that commissioned the portrait of Lucy Hayes presented to the White House upon her leavetaking as First Lady.

**LUCRETIA GARFIELD,** wife of James—

Both Lucretia Rudolph and James Garfield took their religion seriously, accepting the Protestant work ethic without question. They were devoted to education and literature, enjoyed reading books together and attending plays, concerts and lectures. Still, their relationship was a struggle.

During their courting days, he once "told" his diary, "There is no delirium of passion nor overwhelming power of feeling that draws me to her irresistibly [sic]." And her concern was that she loved him more than she did God. Their differences were more of personality than of circumstances. She was shy and reticent, he outgoing and gregarious...with strong, sometimes regrettable interests beyond home and hearth.

The "years of darkness," as the Garfields referred to their early life together became a "truce of sadness," as she forgave his indiscretions. By the time his career had taken them from Ohio to Washington for his House tenure, he could share family life with political career. His journal began to reflect deeper feeling: "she is the best woman I have ever known;" and "she is the light of my life." He was an active father to their five children, too. By the time they reached the White House, "Crete," the pet name he came to call her, was deeply involved in her husband's career. Cabinet appointee James Blaine wrote to Garfield that Mrs. Garfield's backing "is more valuable to me than even the desire of the President-elect himself." Others, though, found her to be too reserved to be a social success in their short, 186-day White House stay.

The Garfield "truce" of course ended in tragedy—no sooner had "Crete" began to recuperate from an illness than her husband was shot and fatally wounded by a crazed assassin. He clung to life for weeks, but then died.

**ELLEN ARTHUR,** wife of Chester—

"Nell" Herndon Arthur died the year before Vice President Arthur vaulted into the Presidency; he was so remorseful for having neglected her for politics that he gave a stained glass window in her memory to St. John's Episcopal Church in Washington, where she had sung in the choir as a young woman. He had it placed in the south side of the building so he could see it from the White House. His youngest sister, Mary McElroy, served as hostess of the White House.

**FRANCES CLEVELAND,** wife of Grover—

Soon after the inauguration of the 48-year-old Grover Cleveland, the widow of his former law partner, Mrs. Oscar Folsome, and her daughter Frances were invited to the White House. Washington society was atwitter, and gossip columnists naturally hailed the mother as the lady to watch. As it turned out it was Frances whom Cleveland was courting—after "waiting for her to grow up." When law partner Oscar died in an accident years before, Cleveland became administrator of the estate and took a guardian-like interest in the 11-year-old Folsome daughter.

She grew up, he proposed, they were married—and they even lived happily ever after. Their wedding in the Blue Room was the first Presidential marriage *in* the White House. The couple set other "firsts" as well: Cleveland was to serve an unprecedented second term after an absence of four years, and a baby girl born to the couple during his second administration was the first to be born to a President in the White House.

"Frank," as the President called his young wife, became one of the most popular women in America. She, like Dolley Madison beforehand, became the First Lady to emulate. Newspapers and magazines of the day were filled with stories about the beautiful and elegant Mrs. Cleveland. But she had a serious side as well. A graduate of Wells College, Frances showed an interest in women's issues of the day, but she, like Lucy Hayes, refused to lend her name to any causes.

**CAROLINE HARRISON,** wife of Benjamin—

Yet another clergyman's daughter was destined to become a First Lady. This time it was Caroline Lavinia Scott, whose father, D. John Witherspoon Scott, was a Presbyterian minister and president and founder of Oxford Female Seminary in Oxford, Ohio. One of his students was Benjamin Harrison, who would win his daughter's heart. And on October 20, 1853, Dr. Scott would perform the marriage ceremony himself.

When Harrison reached the White House in 1889, the venerable old structure was in such disrepair that Caroline ("Carrie") at once found her pet project—a campaign for a *new* White House. Congress granted her $35,000—a sizable amount in those days—to restore the old place instead. She went at her task with vigor, leaving not one drawer, cabinet or closet untouched. In the process she found old, chipped and broken china, which she sorted through—and thus she began the collection of china patterns of former First Ladies that was to become a popular tourist attraction. And, using her own design—based on the four-leafed clover—she ordered a new set of china to add to the collection.

Caroline Harrison also is remembered as a founding member of the Daughters of the American Revolution (DAR) in 1890. She died at the White House in October 1892, with just a few months remaining in her husband's presidency.

**IDA MCKINLEY,** wife of William—

Of all the reclusive, sickly or invalid wives in the White House none was more pitiful or pampered by a husband than Ida Saxton McKinley.

As the beautiful, witty, energetic belle of Canton, Ohio, she once had every reason to expect a full active life and she was determined to spend it with the handsome young lawyer she met at a church picnic, William Mckinley. Married in 1871, they were markedly devoted to one another. After a series of deaths in the family, including that of a daughter, Ida's health began to deteriorate. She suffered phlebitis and began to experience seizures. Although the word was never mentioned in the newspapers, it was whispered her illness was epilepsy.

When McKinley was being groomed as a presidential candidate by the Republican Party, some GOP strategists wondered if his wife were up to the job. By the time the McKinleys reached the White House, however, her health had improved and she was determined to perform her duties as First Lady. Indeed, she sometimes stood in the long reception lines, but more often she received their guests while seated and holding a bouquet of flowers to avoid handshaking. And the President broke with protocol at state dinners by seating his wife at his side so that he could watch over her. If a seizure came on, it is said, he simply took out a handkerchief that he kept in his pocket for this purpose, placed it over her face and continued on with his conversation.

In time, Ida became more petulant, more dependent on him; his devotion to her earned him the title of "saint" by his friends—a term not always used with kindness. When he was shot by an assassin in September 1901, Ida amazed one and all, including her doctors, by the way she rallied, stayed by his bedside and bolstered his spirits for the few days he lingered before death.

**EDITH ROOSEVELT,** wife of Theodore—

A friend from childhood, raised in the same privileged New York society, Edith Kermit Carow was still there, seemingly waiting in the wings, when Teddy Roosevelt's first wife, Alice, died soon after the birth of daughter Alice (who later became the *grand dame* of Washington as the wife of Rep. Nicholas Longworth).

Teddy's second marriage was as happy as his first, if not more so. Edith ("Edie") seemed just the stabilizing influence for the impetuous young politician. She provided the kind of understanding and warm companionship that he needed, both as widower and as a hard-driving husband, father, and career-minded man.

With her husband moving from Vice President to President in the wake of William McKinley's assassination, it was a stunned but well-organized Edith who managed the move from Sagamore Hill in Oyster Bay, headquarters for the lively family of six children in all, to the new White House quarters. As TR put it, Edith was the "ideal great lady and mistress of the White House," but the self-confident First Lady was even more. She often helped the President by sorting his mail, going over papers with his secretary, and scanning the major newspapers.

The Roosevelts brought an aristocratic flavor to the Executive Mansion and Edith solved some of the problems that had long plagued presidential wives—she turned to professional caterers, acquired a social secretary, discussed protocol with Cabinet wives at weekly meetings. She also devised a plan for separating the President's working quarters from their personal residence, and she handled the insatiable curiosity of the press by giving out information and sometimes even pictures.

The elaborate wedding of "Princess Alice" to Nicholas Longworth and the debut of daughter Ethel under the capable management of this First Lady made the Teddy Roosevelt White House a social center of the country. And at times, according to Ike Hoover (chief White House usher), the Teddy Roosevelts produced "the wildest scramble in the history of the White House."

**HELEN TAFT,** wife of William—

The first President's wife to publish her autobiography (Julia Grant's memoirs were not made public until 1975), Helen Herron Taft set other precedents as well. On March 4, 1909, she raised eyebrows as she stepped into a waiting carriage and seated herself next to her husband—newly sworn President William Howard Taft—to ride from the Capitol to the White House. Until now, this was a privilege the in-coming and out-going Presidents had reserved unto themselves. "For me," she wrote in her memoirs, "that drive was the proudest and happiest event of Inauguration Day."

And indeed the new First Lady glorified in her White House role, culmination of a dream she had held since visiting her father's one-time law partner, President Rutherford Hayes, and Lucy Hayes, when she was only 17. Ever since, she had set her sights on the White House—she would marry a man destined for the Presidency. A likely candidate encountered soon after was "that adorable Will Taft," whom she met at a bobsled party in their native Ohio. Theirs was a meeting of the minds that blossomed into love. They were married seven years later, in 1886. Will and "Nellie" were both from Cincinnati, where their families were leading citizens.

Taft's career on the bench won him a Ohio Supreme Court seat at the early age of 29. Though pleased for him, she had her eyes on more political office for them both. Then a big step forward—she became a First Lady as wife of newly appointed Philippines Governor Taft in 1900. She would hone her strong personality and make an imprint on the island's style while reigning at Manila's beautiful Malacanan Palace. It was good "practice" for her ultimate role a decade later as First Lady in the White House.

More than simply a social leader and an elegant party-giver, Helen Taft brought a sense of purpose to the role of First Lady. Overcoming the impact of a stroke, she sponsored musicales and Shakespearean performances on the White House lawn. She arranged to have Potomac Drive converted into a park. And most visibly of all, she planned a flowering touch for the capital city that would rival the cherry-blossom festival of Tokyo. Thus, the famous Japanese cherry trees planted around the Tidal Basin are a memorial to this gracious lady. When she died in 1943 she was buried next to her husband in Arlington Cemetery—the only First Lady to be interred there.

**ELLEN WILSON,** wife of Woodrow—

Her predecessor had set the stage for a more substantive role for President's wives and in the months she lived in the White House, Ellen Louise Axson involved herself in civic activities of her own. Housing reform was her special interest—and she persuaded a group of congressmen to go with her on a tour of back alleys to see for themselves the slum life right in the heart of the capital city. They came, and they saw, and they hurried "Mrs. Wilson's" bill through Congress so she would know of her success before she died in August of 1914.

The daughter of the Reverend S.E. Axson, a Presbyterian minister, Ellen grew up in Rome, Georgia. She believed that on the whole a person should live for others and ". . . not for herself." As a young girl, she went off to what is now called Greenwich Village to study art at the New York Art Student's League. "I prefer painting to politics," she once said—she thought she would have become quite good at art. She instead chose marriage, and her painting was relegated to a back room. Actually, she set up a studio by adding a sky-light in one area of the White House.

For 30 years Ellen was the "polar center" of Wilson's life. Though he had advanced degrees he looked to her to teach him in the fields of art and literature. She was the capable homemaker, she handled the family finances, watched his diet and even sewed for their three daughters to save on household expenses. But she was his right hand in other areas as well, proofreading his academic work and, in politics, going over his speeches with him.

Her last wish was for her husband's happiness and she hoped he would marry again someday.

**EDITH WILSON,** wife of Woodrow—

As First Lady, Edith Bolling Gall Wilson plunged into totally uncharted waters, to become totally immersed in the presidency itself after Wilson suffered a stroke in 1919. She was faced with a dilemma no First Lady had had to face before. Should she ask her husband to resign, or should she insist that he carry on with her help? With the support of Wilson's neurologist, she devised a plan to spare her husband stress and anxiety while the business of government went on. To this end she kept visitors away and screened all documents, papers, memos or even officials he would receive. This was, as she called it, her "stewardship." Critics complained about the "Petticoat Government," others revived that old term, "Presidentress." But she insisted that she was simply protecting her "beloved husband," trying to save his life, even though he was President.

Edith Wilson had shown no interest in politics or government before meeting the recently widowed Wilson in 1915. The widow of Washington businessman Norman Galt, Edith had no children and had devoted time to a family jewelry firm and been active in Washington society. When she and the grieving Wilson met, they were immediately drawn to each other. They were married, despite her objection that not enough time had lapsed since the death of the first Mrs. Wilson, on December 18, 1915. After months of gloom the White House was filled with happiness again.

Although she had demonstrated her abilities as a businesswoman and had exercised real political power during her "stewardship", she showed no sympathy for women's suffrage and never lent her name to any causes.


## FLORENCE HARDING, wife of Warren—

"I have only one hobby—my husband," was the pat answer Florence Kling Harding gave to inquisitive interviewers. The object of her affection, Warren G. Harding, seemed to agree when he once told a reporter that his automobile was his only possession that "Florence did not have a desire to run."

She was the daughter of Marion, Ohio, banker (and richest man in town) Amos Kling. Strong-willed like her father, she often acted against his wishes, as in her first marriage. Educated at the Cincinnati Conservatory, she was able to support herself and her young son when that marriage ended in divorce in 1886.

Enter Warren Harding, a young man with a flair for writing who had managed to buy the local newspaper, the *Daily Star.* Again she went against her father's objections and this time married a man who was some years younger than she. But she believed in her newspaperman and his paper. In no time she was running the business end of the company—and making it pay.

Harding's talent as a public speaker and editorial writer brought him to the attention of political wheeler-dealer Harry Daugherty, who thought Harding "looked like a President." He believed the newspaperman had a future in politics and persuaded his wife to urge him to run for the U.S. Senate. He won by a narrow margin, and the Hardings were off to Washington in March 1915.

Florence reveled in her new status and loved rubbing elbows with the socially prominent Nicholas and Alice Longworth, fellow Ohioans, or millionaire Edward B. McLean and his wife Evalyn Walsh, owner of the famous Hope Diamond. More than a social climber, however, she was an astute political strategist— Daugherty believed that she helped make Harding Senator and, later, President.

Harding—not always the faithful husband—recognized her valuable contributions and with some sense of irony called her "The Duchess," a nickname also used by his poker pals while she mixed the drinks.

Mercifully for both, perhaps, Harding died before the full airing of the Teapot Dome Scandal that darkened his administration. One of his widow's last acts in the White House was to destroy papers— what they were, no one knows now.

**GRACE COOLIDGE,** wife of Calvin—

"Public Female Favorite No. 1," Will Rogers called Grace Anna Goodhue Coolidge and "chuck plumb full of magnetism." A foreign diplomat at a reception said, "To look at her is gladness enough." Grace Coolidge's unpretentious but thoroughly winning ways had all of Washington comparing her to Dolley Madison.

It was a different tune when it came to the taciturn "Cal" Coolidge. In fact, most of Grace's friends—and especially her mother—could not understand what she saw in the shy, usually silent lawyer.

Grace, only child of Andrew and Lemira B. Goodhue, grew up in Burlington, Vermont. The first of the First Ladies to graduate from a coed university, she received her degree from the University of Vermont, then taught at the Clarke School for the Deaf in Northampton, Massachusetts. At the school one morning, while watering flowers in a nearby garden, she happened to notice a strange sight in a nearby window—a man in his underwear shaving with a cocked hat planted on his head. She couldn't help laughing out loud. He noticed her and soon arranged a meeting to explain his incongruous activity. The hat was there to keep a cowlick out of his face while he shaved. The man under the hat was her future husband, of course.

Grace came into her own upon her husband's ascendency to the presidency. Even after his stint as governor of Massachusetts, she and "Cal" were accustomed to their no-nonsense New England frugality, but with the new allotment for entertainment they began inviting political leaders from both parties to the White House for what soon came to be known as the "Coolidge Breakfasts."

Grace Coolidge herself took no part in politics, and her husband did not allow her to give interviews. She played a traditional role—working with the Girl Scouts, hostessing receptions at the White House, managing the family affairs. Years later, reflecting on her White House years she wrote, "This was I and yet not I—this was the wife of the President of the United States and she took precedence over me."

**LOU HOOVER,** wife of Herbert—

Here's a real adventure story! Boy and girl born in Iowa in the same year, 1874, and only 100 miles apart...yet their paths didn't cross until 20 years later—in far-off California.

Daughter of Florence and Charles D. Henry, the future Lou Hoover was a tomboy drawn more to a father who took her camping, horseback riding and hiking than her frail mother. After earning a certificate from a teacher's college, she went to work for her father's bank.

And naturally this didn't satisfy the restless and energetic Lou. One evening she attended a lecture by a Stanford University professor that would change her life; she soon was enrolled at the school as its only woman majoring in geology. And here, in a science lab one morning, she met fellow geology student Herbert Hoover.

Shy and awkward, but extremely bright, he was an orphan raised by Quakers. At the turn of the century mining engineers were in short supply and the young Hoover soon would be working in Australia, followed by China. A telegram proposal of marriage, with honeymoon spent on the way to China, received a quick reply from the adventuresome Lou—yes!

In no time the Hoovers found themselves in the middle of the Boxer Rebellion—they and others from the international community barricaded themselves in the city of Tientsin. During one attack a flying shell fragment struck a nearby staircase while Lou calmly continued with a game of solitaire.

Soon the Hoovers—by now he was a self-made millionaire—settled in London, the world's mining capital during "the golden age of mining." Their "Red Roof" home became the gathering place for the international set. Then, after their two sons were born (1903 and 1907), it was off again—mother and children joined the family breadwinner in France, Russia, Burma, Korea, Japan.

Caught in Europe at the outbreak of World War I, the Hoovers assisted stranded Americans. Volunteering to help distribute food to Belgium and France, already under German occupation, the Hoovers spent four years in relief work. When America entered the war, the Hoovers came back to the United States, Herbert to serve as Food Administrator, and Lou assisting by publicizing ways to conserve food, such as declaring "wheatless" and "meatless" days.

As, next, a postwar Cabinet member's wife, Lou continued her activist role. She advocated physical education for girls or women in schools of all kinds. She spoke out on women's issues, often encouraging women to seek careers. At a Girl Scouts conference, in 1926, she said women who give children as their excuse for not working were simply "lazy".

When the Hoovers moved into the White House, Lou ended some of its more archaic traditions such as leaving calling cards for Cabinet wives or opening the mansion to the public on New Year's day. She startled some onlookers by actually entertaining a black congressman's wife at a small tea—today, the shock would be that the black woman was invited with just 12 other wives for a tea held separately from the large reception for all the congressional wives (except that one black woman).

In general, her entertaining was lavish, "They set the best table that was ever set in the White House," wrote Chief Usher Ike Hoover later. The First Lady used hand signals to communicate with the servants during formal entertaining. Most of her attendants found her silent treatment dehumanizing, and with the grim Depression as backdrop, she appeared stiff, uncaring. As First Lady, too, for whatever reason, she was far less open with the press than she had been in her earlier days in Washington.

**ELEANOR ROOSEVELT,** wife of Franklin—

MRS. ROOSEVELT STILLS THE TUMULT OF 50,000, screamed one headline after Eleanor Roosevelt made a surprise appearance at the 1940 Democratic National Convention in Chicago. She had gone at husband Franklin Delano Roosevelt's request to pacify delegates balking at his choice of Agricultural Secretary Henry Wallace as his running mate.

Amazingly enough, it wasn't all that long since Eleanor had been an awkward, ungainly young woman with little apparent self-confidence. She had left the 1920 Democratic convention in Baltimore because it was so noisy and boring. Now FDR's wife captured the attention of another unruly convention crowd—and held it throughout her talk.

Born into the prominent Roosevelt family of New York herself, Eleanor nonetheless faced childhood adversity. Her mother, Anna Hall Roosevelt, a beauty and favorite of New York society, only made little Eleanor more conscious of her own inadequacies. "She is such a funny child," Eleanor heard her mother say. And then, there was her father...Elliott Roosevelt, debonair younger brother of Theodore Roosevelt, was the light of the young girl's life. But he was an alcoholic, an on-again, off-again figure. By the time she was 10, both parents had died young...Eleanor and her two brothers went to live with their strict grandmother, Mrs. Valentine Hall, once the toast of New York society herself.

A bright spot in Eleanor's lonely life then came when she was sent abroad to Allenswood finishing school outside of London. Under the inspiring tutalage of Marie Souvestre, Eleanor discovered talents within herself and saw new lifestyles from her travels on the Continent.

Much as she dreaded the thought, the still-shy Eleanor was "presented" at New York's Assembly Ball at the Waldorf-Astoria in December 1902. And during the parties of that same debutante season she again met her distant cousin, the handsome and already courtly young Franklin Delano Roosevelt, a student at Harvard. Only 18 at the time, she was thrilled by his show of interest—others were surprised, too. Even more surprising—startling to many—they soon became engaged. By the time FDR's mother, famously haughty as a grande dame herself, accepted the fact that the "apple of her eye," her only son, was determined to marry his less-than-beautiful cousin, Eleanor was teaching at a settlement house in Manhattan. Young FDR was studying law at Columbia.

They were married on St. Patrick's Day, March 17, 1905, with President Teddy Roosevelt giving away his favorite niece. The young couple lived near FDR's mother Sara Roosevelt, a domineering woman who took all the initiative from Eleanor, selecting their apartment furniture, hiring their servants, even selecting nurses after the babies began to arrive. (Eleanor would bear six children in all, five boys and a girl, but one son would die in infancy.)

Meanwhile FDR had become active in New York politics, winning a seat in the New York State Senate. Though Eleanor was not in the least interested in politics, she was impressed with her husband's forward thinking when he openly supported women's suffrage. She dutifully went to Albany to set up housekeeping for her husband and children...and for the first time since her marriage began to see opportunities for herself. "I had to stand on my own feet now," she would later write in her memoirs. "I was beginning to realize that something within me craved to be an individual."

With FDR's appointment in 1913 as Assistant Secretary of the Navy came their first move to Washington and, soon, the eruption of World War I. She jumped at the chance to work for the Red Cross, knitted for servicemen (her knitting would always go with her the rest of life—her hands would never be idle). After America's entry into the war also, she worked at the canteens for servicemen. She even enjoyed socializing now, with their home becoming a gathering place for FDR's political friends.

After the war her activism only increased—Eleanor's interests now included the poor, the disenfranchied, the shell-shocked veterens and, far from last or least, the women's movement.

Then came family tragedy, it appeared. In August 1921, FDR suddenly became ill with poliomyelitis. He would never again walk unaided. His mother wanted him to retire to a quiet life at Hyde Park, the family estate up the Hudson River from New York City. But his secretary Louis Howe thought differently and persuaded his friend in a wheel-chair to go on with his political career. Eleanor concurred.

With Howe's help, Eleanor's political education began in earnest—and she would become the "ears and eyes" of the future Governor of New York and President of the United States. She traveled far and wide on his behalf. She visited institutions, making notes on the conditions at prisons, hospitals and asylums and reporting what she had seen and heard.

When the Roosevelts came to the White House in 1933, Eleanor probably was the most politically astute of any First Lady to occupy the Executive Mansion. She and FDR, of course, would be known for their longest tenure of any White House occupants, before or since. She took on an incredible array of causes and projects all her own—in 1935 she began her syndicated column, called "My Day". She traveled widely for the President, notching 38,000 miles her first year in the White House. Even when on vacation, she was taking notes on the mood of the people around the country.

This time, with FDR AND Eleanor, the American public really got two for the price of one—one of them a First Lady who was almost a super-human partner to the President. She was a spokesperson for the underprivileged, civil rights, unions, and the women's movement. She became the access to the President for "little people" who otherwise had no such means. During World War II, she visited American soldiers around the world, often at recently embattled combat zones. After FDR's death in April 1945, and that war's end, she continued as a champion of political and international causes, serving as a U.S. delegate to the United Nations and as a member of the U.N. Human Rights Commission. In that capacity, she helped to draft the international body's Universal Declaration of Human Rights and then saw it adopted by the body's General Assembly. She kept up her frantic pace until her health gave out—she died in November 1962.

**BESS TRUMAN,** wife of Harry—

When Elizabeth Virginia "Bess" Wallace Truman became First Lady, very little was known about her—and that's the way she wanted it. She had an aversion to publicity; nice ladies didn't seek it out.

Bess Wallace grew up in the comfortable world of Independence, Missouri, where her family stood high in the community. Like Lou Hoover, she was something of a tomboy, a rival to any boy who could whistle through his teeth. She was an excellent horseback rider; she climbed trees and became a local tennis champ. When a bookish young man wearing glasses began calling, Madge Wallace wasn't impressed and thought the young dirt-farmer was not good enough for her daughter. But Harry Truman pursued his "one and only" anyway. After he returned from his U.S. Army combat service in France during World War I with the rank of major, they were married. In their mid-30s at the time, they had been courting for 15 years!

The low profile that Bess Truman maintained in public tended to obscure the important part she really played in her husband's life—and success. She edited his speeches and was on the payrole for his U.S. Senate office as his secretary. Questioned about the arrangement, he told reporters, "She earns every penny of it."

They were a close-knit family, with both Bess and daughter Margaret often joining Truman on his trips. They were right there, for instance, for his famous whistle-stop campaign of 1948, standing with him on his train's rear platform in smalltown after smalltown, smiling and waving after he introduced them to them to the onlooking crowd as the "Boss" (Bess) and the "Boss's Boss" (Margaret).

It was during the Truman Administration that the controversial "Truman Balcony" was added to the South Portico. Architectural purists aside, it was the coolest spot in the town. Far more important in any case, a tinkling chandelier in the Blue Room's ceiling during a reception one evening alerted Truman to trouble above and around them—the old structure, patched and prettied up for decades, needed strengthening, a complete overhaul, or it might come down like a house of cards. The result was complete reconstruction of the White House interior while the Trumans took up residence in Blair House, across Pennsylvania Avenue from No. 1600.

Bess dutifully and graciously set up miniature Red, Blue and Green Rooms in the traditional government guest house, even a State Dining Room, and all replete with White House furniture.

When Bess Truman died in 1982, *The New York Times* headlined, BESS TRUMAN IS DEAD AT 97/WAS PRESIDENT'S 'FULL PARTNER.' The fact is, too, at 97, she had lived longer than any other First Lady.

**MAMIE EISENHOWER,** wife of Dwight—

Just a month after her wedding, Mamie Doud Eisenhower watched her second lieutenant husband pack his gear. "You're not going to leave me this soon after our wedding day, are you?" she cried. His answer stunned her: "My country comes first and always will. You come second." Indeed, adjusting to the many moves of an Army wife was easy compared to the anquish she suffered during their long separations. Duty and country did come first, but "I never got used to his being gone," she said toward the end of her life. "He was my husband. He was my whole life."

She was a young woman living with her parents and three sisters in Denver, Colorado, when she met her young Army lieutenant—not in Colorado, but at Fort Sam Houston in Texas, where the Douds spent the winter months. The West Pointer presented her his class ring on St. Valentine's Day of 1916 to mark their engagement, and they were married that summer.

Next came a series of Army posts—all over the United States, in France, in the Philippines, in the Panama Canal Zone. She went through 27 moves in 37 years!

It was *General* Eisenhower, of course, who catapulted to fame during World War II as Supreme Allied Commander in Europe. Back home, though, Mamie was depressed and feared for "Ike's" safety. Her health deteriorated—she spent a lot of time bedridden. And while she waited, rumors drifted back from England about Ike and Kay Summersby, the young Irish ex-model assigned as his driver. Gossip circulated in Washington, but Mamie rallied and put up a cheerful front, claiming in *Look* magazine there was nothing improper between her husband and Summersby, because, "I know Ike."

The war over, cries of "I like Ike" echoed across the land, and everyone loved the lady in pink by his side. Ike won election in 1952 by a landslide. And when they moved into the White House, Mamie quickly became a new favorite of the public. As the media soon learned, she was always good for a saucy quote. She had taken language classes with Bess Truman and other VIP women. "None of us ever really studied," said the new First Lady. She made no bones about their sleeping in a double bed together, saying that she liked to be able to reach over during the night and pat Ike's familiar "bald pate."

She told reporters, "I don't understand politics." Yet she charmed everyone with her friendliness and good humor. Told that a poll had picked her husband as the greatest American, she smiled and exclaimed: "They didn't have to go to all that trouble. I could have told them."

The fashion industry experienced a shot in the arm with Mamie's interest in clothes, not to mention the fact that her coiffure sent fashionable ladies rushing to the salons to have their hair cut, colored and in many cases "banged", like hers.

As Mamie later came to realize, times change—after brief hiatus for Bess Truman and Mamie herself, the role of a President's wife would revert in some degree to Eleanor Roosevelt's sometimes frantic activism. So it was that Mamie told Rosalynn Carter when they met 20 years later, "I stayed busy all the time and loved being in the White House, but I was never expected to do all the things you have to do." All the same, while not so much an activist as more recent First Ladies, Mamie did her dutiful bit in the White House—she and Ike entertained more heads of state and foreign leaders than most, if any, previous occupants of the White House.

## JACKIE KENNEDY, wife of Jack—

"Fantastically chic," pronounced *The New York Times.* "Stunning egghead," said *Newsweek.*

Jacqueline Lee Bouvier Kennedy changed forever the way we Americans look at our First Ladies.

Long before she met Jack Kennedy she stood out from the crowd. "Queen Deb of the Year is Jacqueline Bouvier," columnist Igor Cassini wrote in *The New York Journal-American,* "a regal brunette who has classic features and the daintiness of Dresden porcelain." Born into the "right" social circles, she was the daughter of John Vernon Bouvier III and his wife Janet Lee, who later obtained a divorce and married wealthy Washington attorney Hugh D. Auchincloss in 1942.

Jackie attended Chapin School in New York, Miss Porter's in Connecticut, then Vassar, all precocious prestige schools. She spent a year abroad studying at the Sorbonne in Paris, where she became fluent in French and developed a lifelong love of French art and literature. She finished her education at George Washington University in the Nation's capital and later became *The Washington Times-Herald*'s "Inquiring Camera Girl." By the time she got around to interviewing the handsome young congressman from Massachusettes (and Dick Nixon, for that matter), young Jack Kennedy already was squiring her around town.

"It was a very spasmodic courtship," Jackie once told an interviewer. She held up a post card from Bermuda that read: "Wish you were here. Cheers, Jack."

"And that was my entire courtship correspondence with Jack!"

After Jack was elected to the Senate in 1952, they announced their engagement. Their wedding in Newport, Rhode Island, a year later was the social event of the season. With all the Kennedy politicos attending, it was a political event as well. After a honeymoon in Acapulco, the young couple settled down in Georgetown.

There, differences soon surfaced. Although Jackie took a course in American history to please her husband, she didn't find politics interesting. "Jackie is superb in her personal life," Jack once said to a friend, "but do you think she'll ever amount to anything in her political life?" To which, Jackie shot back: "Jack is superb in his political life, but do you think he will ever amount to anything in his personal life?"

The public, for its part, clamored for appearances by the glamorous wife of presidential candidate Kennedy in 1960—politically attuned or not, she was a true asset to his victorious campaign (against Dick Nixon).

As First Lady, Jackie quite naturally found a project that would compliment her interest in art. First, she convinced Congress to designate the White House a national historic site, as a museum, really, then she began the most extensive restoration of its furnishings, antiques and objects d'art ever attempted. She spent months of study and hard work—she even scavenged through old cupboards, storerooms and forgotten crannies at the White House. She persuaded museum directors, various designers and art historians to sign on to her committees and solicited anyone who owned original pieces from the mansion. When the project was near completion, television cameras followed the First Lady as she took the Nation on a tour of the White House, which she indeed had transformed into a living museum.

Jackie of course forever will be remembered as the tragic figure at the funeral of her still-young husband, killed by an assassin's bullets in 1963, ten years after their marriage. She set grim and certainly unwilling precedent as the first President's widow to attend the swearing-in of his successor. Who can ever forget the awful image? A still-bloodstained Jackie standing by in Air Force One as Lyndon Baines Johnson was sworn in at Love Field in Dallas.

**LADY BIRD JOHNSON,** wife of Lyndon—

Lady Bird and Lyndon Baines Johnson. . . like those of Jack and Jackie Kennedy, their names go well together, don't they? LBJ. . .it would be a monogram for the entire family. It even would be a President's initials, too. And who would have guessed. . .way back in 1934?

Home on a visit from Washington, where he served a Texas congressman as secretary, LBJ was introduced by a friend to "a lovely girl with ideals, principles, intelligence and refinement"—his own description in one of the love letters that soon followed. Their's was a "whirlwind" courtship, as Lady Bird later recalled. Her Aunt Effie, who had helped raise Lady Bird in both Texas and Alabama after her mother's early death, responded cautiously toward the tall, overpowering suitor, but the girl's father, Thomas Jefferson Taylor, took an instant liking to the frequent visitor: "This time you brought home a man," he told daughter Claudia Alta Taylor. Two months later, on November 17, 1934, they were married in San Antonio. From that day on, Lady Bird was LBJ's staunchest supporter. It was money that she had borrowed against her inheritance, in fact, that staked the start of his own political career.

"Busy as a man with one hoe and two rattlesnakes," was an expression typical of the down-country girl who now joined LBJ in the Nation's capital, but the thought also was fair comment on the life she had entered as the wife (and occasional office-staffer) of a young congressman in a hurry (first elected to the House in 1938 and to the Senate 10 years later). She served him coffee in bed, brought him his morning paper, changed her fashions from "muley-looking" to bright yellows and reds, wore high heels, which her man preferred, laid out his clothes and even polished his shoes at times. She ran his office when he briefly donned a uniform during World War II before all congressmen were called back to their legislative duties...and kept her opinions about the later Vietnam quagmire to herself. She learned always to have a well-stocked refrigerator, since LBJ often brought a crowd of political cronies in for pot-luck supper. And she never lost her equalibrium.

"She is a lot like Melanie in *Gone With the Wind,* except with more drive," daughter Lynda Bird (Mrs. Charles Robb) once said. Added younger daughter Luci Baines (Mrs. Ian Turpin): "She's really the knot of the family."

No one, of course, could ever help but notice the L and B initials that permeate the family. "Why, she's as pretty as a ladybird," was the proud proclamation of a nursemaid when Claudia was born. And Lady Bird it was from there on. LBJ was so delighted over their matching initials, he monogramed every one in the family, and every *thing,* including pets and their ranch.

She came to the White House under tragic circumstances and yet made the transition with grace and dignity. When her husband was elected in his own right (1964), the First Lady from Texas set out to find her own project. And here, her nickname may have been prophetic, for her lifelong interest had been nature and its beauty. And so, among various beautification and nature projects, one lasting contribution would be The First Lady Committee for a More Beautiful Capital, an idea that quickly spread across the Nation. Her memoir, *A White House Diary,* published in 1970, is considered the most complete account of life in the White House by a First Lady.

**PAT NIXON,** wife of Richard—

To pay her way to New York and back when she was only 20, Pat Ryan drove a couple across the country from California. The couple were ailing, the roads were curvy, the car was cranky and, as she told a reporter later, she became, "driver, nurse, mechanic and scared." A prelude to her life with Richard Nixon, whom she married on June 21, 1937?

Christened Thelma Catherine Ryan, she was born on a March 16— her father swung her up into his arms and called her his "St. Patrick's babe." And so, "Pat" it would be. Her mother died when Pat was only 13, leaving her to care for her father and two brothers. "Life was sort of sad," she would recall, "so I had to cheer everybody up." Her father soon died from silicosis, a lung disease he had contracted as a miner in Ely, Nevada. In New York she worked as an X-ray technician in a hospital treating patients with the same lung condition. "Haunting" as this experience was, she did it because she wanted to help. "That is what gives one the deepest pleasure in the world— helping someone," she once explained.

She was able to save enough money to return home and graduate, *cum laude,* in 1937 from the University of Southern California. She took a job at Whittier (California) High School, and there she met a young graduate of Duke University Law School as they both sought parts in a local theatre production. Richard M. Nixon was immediately drawn to her, but she had her doubts at first. They continued to date, and at last he persuaded her to marry him. She did so in a Quaker service, since she had converted to his faith. As they drove off to Mexico for a honeymoon, the car this time was hers; she had helped pay for it.

They did not live happily ever after. In the future congressman's early days of campaigning in California, Pat pitched in every way she could—so much so that they were called the "Dick and Pat team." But politics can be wearing—and rough. In 1952, vice presidential candidate Nixon was questioned about his use of certain campaign funds; there was some doubt that Dwight Eisenhower would keep Nixon as his running mate. After making his famous televised "Checkers" speech, Nixon remained on the ticket and became Vice President.

From then on, however, as Nixon himself would write later, Pat "would hate politics and dream of the day when I would leave it behind."

That day would be a long time in coming, yet Pat weathered each and every storm that seem to plague her husband's career. Evermore careworn in appearance, she yet maintained her dignity. And as First Lady, she returned to the "helping" theme of her young adulthood by encouraging volunteerism. She broke new ground by inviting visitors for non-denominational religious services in the East Room. She encouraged further acquisition of antiques and art for the White House Collection and brought in musical artists of all kinds for performances in the White House.

She was one of the most traveled First Ladies, going to 83 nations (some crowds not so friendly, some, like the mob in Caracas, Venezuela, downright life threatening). She criss-crossed the United States many times. "I do or die," Pat was frequently quoted as saying, "I never cancel out." She must have died a lot when Nixon had to resign in 1974, but still she clung to her sense of dignity.

**BETTY FORD,** wife of Gerald—

"I take a Valium every day," was the candid statement Betty Ford made in an interview as the suddenly newsworthy wife of newly appointed Vice President Gerald Ford. That sent the reporters scurrying for the phones, but it was only the beginning for this beautiful bombshell who was catapulted into the limelight by the sweeping events of the early 1970s.

First, of course, her "Jerry" was appointed by President Nixon to fill the vacancy left by the resignation of Vice President Spiro Agnew—an unprecedented event. That was in the fall of 1973...with more, much more, to come. And suddenly, Betty found herself surrounded by the media; it seemed that everyone wanted to know about the woman that *Good Housekeeping* said "nobody knows." In fact, she had been around Washington a long time.

Jerry and Betty married in October 1948 in Grand Rapids, Michigan, their hometown. In November, first-time House candidate Jerry sailed into office, and the newlyweds were off to Washington. There, she was the dutiful wife doing all the right things, from teaching Sunday school to joining the appropriate wives' clubs and balancing home and hearth with four children (three sons and a daughter).

Health problems and "single-parenting" (Jerry was always away politicking or working) added to the strains—her successful bout with dependency after they left Washington would gain her the respect of the Nation. She went on to found the Betty Ford Center for Drug and Alcohol Rehabilitation, which opened in 1982 in Rancho Mirage, California.

Her mother many years earlier said daughter Elizabeth Ann "popped out of a bottle of champagne." The future First Lady's happy parents were Hortense and William Bloomer; her father died when she was 16 and she modeled to help out with the family finances. But she was able to attend the Bennington School of dance in Vermont for two summers. Here, she was thrilled to study under the famous Martha Graham, to experience "the ecstasy of being able to dance eight hours a day." In 1975, as First Lady, she had the gratification of appearing as the honored guest at the dedication of a fine arts center at Bennington College.

Only months before, she and Jerry had been surbanites in Alexandria, Virginia—even after he moved from Minority House Leader to Vice President. Then, just as suddenly, came President Richard Nixon's resignation in August 1974. Jerry Ford suddenly, breathtakingly, had vaulted, in less than a year, from House seat to President.

In the White House soon after, Betty Ford quickly established her reputation as the honest and outspoken First Lady. She called the Supreme Court's ruling allowing abortion "a great, great thing." She thought it would not be surprising if the young people of the 1970s tried marijuana, and while she wouldn't condone her daughter Susan having an affair, she wouldn't make her leave home over the issue, either. Such talk shocked many, but endeared her to many others who agreed.

She lobbied for the Equal Rights Amendment, and when that failed to pass she continued to work for women's causes, often by "pillow-talking" with her husband the President about appointments of women to more and higher positions in government.

**ROSALYNN CARTER,** wife of Jimmy—

A "steel magnolia blossom," is how *New York Times* reporter Judy Klemesrud saw this energetic campaigner from Plains, Georgia. And the name stuck, all the way to the White House.

Rosalynn Smith and Jimmy Carter grew up in the same little southwest Georgia town, alongside peanuts and cotton. Church activities were the center of life, both spiritual and social. She was a Methodist and he a Baptist. Her father, whom she adored, thought she could do anything and encouraged her every endeavor. When she was only 14, however, he died, an event leaving her "devastated," she wrote later, adding, "My childhood really ended at that moment."

To make ends meet, her mother took in sewing, doing piecework for others. Rosalynn worked in the town beauty parlor and helped with the chores at home. When time came for college, she was able to attend a junior college, Georgia Southwestern.

Enter Jimmy, home from Annapolis. Rosalynn had seen his picture on the dresser of his sister Ruth, her best friend, but she thought the handsome midshipman was "out of reach" for her. His sister played matchmaker anyway and packed a picnic for the three of them. He agreed to go along, he liked her, he kissed her—and later he told his mother, "She's the girl I want to marry."

Two years later, 1946, they were married. After that, it was goodbye Plains, hello world.

Her opportunities widened as the Navy moved them to places she only dreamed about before. When her husband was off on sea duty, she was left with decisions and responsibilities—and she grew in her new role as head of the household and mother of three growing boys. (Daughter Amy was born later.)

When Carter's father died in 1954, they left the Navy and returned to the family company. Rosalynn hated to go back to the limiting world of Plains. Only when she began to take over the bookkeeping of the wholesale peanut business did she feel she was doing something important.

Then her husband entered politics and a whole new world challenged the little girl from Plains, now dramatically coming into her own as the wife of an increasingly popular local politician. At first she was shy and afraid of making speeches for her husband, but when she realized that stumping the countryside—and later the whole country—was the name of the game, she played a major role in her husband's campaigns as he rose from the state house to the governor's mansion and finally to Number 1600 Pennsylvania Avenue.

To the White House she then brought a strong sense of purpose with an agenda of her own. Heading a long list was her interest in mental health; she persuaded Jimmy to appoint a Commission on Mental Health. She lobbied for the ERA, as Betty Ford had, and worked to improve the quality of life for the aged.

In her partnership role, she sat in on Cabinet meetings, rare for a First Lady...controversial, too. She perhaps is best remembered, though, for her ambassadorial good-will tour of South America...if not also for her bitterness over the defeat of her husband in the 1980 election. "Nothing is more thrilling than the urgency of a campaign..." she once said. The tremendous energy it takes, she added, makes victory "so sweet" but also it makes "a loss so devastating."

**NANCY REAGAN,** wife of Ronald—

"Nothing can prepare you for living in the White House..." wrote Nancy Davis Reagan, who along with the 40th President of the United

States spent eight years in the Executive Mansion. In fact, Nancy's life story reads pretty much like a Hollywood script and indeed could have served as preparation, as a dress rehearsal, for her strut upon the Washington stage.

As a child living with an aunt and uncle in Bethesda, Maryland, Anne Frances Robbins ("Nancy") longed to be with her stage-actress mother, Edith Luckett. Then, as in a dream come true, her divorcee mother married Dr. Loyal Davis, prominent neurosurgeon and chairman of the Department of Surgery at Northwestern University—Nancy went to live with them and became very fond of "Dr. Loyal," as she called him. In 1929 he legally adopted her. She later went from those comfortable circumstances to Smith College, where she majored in drama. After a debut in Chicago, she went to New York and with her mother's connections in the theatre landed a few parts. Then a screen-test in Hollywood came her way and earned her a seven-year contract with Metro-Goldwyn-Mayer. It was like "walking into a dream world," she later wrote, but, "You could get a severe case of insecurity when you came into makeup in the morning and found yourself seated between Elizabeth Taylor and Ava Gardner."

Now the background music reaches a crescendo—actor Ronald Reagan, then president of the Screen Actors Guild, arrives on the scene. "From the moment I met him, Ronald Reagan has been the center of my life," she wrote in her memoirs, *My Turn*. "I have been criticized for saying that, but it's true."

She and "Ronnie" married in the Little Brown Church in California's San Fernando Valley on March 4, 1952. She soon allowed her contract with M-G-M to lapse to become fulltime wife and, later, mother to Patti and Ron (born in 1952 and and 1958, respectively).

In 1966 the Reagan made his sucessful bid for the governorship of California, and Nancy was praised for the style and elegance of her clothes. A writer for *Look* magazine compared her to Jacqueline Kennedy— "she has the same spare figure, the same air of immaculate chic."

When the former First Lady of California came to Washington in 1981, she utilized her keen interest in interior design for an extensive refurbishing of the White House. She was surprised to win few kudos from the press, even though no public funds had been expended—in fact, a ridiculed and costly new set of china was a private gift. Nancy not only had a trouble winning over the press, she became a public relations problem for the administration. Even the gallantry she displayed in response to her husband's brush with death after he was shot by a would-be assassin did not seem to win her complete acceptance by the press, which always insisted upon treating her as a controversial figure.

In Reagan's second term, the critics did give her credit for her drug abuse project and her support of Foster Grandparents, a program she had begun while First Lady of California. But when it became clear that Nancy was playing a substantial role in the administration, she was criticized for that, too. Before she could "retire" in 1989 with her beloved "Ronnie", the press kept up its old negative fire. It was "Fancy Nancy" here, and "frivolous clotheshorse" or "chum of the rich" there.

For all of this, Nancy still could reflect philosophically on her eight years as First Lady. If nothing can prepare you for living in the White House, she now could also say, "nothing can prepare you for leaving it."

**BARBARA BUSH,** wife of George—

A happy grandmother, yes, and much more. One of the most popular First Ladies in modern times, even Barbara Pierce Bush once was a little girl, the daughter of Marvin and Pauline Pierce. Her father was president of the McCall Corporation, and after a happy, well-to-do childhood in suburban Rye, New York, she was off to the Ashley Hall School for girls in South Carolina.

She met fellow "preppie" George Bush, a senior at Phillips Academy in Andover, Massachusetts, at a Christmas dance when she was 16. Just 18 months later, they became engaged and he was off to the wars—to World War II, that is. Soon, at age 18, he would be the youngest man ever to win the U.S. Navy's aviator's wings of gold.

While his anxious fiancée waited at home for her hero's return, young George really was a hero—he experienced combat as a carrier-based pilot in the Pacific, and was rescued when his Avenger torpedo plane was knocked into the sea by anti-aircraft fire. About the time he returned from the warzone, safe and sound, after all, she dropped out of Smith College and they married...in January of 1945.

After he completed his academic career at Yale University, they moved to Texas, where over the next few years he would be active in the oil business. Barbara Bush had started a career, too—as a mother, eventually, of six children. One of them, Robin, sadly, died of leukemia at age 4, a traumatic experience for the still-young couple. "Because of Robin, George and I love every living human more," Barbara Bush later said.

Himself the son of a U.S. Senator (Prescott Bush of Connecticut), George Bush soon would be jumping into Texas politics—he lost a race for the Senate in 1964, but bounced back two years later by winning a House seat from the Houston area.

With Barbara often by his side, he underwent another Senate debacle in 1970, then plunged into a series of public service and political posts that eventually gave him what many political pundits termed the "longest resumé in the Western World." So it was that Barbara Bush soon found herself in long-estranged Communist China as wife of the new U.S. representative to that "People's Republic."

In the decade of the '70s she also honed her political and social skills as wife and helpmate to the American ambassador to the United Nations, to the chairman of the Republican National Committee, the director of the Central Intelligence Agency, and—in 1980—a Republican primary contender for President. And later that year, the official GOP nominee for Vice President. Every one of these titleholders was her own husband, George Bush.

She and George closed out the decade, of course, with his election as Vice President on the ticket headed by Ronald Reagan. Then began almost another decade in which Barbara held down a delicate political role as the wife of the man expected to seek the presidency after Reagan but also expected to "make no waves" in the interim. They had to wait eight long years for their turn, but even so Barbara at last entered the White House in 1989 without the slightest appearance of impatience or self-consciousness.

Happy wife and helpmate, yes, and much more. She tried "to do some good every day," she once said, and many benefitted from her good works. In May of 1989 she invited literacy and education experts to the White House to help organize the Barbara Bush Foundation for Family Literacy, which she then served as the honorary chairman. An advocate of volunteerism, she also supported many other groups and causes, such as the Girl Scouts of America, the Leukemia Society of America, Reading Is Fundamental, and she encouraged school volunteer programs. She lent her support to the aged and homeless, and to victims of AIDS. At the 1992 GOP National Convention, she also went to bat for her beleaguered-appearing incumbent husband, "batting" down negative barbs in interviews and even addressing the Houston convention—and by extension, the Nation—herself.

But Barbara Bush always found time for her family, too. She especially enjoyed having her crew up to Kennebunkport, Maine, the Bush summer home, for long walks along the shore or a game of tennis. And don't forget Millie, her famous springer spaniel that once even "wrote" a book (with the proceeds going to Barbara's literacy cause).

**HILLARY CLINTON,** wife of Bill—

They said the same things about Edith, Eleanor, Rosalynn, and others, you know, then it was Hillary's turn!

Even in 1993, at the very end of the 20th century, America went into a fresh tailspin over an "uppity" new woman in the White House.

Consider that at Wellesley this product of Chicago's middle-class suburbs already had cast aside her family's Republicanism, had upset the applecart of tradition by insisting that a student speak at commencement exercises. And who else but Class President (1967) Hillary herself, with a sharp attack upon the words of the great day's previous speaker, a Republican Senator?

Consider, too, that she soon had a cum laude degree from Yale Law in her feminist pocket and was off to Washington—not only joining the new wave of Baby Boomer women professionals on the move, but also plunging into combative politics as she signed on with the House Judiciary Committee staff (Democratic side, that is) busily drawing up papers for the impeachment of a President, Richard M. Nixon.

Marriage and a move to Arkansas proved vital to her list of accomplishments as she joined a prestigious law firm in Little Rock and became First Lady of the state.

She pursued many other interests, including activities on behalf of the non-profit National Center on Education and the Economy, as a skilled and effective crusader for her many liberal causes. True to her concerns for the poor, women and children—her law school thesis had been on the rights of children—she worked for the Children's Defense Fund, eventually serving five years as the fund's chairperson. She received national recognition when the National Law Journal twice named her one of the top 100 lawyers in the country. (She also out-earned her governor-husband Bill by a factor of 4 to 5 times his own salary per annum.)

But not all was always hunky-dory for the little woman from Illinois, nee Hillary Rodham, who chose to hitch her wagon to Arkansas and politically ambitious Bill. Controversial she was from the start, chosing to retain her maiden name and refusing to change her rebellious Sixties look—sometimes wearing headbands, "Rodham" was given a large share of the blame for husband Bill Clinton's defeat for a second term as Governor.

But she is also credited for learning fast, as maiden name and headband disappeared in time for her husband's third and once-again successful gubernatorial run. (He would serve a total of five terms in all.)

By the end of the 1992 presidential campaign, an entire country knew what Arkansas already knew—Hillary was a political force, with or without husband Bill.

Probably the most scrutinized wife of a presidential candidate ever, Hillary herself has tried to explain that her high and often controversial visibility really isn't her doing. In an interview with *Newsweek,* she said: "I feel like there is this great national conversation going on of which I am a part, but it is not so much about me personally but about all the changes going on in the country—about women and our roles, the choices we make in our lives."

Americans have had controversial, "activist" First Ladies before—Edith Wilson, Eleanor Roosevelt, Rosalynn Carter come to mind. But they were individuals (and phenomena) ahead of their times, it could be said. Edith Wilson, of course, was accused of running the government while her husband Woodrow was incapacitated by a stroke; Eleanor Roosevelt was famous for her politicking, both by FDR's side and on behalf of her own liberal causes; and Rosalynn ruffled some onlooker feathers by taking part in Jimmy Carter's political strategy sessions, even Cabinet meetings, or by representing him on trips abroad.

Would Hillary be another individual phenomena like those First Ladies? Or was she simply a product of her own times, as she tried to assert? As she "took office" early in 1993 by husband Bill's side (with an unprecedented West Wing office at that!) America could only wait and see.

# Acknowledgements and Further Readings

Before coming to heartfelt personal thanks for the help and encouragement received in compiling, writing and publishing the foregoing, please allow us a grateful tip of the hat to a faceless crowd we don't even know—those many authors and historians who wrote about the White House or its occupants in the past. For us, as researchers of secondary, previously published sources only, their works have been vital information. We've cited many of them in the text herein—and we would urge readers interested in following up in greater depth than we offer to pursue those very books, most of them available in the average public library or corner bookstore.

As is apparent, many of the previously published sources we've cited for fact or occasional quote were "one-shot" books such as biographies of this or that President or First Lady. Others were "insider" books by former staffers or residents of the White House, good for their detailed focus, like the biographies, but quite naturally subject to limitation in time frame. The general White House histories were of course useful, but by their nature—as general books or overviews—they cannot often "zoom in" for sustained close look.

One source, however, does both, and we cannot recommend it too highly, and that is the utterly engrossing, wonderfully researched and written two-volume history of the White House by William Seale, *The President's House* (White House Historical Association, with the cooperation of the National Geographic Society, Washington, D.C., 1986—available from the Association, 740 Jackson Place NW, Washington, DC 20503). No general history of the White House yet published can match Seale's work for both overview and illuminating, anecdotal detail, much of which he found in his own research of old records and other primary sources. Plus, it's simply "a great read."

We can, at the same time, also steer readers to two other overview books, each a single volume, that we found to be knowledgeable in detail and highly readable as well—Bess Furman's *White House Profile* (New York and Indianapolis, 1951) and Amy LaFollette Jensen's *The White House and Its Thirty-Five Families* (New York, 1970).

Among the more focused secondary sources we consulted, a personal favorite was *Starling of The White House* by retired Secret Service Agent Edmund Starling, with Thomas Sugrue (New York, 1946), and we thank longtime friend William Fishback, Special Adviser to the President, University of Virginia, for lending his copy of this slim but indispensable volume. Another "insider" book that sat well here was former Chief Usher J.B. West's *Upstairs at The White House: My Life With the First Ladies,* written with Mary Lynn Kotz (New York, 1973). Two more classic, "insider" books of the modern period are Chief Usher Irwin W. "Ike" Hoover's *Forty-two Years in The White House* (Boston, 1934) and Lillian Parks' *My Thirty Years Backstairs at The White House* (New York, 1961).

Most of our other sources have been named in passing already, but two more that were especially useful in researching for our First Ladies section were: *First Ladies* by Betty Boyd Caroli (New York, 1987) and *Presidential Wives: An Anecdotal History* by Paul F. Boller, Jr. (New York, 1988). A third in this category was *All The Presidents' Ladies: Anecdotes of the Women Behind the Men in The White House,* Peter Hay (New York, 1988).

We hasten to point out also that the same White House Historical Association mentioned earlier, located on Lafayette Square in front of the White House itself, offers not only the two-volume history by Seale but also a series of smaller, beautifully illustrated books about the First Ladies, the Presidents, the White House. For us, they were excellent fact sources but also a pleasure simply to read or browse through, looking at the paintings reproduced on their glossy pages. A related source for two or our vignettes (Rose Garden and Paul Jennings memoir) was the Association's White House History journal, Vol. I, No. 1 (1983).

Much of our material came from general, widely shared sources too ubiquitous to mention here—American histories, for example— but a few more specific works that have gone unmentioned in full thus far were: *Presidential Style: Giants and a Pygmy in The White House,* by Samuel and Dorothy Rosenman (New York, 1976); *Hidden Illness in The White House,* by Kenneth Crispell and Carlos Gomez (Durham, N.C., 1988); *Presidential Transitions: Eisenhower Through Reagan* by Carl M. Brauer (New York, 1986); *A Thousand Days: John F. Kennedy in The White House* by Arthur Schlesinger, Jr. (New York, 1965); *The Adams Chronicles: Four Generations of Greatness,* by Jack Shepherd (Boston, 1975); *'Marse Henry: A Biography of Henry Watterson* by Isaac F. Marcosson (New York, 1951); *The Abraham Lincoln Encyclopedia* by Mark E. Neely, Jr. (New York, 1982); *Plain Speaking: An Oral Biography of Harry S. Truman,* by Merle Miller (New York, 1980); *As He Saw It* by Elliott Roosevelt (New York, 1946); *F.D.R.: An Intimate History,* by Nathan Miller (New York, 1983); *The Flying White House: The Story of Air Force One,* by J.F. terHorst and Col. Ralph Albertazzie (New York, 1979).

So much for our sources—faceless they may be, but we do thank them, one and all.

Among our personal and far-from-anonymous helpers and stalwart supporters, we'd especially like to thank my colleagues at Empire Press, Leesburg, Virginia, for their help in assembling, typesetting and design—a gang led by Composition Manager Ralph Scherer and including his typesetting partner Janet Scherer plus editorial guru Bill Vogt; general EP gurus Ken Phillips and Roberta Phillips, advertising moguls Gregg Oehler and Tamra Seneff, picture researcher Delinda Hanley, who tracked down our cover engraving...and down at our Charlottesville (Va.) home base, Ruth Estep for handling, organizing, keeping track of and typing this manuscript of many, many fragmented parts, and our ever-patient printers, Papercraft of Charlottesville, with a large cast of experts at whatever it is that they do to make sense of the package dropped into their laps, Shirley Cunningham for organizing the vignettes author and proofreading par excellence, and far from last or least, our cover designer, Stephen S. Vann, art director at Empire Press. And finally to our families, thanks for putting up with so many recent time-outs while we tried to finish our book on timely schedule. And, now, at last, it actually is done. With these very lines!

—C.B.K. and on behalf of I.S., too

# *Index to Presidents*

# *Index to Presidents*

# Index to First Ladies

*(and presidential spouses)*

# END NOTE

Sometimes it's nice *not* to be an expert, and so it has been a combination of thrill, pleasure and on-going fascination for us to research and write our foregoing account of life in the White House and brief biographies of the women who have come and gone over the same two centuries-plus as First Ladies. While we still would not claim to be expert on the subject, we surely have learned a lot, and we hope our readers will catch some of the enthusiasm with which we sat down and began writing some months ago. For those who might have expected more "inside" views of the most recent or current White House occupants, let us acknowledge that the body of our book addresses history in more detail than it does our own times, although every President does figure in one story or another herein. We felt the most recent were still "in the news" and well known, whereas their predecessors no longer are so well known. Paradoxically, our First Ladies section provides greater detail on the more recent First Ladies, in part because they have tended to be more active in their White House roles, in part also because they are better documented than many of their predecessors. Whatever the case or the reader's own interest in these matters, we hope the reader can share our interest in the subject, perhaps even the frequent thrill that we experienced while putting it all together.

C. Brian Kelly
Ingrid Smyer
August 1992

## About The Authors

C. Brian Kelly, a newspaper reporter for 20 years and more recently editor of the popular-history magazines *Military History* and *World War II,* is a lecturer at the University of Virginia and author of the first book in Montpelier Publishing's *Best Little Stories* series, titled *Best Little Stories From World War II.* Ingrid Smyer, free-lance writer, occasional editor, political and community activist, is co-publisher with Kelly of Montpelier Publishing, located in Charlottesville, Virginia.